De cabo a rabo

*The Most Comprehensive Guide to Learning
Spanish Ever Written*

Vocabulario/Gramática

David Faulkner

Now available for FREE at DavidFaulknerBooks.com:
De cabo a rabo: Vocabulario
Audiobook

For additional support, visit SpanishForTheLoveOfIt.com.

**Flashforward
Publishing**

De cabo a rabo: Vocabulario/Gramática

The Most Comprehensive Guide to Learning Spanish Ever Written

Published by Flashforward Publishing

Boulder, CO

ISBN: 978-0-9964497-9-3 (softcover)
ISBN: 978-1-953825-02-5 (softcover)
ISBN: 978-0-9964497-1-7 (hardcover)

FOREIGN LANGUAGE STUDY / Spanish

QUANTITY PURCHASES: Schools, companies, professional groups, clubs, and other organizations may qualify for special terms when ordering quantities of this title. For information, please contact the author through DavidFaulknerBooks.com.

Flashforward
Publishing

Querid@ estudiante,

Whether you are completely new to Spanish, or have been studying it for years, if you're looking to grow your Spanish vocabulary and improve your understanding of Spanish grammar, you've come to the right place. I have broken *Vocabulario* down into 30 themed units, which go hand in hand with 30 manageable units in *Gramática*. Here, in this combo book, you get both great titles.

My goal has been to create the most original, most user-friendly, and most comprehensive Spanish-learning guides, leaving behind all the fluff typically found in your average language books. These guides are my life-long obsession with the Spanish language, on paper, accessible to all who want to improve and polish their Spanish language skills.

I have drawn on my personal experiences traveling and living in several Spanish-speaking countries on three continents. I have also drawn on my experiences in the classroom studying under professors from just about every Spanish-speaking country in the world. I have pushed my limits of linguistic understanding (as well as theirs) in an attempt to understand every aspect, subtlety, and nuance of the language. I have tried to make this "De cabo a rabo – Spanish" series multi-regional—if not universal—in order to give you the greatest chance of communicating effectively with any native Spanish speaker in the world.

Vocabulario/Gramática provides you with a lifetime's worth of input, but it cannot train your ear, nor does it provide opportunities for output or give you feedback. For unit-by-unit practice, you'll want to pick up a copy of the third book in the "De cabo a rabo – Spanish" series: *Actividades*. With over 250 fun and challenging written exercises that guide you through *Vocabulario/Gramática*, *Actividades* will have you thinking about the language in ways you never considered, regardless of your skill or knowledge level.

In addition to *Vocabulario/Gramática* and *Actividades*, to truly master the language, you will need to hear it. As a thank-you to you for your support, I have made *Vocabulario – Audiobook* available for free on my website, providing you pronunciation practice with every Spanish vocabulary entry, read by native speakers from six different countries. In addition to this audio program, you'll want to get your ears on as much authentic audio as you can handle and, to help you along, I have an ever-growing collection of unit-by-unit audiovisual enrichment recommendations for you on my website that I'm certain you'll find educational as well as entertaining.

Whatever your motivation to improve your Spanish may be, I hope these guides continue to serve you well for many years to come. Mastering a new language is one of the most difficult things you could ever attempt, and it requires persistence, humility, and patience. Don't be discouraged if understanding certain concepts escapes you the first, second, or even third time around. Every time you come back and review them, with new experiences under your belt, you will see them with new eyes and, one day, they'll finally click. "When the student is ready, the teacher will appear," and every time you re-read one of these units, even though the wording hasn't changed, you will likely learn something you hadn't previously picked up on. With that, I wish you great success!

Un abrazo,

David

P.S. Don't miss **De cabo a rabo: Vocabulario – Audiobook** FREE at DavidFaulknerBooks.com. For additional support, visit SpanishForTheLoveOfIt.com.

Vocabulario

Unidad 1 – ¡Mucho gusto!

greetings and good-byes

Hola – Hello

Adiós – Bye

Hasta luego – See you later (until later)

Buenos días – Good morning

Buenas tardes – Good afternoon

Buenas noches – Good night / Good evening

to ask how someone is/feels

¿Cómo estás (tú)? – How are you? (familiar)

¿Cómo está (usted)? – How are you? (formal)

¿Qué tal? – How are things?

to answer how you are/feel

(muy) bien – (very) well

(muy) mal – (very) bad

regular – okay / fine

más o menos – okay / fine (more or less)

to show good manners

(muchas) gracias – thank you (very much)

de nada – You're welcome.

por favor – please

(Usted es) muy amable – You are very kind.

perdone / disculpe – excuse me

con permiso – excuse me (to pass by someone)

to ask someone's name and tell your name

¿Cómo te llamas (tú)? – What is your name?

    (Yo) me llamo _____. – My name is _____.

¿Cómo se llama usted? – What is your name?

el nombre – name

to reciprocate a question

¿Y tú? – And you? (familiar)

¿Y usted? – And you? (formal)

introductions

Te presento a ____. – Let me introduce you to ____.

¡Mucho gusto! – It's a pleasure!

¡El gusto es mío! – The pleasure is mine!

Preséntate. – Introduce yourself.

¡Encantado! / ¡Encantada! – Delighted!

¡Igualmente! – Likewise!

titles of respect

señor (Sr.) – Mr. / sir

señora (Sra.) – Mrs. / ma'am

señorita (Srta.) – Miss.

to request and give other personal information

¿Cuál es tu número de teléfono? – What is your phone number?

    Mi número (de teléfono) es _____. – My (phone) number is _____.

¿Cuándo es tu cumpleaños? – When is your birthday?

    Mi cumpleaños es el _____. – My birthday is (the) _____.

¿Cuántos años tienes? – How old are you?

    (Yo) tengo _____ años. – I am _____ years old.

¿De dónde eres? – Where are you from?

    (Yo) soy de _____. – I am from _____.

(Hable) más despacio. – (Speak) more slowly.

(Yo) no comprendo. – I don't understand.

to say when something takes place

el / la – the
el día (*masculino*) – the day
la semana – the week
el mes – the month
el año – the year
un / una – a(n)
un día – a day
una tarde – an afternoon
hoy – today
mañana – tomorrow

próximo/a – next
el próximo lunes – next Monday
la próxima semana – next week
en – in
en dos meses – in two months
en tres días – in three days
en la mañana – in the morning
la mañana (esta mañana) – the morning (this morning)
la tarde (esta tarde) – the afternoon (this afternoon)
la noche (esta noche) – the night (tonight)

el lunes – (on) Monday
el martes – (on) Tuesday
el miércoles – (on) Wednesday
el jueves – (on) Thursday
el viernes – (on) Friday
el sábado – (on) Saturday
el domingo – (on) Sunday

enero – January
febrero – February
marzo – March
abril – April
mayo – May
junio – June

julio – July
agosto – August
septiembre – September
octubre – October
noviembre – November
diciembre – December

los números y las fechas – numbers and dates

el + *number* + de + *month*
el diez de abril – the 10th of April

el uno de – the first of
el primero de – the first of

cero (0)	diez (10)	veinte (20)	treinta (30)
uno (1)	once (11)	veintiuno (21)	treinta y uno (31)
dos (2)	doce (12)	veintidós (22)	
tres (3)	trece (13)	veintitrés (23)	
cuatro (4)	catorce (14)	veinticuatro (24)	
cinco (5)	quince (15)	veinticinco (25)	
seis (6)	dieciséis (16)	veintiséis (26)	
siete (7)	diecisiete (17)	veintisiete (27)	
ocho (8)	dieciocho (18)	veintiocho (28)	dos mil (2000)
nueve (9)	diecinueve (19)	veintinueve (29)	dos mil dieciocho (2018)

¿Cuántos/as _____ hay? – How many _____ are there?
¿Cuántos días hay en febrero? – How many days are there in February?
   Hay _____. – There is/are _____.

¿Cuál es la fecha de hoy? – What is today's date?
¿Qué día es hoy? – What day is today?
   Hoy es _____. – Today is _____.

interrogative words

¿Qué? – What?
¿Dónde? – Where?
¿Cuál? *pl.* ¿Cuáles? – Which? / What?
¿Cuándo? – When?

¿Por qué? – Why? / For what?
¿Quién? *pl.* ¿Quiénes? – Who?
¿Cómo? – How? / What?
¿Cuánto/a? – How much?
¿Cuántos/as? – How many?

Unidad 2 – lo básico

las actividades – activities
ayudar en casa – to help around the house
cocinar – to cook
dibujar – to draw
escuchar música – to listen to music
estar con amigos – to be with friends
escribir – to write
estudiar – to study
hablar (por teléfono) – to talk (on the phone)
hacer – to do
ir a la escuela – to go to school
ir al cine – to go to the movies
leer – to read
nadar – to swim
patinar – to skate
pintar – to paint
practicar deportes – to play sports
trabajar – to work
tocar la guitarra – to play the guitar
ver la televisión (tele) – to watch T.V.

to say what you like
(A mí) me gusta _____. – I like _____.
Me gusta más _____. – I like _____ more.
Me gusta mucho _____. – I like _____ a lot.
(A mí) sí me gusta _____. – I do like _____.
A mí también (me gusta). – I like it too.

to say what you don't like
(A mí) no me gusta _____. – I don't like _____.
No me gusta mucho _____. – … very much.
No me gusta nada _____. – … at all.
_____ tampoco – _____ either / neither
A mí tampoco (me gusta). – I don't (like it)
                                    either.

to ask what someone likes to do
¿Qué te gusta hacer? – What do you like to do?
¿Y a ti? – And you?

to ask what someone is like
¿Eres _____? – Are you _____?
¿Cómo eres? – What are you like?
¿Cómo es ella? – What is she like?

to say what you or someone else is like
(Yo) soy _____. – I am _____.
(Ella) es _____. – She is _____.

las características – personality traits
amable – kind
artístico/a – artistic
atrevido/a – daring
callado/a – quiet
deportista – jock / plays sports
desordenado/a – disorganized / messy
divertido/a – fun
generoso/a – generous
gracioso/a – funny
honesto/a – honest
impaciente – impatient
ordenado/a – organized / neat
paciente – patient
perezoso/a – lazy
prudente – cautious
serio/a – serious
sincero/a – sincere
sociable – sociable
tacaño/a – cheap / stingy with money
trabajador/a – hard working

to verify a statement
¿De veras? – Really?
¿En serio? – Seriously?

other useful words and expressions
el (*masculino*), la (*femenino*) – the (*singular*)
los (*masculino*), las (*femenino*) – the (*plural*)
sí – yes
no – no / not
quizá – maybe
y – and
o – or
o _____ o _____ – either _____ or _____
ni _____ ni _____ – neither _____ nor _____
a veces – sometimes
muy – very
pero – but
por eso – that's why / for that
pues – well / then
también – also
tampoco – neither / either
la pregunta – question
Tengo una pregunta. – I have a question.
¿Qué significa ____? – What does ____ mean?
¿Cómo se dice ____ en español/inglés?
      – How do you say ____ in Spanish/English?

Unidad 3 – la escuela y el trabajo

la escuela – school
el almuerzo – lunch
el arte – art
las ciencias – science
las ciencias sociales – social sciences
la clase de _____ – _____ class
la educación física – P.E.
el español – Spanish
el inglés – English
las matemáticas – math
la música – music
difícil – difficult
fácil – easy
enseñar: enseña – to teach: teaches
la tarea – homework / task

la hora – hour / time of day
¿Qué hora es? – What time is it?
es / son – it is
de la mañana – in the morning
de la tarde – in the afternoon
de la noche – at night

treinta y dos (32)
treinta y tres (33)
treinta y cuatro (34)
treinta y cinco … treinta y nueve (35 – 39)

school/office supplies
la agenda – daily planner
el archivador – filing cabinet
la calculadora – calculator
el calendario – calendar
la carpeta – file folder
la computadora (compu) – computer
el cuaderno – notebook
el diccionario – dictionary
el escritorio – desk
el horario – schedule
el lápiz, *pl.* los lápices – pencil(s)
el libro – book
el marcador – marker *marcadores*
la mochila – backpack
el papel – paper
la pluma / el bolígrafo – pen
la regla – ruler / rule
el reloj – clock
la silla – chair

pizarron blanco

to ask and tell when something takes place
la hora – hour / time of day
empezar: empieza – to start: it starts   *empezar*
terminar: termina – to end: it ends   *empieza*
¿A qué hora? – At what time?
¿A qué hora empieza? – What times does it start?
¿A qué hora termina? – What time does it end?
   (Termina) a la una – (It ends) at one o'clock
a las dos, tres … doce – at 2:00, 3:00 … 12:00
a mediodía – at noon / midday (not exact time)
a medianoche – at midnight / in the middle of the night
el semestre – semester
el primer semestre – first semester
el segundo semestre – second semester
la primera semana – the first week

Es la una (y veinte). – It is 1:00 o'clock (1:20).
Son las dos, tres, doce (y cuarenta). – It is _____ (:40).
(y) cuarto – quarter (15 minutes)
(y) media – half (30 minutes)
Son las once y media de la noche. – It's 11:30 PM.

cuarenta (40)
cuarenta y uno … cuarenta y nueve (41 – 49)
cincuenta (50)
cincuenta y uno … cincuenta y nueve (51 – 59)

el horario – schedule
la cita – appointment
la escuela – school
la reunión – meeting
el trabajo – work / job
importante – important

people at school or at work
el colega / la colega – colleague
el consejero / la consejera – counselor
el compañero / la compañera – companion / mate
el director / la directora – principal / director
el empleado / la empleada – employee
el estudiante / la estudiante – student
el jefe / la jefa – (the) boss
el maestro / la maestra – (the) teacher
el mentor / la mentora – mentor
el tutor / la tutora – tutor
con – with
Mucho gusto en conocerte. – It's a pleasure to meet you.

mucho gusto en conocerte

la posesión – possession

tener: (yo) tengo – to have: I have
    (tú) tienes   you have
mi(s) – my   nuestro/a(s) – our
tu(s) – your   vuestro/a(s) – your
su(s) – his / her   su(s) – their
    – your (Ud.)   – your (Uds.)

mi jefe – my boss   mis maestros – my teachers
tu jefe – your boss   tus colegas – your colleagues
nuestro jefe – our (male) boss
nuestra jefa – our (female) boss
su jefa – his/her/their (female) boss

Tengo mis cuadernos en mi mochila. – I have my notebooks in my backpack.

to ask and say people's names

¿Cómo te llamas? – What is your name? (What do you call yourself?)
    Yo me llamo _____. – My name is _____. (I call myself _____.)
¿Cuál es tu nombre? – What is your name?
    Mi nombre es _____. – My name is _____.
¿Cómo se llama él/ella? – What is his/her name? (What does he/she call himself/herself?)
    Él/ella se llama _____. – His/her name is _____. (He/she calls himself/herself _____.)
¿Cuál es su nombre? – What is his/her name?
    Su nombre es _____. – His/her name is _____.
¿Cómo se llama tu jefa? – What is your boss's name?
¿Cuál es el nombre de tu jefa? – What is your boss's name?
presentar – to present / to introduce (a person)   "Te presento a mi amigo."
el apodo / el sobrenombre / el mote – nickname   *Andie es mi apodo - mi mote*

to say what something is for (its purpose)

para – for
Tengo un lápiz para la clase. – I have a pencil for the class.
¿Tienes tu computadora para la reunión? – Do you have your computer for the meeting?

to ask and say what people need

necesitar: (yo) necesito – to need: I need
    (tú) necesitas   you need

Necesito un cuaderno para la reunión. – I need a notebook for the meeting.
¿Necesitas una agenda para el trabajo? – Do you need a daily planner for work (for the job)?

quantity

mucho/a – a lot of / much
muchos/as – a lot of / many
poco/a – a little
pocos/as – a few
un/una – a(n)

¿Tienes mucha tarea? – Do you have a lot of homework?
¿Tienes muchas plumas? – Do you have a lot of pens?
Tengo poca tarea. – I have a little homework.
Tengo una pluma. – I have a pen. / I have one pen.

other useful words and expressions

favorito/a – favorite
más – more / most / else (¿Qué más? – What else?)
menos – less / fewer / least
de – of / from
de la escuela – from the school
a – to (direction)
a la escuela – to the school
de lunes a viernes – from Monday to Friday
           – Monday through Friday

to show regret or empathy

Lo siento (mucho). – I'm (so) sorry.

location

aquí – here
    Aquí está. – Here it is.
allí – there
    Allí está. – There it is.

Unidad 4 – los pasatiempos

to describe how someone is or feels

estar – to be (physical states and emotions)

¿Cómo estás? – How are you?

    Estoy enfermo/a. – I am sick.

        aburrido/a – bored

        cansado/a – tired / worn out

        contento/a – happy

        deprimido/a – depressed

        emocionado/a – excited

        frustrado/a – frustrated

        harto/a – fed up

        listo/a – ready

        nervioso/a – nervous

        ocupado/a – busy

        preocupado/a – worried

        triste – sad

to ask and say where someone is

estar – to be (location)

¿Dónde estás? – Where are you?

    Estoy en el parque. – I am at the park.

-ar verbs (regulars)

alquilar / rentar (videos) – to rent (videos)

bailar – to dance

caminar – to walk

cantar – to sing

cocinar – to cook

enseñar – to teach

escuchar (música) – to listen to (music)

esquiar – to ski

estudiar – to study

fumar – to smoke

hablar – to speak / to talk

limpiar (la casa) – to clean (the house)

manejar (un carro) – to drive (a car)

mirar (la tele) – to watch (T.V.) / to look at

montar (en bicicleta) – to ride (a bicycle)

nadar – to swim

pasar (tiempo) – to pass / to spend (time)

pescar – to fish

pintar – to paint

platicar / charlar – to talk / to chat

preparar (la cena) – to prepare (dinner)

tocar – to touch / to play an instrument

trabajar – to work

usar (la computadora) – to use

viajar – to travel

-er/-ir verbs (regulars)

aprender – to learn

abrir – to open

comer – to eat

correr – to run

asistir (a clase) – to attend (class)

beber (jugo) – to drink (juice)

escribir (una carta) – to write (a letter)

leer (un libro) – to read (a book)

vivir (en la ciudad) – to live (in the city)

-ar/-er/-ir verbs (irregulars)

ir – to go

    a una fiesta – to go to a party

    de compras – to go shopping

jugar (u → ue) – to play

    (al) básquetbol – to play basketball

    (al) béisbol – to play baseball

    (al) fútbol – to play soccer

    (al) fútbol americano – to play football

    (al) tenis – to play tennis

    (a los) videojuegos – to play videogames

    (al) voleibol – to play volleyball

pensar (e → ie) (que) – to think (that)

poder (o → ue) – to be able

preferir (e → ie) – to prefer

querer (e → ie) – to want

saber (yo sé) – to know (information)

tener (yo tengo) (e → ie) – to have

ver (yo veo) – to see / to watch

to ask and say where someone is going

ir: (yo) voy – to go: I'm going / I go

    (tú) vas   you're going / you go

a – to

al (a + el) / a la – to the

de – from / of

del (de + el) / de la – from the

el campo – field / countryside

el centro comercial – mall

el gimnasio – gym

el parque – park

el parque de diversiones – amusement park

la piscina / la alberca – swimming pool

la playa – beach

¿Adónde? – Where to? / To where?

¿Adónde vas? – Where are you going?

    Voy a la playa. – I am going to the beach.

to say with whom you do an activity
con – with
   conmigo – with me
   contigo – with you
   con él, ella, Ud. – with him, her, you
   con nosotros/as – with us
   con vosotros/as – with you (all) (Spain)
   con ellos/as, Uds. – with them, you (all)
sin – without
   sin mí – without me
   sin ti – without you
   sin él, ella, Ud. – without him, her, you
   sin nosotros/as – without us
   sin vosotros/as – without you (all) (Spain)
   sin ellos/as, Uds. – without them, you (all)
el amigo / la amiga – friend
la familia – family
solo/a – alone
juntos/as – together

to extend, accept, or decline invitations
tal vez – perhaps
posiblemente – possibly
probablemente – probably
poder: (yo) puedo – to be able: I can
        (tú) puedes   you can
querer: (yo) quiero – to want: I want
         (tú) quieres   you want
¡Cómo no! / ¡Por supuesto! – Of course!
¡Claro que sí! – Of course!
¡Claro que no! – Of course not!
de nada / por nada – You're welcome.

to say when you do an activity
la estación, *pl.* las estaciones – season(s)
la primavera – spring
el verano – summer
el otoño – fall / autumn
el invierno – winter
el lunes, el martes . . . – (on) Monday, Tuesday
los lunes, los martes . . . – (on) Mondays, etc.
el fin de semana – (on) the weekend
los fines de semana – (on) the weekends
después de (la escuela) – after (school)
(en / por) la mañana – (in) the morning
              la tarde – (in) the afternoon
              la noche – (at) night
generalmente – generally
hoy no – not today
mañana – tomorrow
todos los días – every day

las exclamaciones – exclamations
¡No me digas! – You don't say!
¡A poco! – No way! / Say it ain't so!
¡Genial! – Awesome! / Sweet!
¡Qué lástima! – What a pity!
¡Qué pena! – What a shame! / How sad!

other useful words and phrases
la voz, *pl.* las voces – voice(s)
algo – something
nada – nothing
       – anything (in a negative sentence)
     Ej. No tengo nada.
el pasatiempo – pastime
que – that
porque – because
¿por qué? – why?
¿por qué no? – why not?
ir + a + *infinitivo* – to be going *to* _____
para + *infinitivo* – in order *to* _____
   para nadar – in order to swim
después de + *infinitivo* – after _____*ing*
   después de nadar – after swimming
antes de + *infinitivo* – before _____*ing*
   antes de nadar – before swimming
sin + *infinitivo* – without _____*ing*
   sin nadar – without swimming

Unidad 5 – la comida

las comidas – meals
comer – to eat (lunch)
beber / tomar – to drink
desayunar – to eat breakfast
almorzar (o → ue) – to eat lunch
cenar – to eat dinner / to dine
la cena – dinner
la comida – food / lunch
la (comida) chatarra – junk (food)
el desayuno – breakfast
la merienda – afternoon snack
la botana – snack
el aperitivo – appetizer
los refrigerios – refreshments

la comida – food
el arroz – rice
el atún – tuna
el bistec – steak
la carne – meat (often beef)
el cereal – cereal
la ensalada – salad
las frutas – fruits
   el aguacate / la palta – avocado
   el arándano – blueberry / cranberry
   la ciruela – plum
   el durazno / el melocotón – peach
   la frambuesa – raspberry
   la fresa / la frutilla – strawberry
   el limón – lemon / lime
   la manzana – apple
   el melón – melon (cantaloupe, honeydew)
   la naranja – orange
   la nectarina – nectarine
   la pera – pear
   la piña – pineapple
   el plátano / la banana – banana
   la sandía – watermelon
   el tomate – tomato
   la toronja – grapefruit
   la uva – grape
   la zarzamora (mora) – blackberry
los frutos secos / las nueces – nuts
   la almendra – almond
   el anacardo – cashew
   el cacahuate / el maní – peanut
   la nuez – walnut
   el pistacho – pistachio

el guisado – stew
la hamburguesa – hamburger
la hamburguesa con queso – cheeseburger
el huevo – egg
el jamón – ham
la mayonesa – mayonnaise
la mostaza – mustard
el pan – bread
   el pan tostado – toast
la papa / la patata – potato
   las papas al horno – baked potatoes
   las papas fritas – french fries
el pescado – fish
el pollo – chicken
el puerco – pork
el queso – cheese
la sal y la pimienta – salt and pepper
el sándwich / la torta – sandwich
   de jamón – ham sandwich
   de queso – cheese sandwich
la sopa – soup
   de pollo – chicken soup
   de tomate – tomato soup
   de verduras – vegetable soup
las verduras / los vegetales – vegetables
   el ajo – garlic
   el apio – celery
   la berenjena – eggplant
   el brócoli / el brécol – broccoli
   la calabaza – pumpkin / squash
   el calabacín – zucchini
   la cebolla – onion
   los chícharos / los guisantes – peas
   el chile – chili pepper
   la col / el repollo – cabbage
   la col rizada – kale
   la coliflor – cauliflower
   los espárragos – asparagus
   las espinacas – spinach
   las habichuelas verdes – green beans
   la lechuga – lettuce
   el maíz – corn
   el pepinillo – pickle
   el pepino – cucumber
   el pimiento – bell pepper
   los repollitos de Bruselas – Brussels sprouts
   la zanahoria – carrot
el yogur – yogurt

las bebidas – drinks
el agua (*femenino*) – water
el café – coffee
el jugo de naranja – orange juice
el jugo de manzana – apple juice
la leche – milk
el licuado / el batido – smoothie
la limonada – lemonade
el refresco / la gaseosa – soft drink
el té (caliente) – (hot) tea
el té helado / el té frío – iced tea

el postre – dessert
el chocolate – chocolate
el helado – ice cream
la paleta – popsicle
el pastel – cake

las descripciones – descriptions
bueno/a (para la salud) – good (for your health)
malo/a (para la salud) – bad (for your health)
delicioso/a / sabroso/a – delicious / tasty
asqueroso/a – disgusting
auténtico/a – authentic

likes or preferences
más o menos – more or less
me encanta(n) – I love it (them)
me gusta(n) – I like it (them)
preferir (e → ie) – to prefer

la opinión – opinion
creer – to believe / to think
Creo que sí. – I believe so. / I think so.
Creo que no. – I don't think so.
¡Qué asco! – How disgusting!
¡Guácala! – Yuck!

la frecuencia – frequency
nunca – never
    – ever (in a negative sentence)
    Ej. Ella no quiere ir nunca.
siempre – always
todos los días – every day
una vez – once / one time
dos veces – twice / two times
muchas veces – a lot / many times
de vez en cuando – from time to time
normalmente – normally

¿Cuándo?
ahora – now
a tiempo – on time
durante – during
mientras – while
pronto – soon
tarde – late
temprano – early

otras palabras y expresiones útiles
algo – something
nada – nothing
    – anything (in a negative sentence)
    Ej. No quiero nada.
alguno/a(s) – some
algún – some (before *singular*, *masculine noun*)
    algún restaurante – some restaurant
ninguno/a – none (effectively no *plural* form)
        – any (in a negative sentence)
    Ej. No quiero ninguna bebida.
ningún – no (before *singular*, *masculine noun*)
    ningún restaurante – no restaurant
        – any (in a negative sentence)
    Ej. No quiero ir a ningún restaurante.
unos / unas – some
como – like / as
¿no? / ¿verdad? – right?
si – if / whether (no accent mark)
la experiencia – experience
tener hambre – to be hungry
tener sed – to be thirsty
los dos / las dos – both
mismo/a – same

Unidad 6 – la gente y las descripciones

la familia – family
los abuelos: el abuelo – grandpa
                la abuela – grandma
los hermanos: el hermano – brother
                 la hermana – sister
los hijos: el hijo – son
            la hija – daughter
los nietos: el nieto – grandson
             la nieta – granddaughter
los padres: el padre (papá) – father (dad)
              la madre (mamá) – mother (mom)
los primos: el primo – cousin
             la prima – cousin
los tíos: el tío – uncle
           la tía – aunt
el hijo único / la hija única – only child
los gemelos / las gemelas – twins

las descripciones – descriptions
ser + *adjetivo* – to be _____
alto/a – tall
antipático/a – mean
bajo/a – short
bonito/a – pretty / good-looking
cariñoso/a – affectionate
delgado/a – thin
feo/a – ugly
gordo/a – fat
grande – big / large
guapo/a – good-looking (handsome, gorgeous)
inteligente – intelligent
joven, *pl.* jóvenes – young
mayor, *pl.* mayores – older / greater
menor, *pl.* menores – younger / lesser
pelirrojo/a – redhead
pequeño/a – small
simpático/a – nice
viejo/a – old
tener + *sustantivo* – to have _____
el pelo – hair
   canoso – gray   corto – short
   castaño – brown   largo – long
   negro – black   liso – straight
   rubio – blonde   rizado – curly
los ojos – eyes
   azules – blue eyes
   verdes – green eyes
   marrones – brown eyes

la gente – people
el / la adolescente – adolescent / teenager
el / la adulto/a – adult
el bebé – baby (regardless of gender or sex)
el chico / el muchacho – boy
la chica / la muchacha – girl
el hombre – man
la mujer – woman
el / la niño/a – child
la persona – person (regardless of gender or sex)

to ask and say what someone is like
¿Cómo es Laura? – What is Laura like?
   Ella es _____. – She is _____.
¿Cómo son Laura y Paco? – What are they like?
   Son _____. – They are _____.

to make comparisons
más + *adjetivo* + que – more _____ than
menos + *adjetivo* + que – less _____ than
mayor que – older than
menor que – younger than

la edad – age
¿Cuántos años tiene él? – How old is he?
   Él tiene ___ años. – He is ____ years old.
sesenta (60)   noventa (90)
setenta (70)   cien (100)
ochenta (80)   ciento uno (101)

las mascotas – pets
el gato – cat
el perro – dog

la posesión – possession
de – of
de mi hermano – my brother's (of my brother's)
el gato de mi tío – my uncle's cat
tener (yo tengo) (e → ie) – to have

el número – number
¿Cuántos/as? – How many?
alguien – someone
nadie – no one
   – anyone (in a negative sentence)
   Ej. No hay nadie aquí.
sólo / solo / solamente – only
todos/as – every / all / everyone

Unidad 7 – la ropa

articles of clothing
la blusa – blouse
la bolsa – bag / purse
el calcetín, *pl.* los calcetines – sock(s)
la camisa – shirt
la camiseta – T-shirt
la chaqueta / la chamarra – jacket
la corbata – tie / necktie
la falda – skirt
los jeans – jeans (pronounced as in English)
los pantalones (cortos) – pants (shorts)
la ropa – clothing / clothes
la sudadera – sweatshirt
el suéter – sweater
el traje – suit
los (zapatos de) tenis – tennis shoes
el vestido – dress
los zapatos – shoes

las descripciones – descriptions
el color – color
¿De qué color es _____? – What color is _____?
amarillo/a – yellow
anaranjado/a – orange
azul, *pl.* azules – blue
blanco/a – white
gris, *pl.* grises – gray
marrón, *pl.* marrones – brown
morado/a – purple
negro/a – black
rojo/a – red
rosado/a – pink
verde – green
nuevo/a – new
¡Qué + *adjetivo*! – How _____!

specific items
ese (*masc.*) / esa (*fem.*) / eso (*neutro*) – that
esos / esas – those
este (*masc.*) / esta (*fem.*) / esto (*neutro*) – this
estos / estas – these
otro/a – other / another

places to shop for clothing
el almacén – warehouse
la tienda de descuentos – discount store
la tienda de ropa – clothing store
la zapatería – shoe store

de compras – out shopping
buscar – to look for
comprar – to buy
contar (o → ue) – to count
costar (o → ue) – to cost
desear – to want / to desire
encontrar (o → ue) – to find
llevar – to wear
pagar – to pay
venir (yo vengo) (e → ie) – to come
para – for (intended recipient)
    para mí – for me
    para ti – for you
    para él, ella, Ud. – for him, her, you
por – for (in exchange for)
    por $15 – for $15
el precio – price
el dinero – money
ciento un(o)/una, etc. – one hundred one, etc.
¿Cuánto cuesta _____? – How much does _____ cost?
    Cuesta _____. – It costs _____.
¿Cuánto cuestan _____? How much do _____ cost?
    Cuestan _____. – They cost _____.
el dólar, *pl.* los dólares – dollar(s)
4 dólares con 5 centavos – 4 dollars and 5 cents
la ganga – bargain
¡Qué ganga! – What a bargain!
barato/a – cheap / inexpensive
caro/a – expensive
gratis / gratuito/a – free (no cost)

la gente – people
el dependiente / la dependienta – store clerk
el / la joven, *pl.* los / las jóvenes – youngster(s)

location
por aquí – this way / around here
por allí – that way / around there
por todas partes – everywhere
por ninguna parte – nowhere / anywhere (negative)

to make comparisons
más + *adjetivo* + que – more _____ than
menos + *adjetivo* + que – less _____ than
mejor que – better than
peor que – worse than
tan + *adjetivo* + como – as _____ as
tanto/a + *sustantivo* + como – as much _____ as

los números cardinales – cardinal numbers

(1) uno	(30) treinta	(200) doscientos
(2) dos	(31) treinta y uno	(268) doscientos sesenta y ocho
(3) tres	(32) treinta y dos	(300) trescientos
(4) cuatro	(33) treinta y tres	(383) trescientos ochenta y tres
(5) cinco	(34) treinta y cuatro	(400) cuatrocientos
(6) seis	(35) treinta y cinco	(405) cuatrocientos cinco
(7) siete	(40) cuarenta	(500) quinientos
(8) ocho	(41) cuarenta y uno	(520) quinientos veinte
(9) nueve	(42) cuarenta y dos	(600) seiscientos
(10) diez	(43) cuarenta y tres	(699) seiscientos noventa y nueve
(11) once	(44) cuarenta y cuatro	(700) setecientos
(12) doce	(45) cuarenta y cinco	(777) setecientos setenta y siete
(13) trece	(50) cincuenta	(800) ochocientos
(14) catorce	(51) cincuenta y uno	(801) ochocientos uno
(15) quince	(52) cincuenta y dos	(900) novecientos
(16) dieciséis	(53) cincuenta y tres	(914) novecientos catorce
(17) diecisiete	(54) cincuenta y cuatro	(1,000) mil
(18) dieciocho	(60) sesenta	(1,928) mil novecientos veintiocho
(19) diecinueve	(66) sesenta y seis	(2,000) dos mil
(20) veinte	(70) setenta	(2,004) dos mil cuatro
(21) veintiuno	(77) setenta y siete	(3,000) tres mil
(22) veintidós	(80) ochenta	(4,000) cuatro mil
(23) veintitrés	(88) ochenta y ocho	(10,000) diez mil
(24) veinticuatro	(90) noventa	(25,000) veinticinco mil
(25) veinticinco	(99) noventa y nueve	(50,000) cincuenta mil
(26) veintiséis	(100) cien	(100,000) cien mil
(27) veintisiete	(101) ciento uno	(1,000,000) un millón
(28) veintiocho	(110) ciento diez	(1,000,000,000) mil millones
(29) veintinueve	(132) ciento treinta y dos	(1,502,000,000) mil quinientos dos millones

¡Ojo! un vestido (1), veintiún vestidos (21), treinta y un años (31), ciento un dólares (101)

una camisa (1), veintiuna camisas (21), treinta y una semanas (31), doscientas una cosas (201)

(1/2) la mitad	(1/3) un tercio	(1/4) un cuarto	(1/5) una quinta parte
una mitad	(2/3) dos tercios	(3/4) tres cuartos	(2/5) dos quintas partes

direct-object pronouns

lo – it (*masculino*)	los – them (*masculino*) (*masculino* and *femenino*)
la – it (*femenino*)	las – them (*femenino*)

otras palabras y expresiones útiles

la fiesta – party

¿Qué tal? – How are things?

¿Qué tal _____? – How about _____?

¿Cómo te queda? – How does it fit you?

   Me queda bien. – It fits me well.

¿Qué te parece? – What do you think (of it)?

   Me parece bien. – It seems good to me.

¡Feliz cumpleaños! – Happy birthday!

igual / lo mismo – the same

(me) da igual – it's all the same (to me)

¡Vaya! / ¡Anda! – Wow!

A ver … – Let's see …

cuando – when

hasta – until

para + *infinitivo* – in order *to* _____

perdone (Ud.) / disculpe (Ud.) – excuse me

Unidad 8 – las vacaciones

las vacaciones – vacation
estar de vacaciones – to be on vacation
ir de vacaciones – to go on vacation

places to visit on vacation
la catarata / la cascada – waterfall
la catedral – cathedral
el centro – center
la ciudad – city
el lago – lake
los lugares de interés – places of interest
el mar – ocean / sea
la montaña – mountain
el museo – museum
el país – country
la pirámide – pyramid
el río – river
la selva tropical – rain forest
las ruinas (el sitio arqueológico) – ruins

las actividades – activities
andar / pasear – to go (around, about) / to walk
bajar – to go down / to lower
bucear – to SCUBA dive
descansar – to rest
esquiar (i → í) – to ski
explorar – to explore
llevar – to carry / to wear
los recuerdos – souvenirs
sacar fotos – to take photos
    la fotografía (foto) – photograph (photo)
subir – to go up / to rise / to raise
tomar el sol – to sunbathe
visitar – to visit

planning a vacation
pensar (e → ie) + *infinitivo* – to plan *to* _____
regresar – to return / to go back
entrar (en) – to enter (into)
salir (de) – to leave (from)
    (yo) salgo – I leave
querer (e → ie) + *infinitivo* – to want *to* _____
poder (o → ue) + *infinitivo* – to be able *to* _____
ir + a + *infinitivo* – to be going *to* _____
necesitar – to need
traer – to bring
    (yo) traigo – I bring
repetir (e → i) – to repeat

things to take on vacation
el abrigo – coat
las gafas de sol – sunglasses
las botas – boots
el bronceador – suntan lotion
la bufanda – scarf
la cámara – camera
la gorra – baseball cap
los guantes – gloves
el impermeable – rain jacket
la maleta – suitcase
el (los) paraguas – umbrella(s) (for rain)
el parasol – umbrella to block the sun
el pasaporte – passport
la toalla – towel
el traje de baño – bathing suit

el tiempo – weather
¿Qué tiempo hace? – What's the weather like?
Hace buen tiempo. – It's good weather.
Hace calor. – It's hot.
Hace fresco. – It's cool. / It's chilly.
Hace frío. – It's cold.
Hace mal tiempo. – It's bad weather.
Hace sol. – It's sunny.
Hace viento. – It's windy.
Hace 32 grados. – It's 32 degrees.
Está nublado. – It's cloudy.
Llueve. – It's raining. / It rains.
Está lloviendo. – It's raining.
Nieva. – It's snowing. / It snows.
Está nevando. – It's snowing.
la lluvia – rain
la nieve – snow
la nube – cloud
el sol – sun
el viento – wind

¿Adónde vas?
a ninguna parte – nowhere / anywhere (negative)
a todas partes – everywhere
aquí (precise) / acá (vague) – here
allí / ahí (precise) / allá (vague) – there

ongoing action
estar + *gerundio* (-*ing* form) – to be _____*ing*
¿Qué estás haciendo? – What are you doing?
    Estoy descansando. – I am resting.

Unidad 9 – la casa y los quehaceres

to say where someone lives
cerca (de) – near / close (to)
lejos (de) – far (from)
al lado (de) – next to / to the side (of)
vivir – to live
en – in / on / at

houses or apartments
el alquiler / la renta – rent
el apartamento – apartment
el baño – bathroom
la casa (de _3_ pisos) – (_3_ story) house
el césped / el sacate (zacate) – lawn
la cocina – kitchen
el comedor – dining room
el cuarto – room
el dormitorio / la habitación / la recámara
    – bedroom
el elevador / el ascensor – elevator
las escaleras – stairs / staircase
el garaje / la cochera – garage
el jardín (delantero, trasero) – (front, back) yard
el lavadero – laundry room
la pared – wall
el pasillo – hallway (hall)
el patio – patio
el (primer, segundo) piso – (first, second) floor
el porche – porch
la sala – living room
la sala de estar – family room
el sótano – basement

household items
la alfombra – carpet
la bañera / la tina – bathtub
la cama – bed
la chimenea – chimney / fireplace
el coche / el carro – car
la cómoda – dresser
    el cajón, *pl.* los cajones – drawer(s)
el (los) cortacésped – lawnmower(s)
la cortina – curtain
las cosas – things / stuff
el cuadro – picture (usually framed)
la ducha – shower
los electrodomésticos – appliances
la escoba – broom
el escritorio – desk

el espejo – mirror
el estante – shelf / bookshelf
el estéreo – stereo
    la bocina / el parlante – speaker
la estufa – stove
el fregadero – kitchen sink
el guardarropa / el clóset – closet
el horno – oven
el (horno de) microondas – microwave (oven)
el inodoro / el retrete / la taza – toilet
la lámpara – lamp
el lavabo / el (los) lavamanos – bathroom sink(s)
la lavadora – washing machine
el (los) lavaplatos – dishwasher(s)
la mesa – table
los muebles – furniture
el piso / el suelo – floor
el póster, *pl.* los pósters / el cartel – poster(s)
la puerta – door
el reproductor de CD/DVD – CD/DVD player
el refrigerador (refri) – refrigerator (fridge)
la secadora – clothes dryer
la silla – chair
el sillón, *pl.* los sillones – armchair(s)
el sofá (*masculino*) – couch / sofa
el tapete – rug
el televisor – TV set
la ventana – window

las descripciones
antiguo/a – old / antique
bastante – quite / rather (*adverb*)
cómodo/a – comfortable
cuadrado/a – square
de cuero – (made) of leather
de madera – wooden / (made) of wood
de metal – (made) of metal
de plástico – (made) of plastic
de vidrio – (made) of glass
grande – large / big
incómodo/a – uncomfortable
limpio/a – clean
moderno/a – modern
nuevo/a – new
pequeño/a – small
real – real / royal
redondo/a – round
sucio/a – dirty

los colores – colors
amarillo/a – yellow
anaranjado/a / naranja – orange
azul – blue
blanco/a – white
gris – gray
marrón, *pl.* marrones – brown
morado/a – purple
    claro – light purple
    oscuro – dark purple
negro/a – black
rojo/a – red
rosado/a / rosa – pink
verde – green
    claro – light green
    oscuro – dark green

los quehaceres (de la casa) – chores
arreglar – to fix / to straighten / to tidy
ayudar – to help
barrer – to sweep
cortar (el césped) – to cut / to mow (the lawn)
desempolvar – to dust
hacer – to do / to make
    (yo) hago – I do / I make
hacer la cama – to make the bed
lavar (la ropa, los platos)
    – to wash (clothes, dishes)
limpiar (el baño) – to clean (the bathroom)
pasar la aspiradora – to vacuum
planchar (la ropa) – to iron (clothes)
poner – to put / to place / to set
    (yo) pongo – I put / I place / I set
poner la mesa – to set the table
preparar – to prepare
    el desayuno – to prepare breakfast
    el almuerzo – to prepare lunch
    la cena – to prepare dinner
quitar la mesa – to clear the table
sacar la basura – to take out the trash
usar – to use

las preferencias – preferences
preferir (e → ie) – to prefer
querer (e → ie) – to want

la obligación – obligation
tener que + *infinitivo* – to have *to* _____
deber + *infinitivo* – to ought *to* (should) _____
necesitar + *infinitivo* – to need *to* _____

la frecuencia – frequency
¿con qué frecuencia? – how often?
a menudo / muchas veces – often
a veces – sometimes
cada – each / every
(casi) nunca – (almost) never
(casi) siempre – (almost) always
constantemente – constantly
de vez en cuando – from time to time
frecuentemente – frequently
generalmente – generally
normalmente – normally
(casi) todos los días – (almost) every day
los lunes – (on) Mondays
los fines de semana – (on) the weekends
después de + *infinitivo* – after _____*ing*
antes de + *infinitivo* – before _____*ing*

otras palabras útiles
hay – there is / there are
    un / una – a(n)
    uno / una – one
    dos – two
    tres – three
ándale (pues) – get to it (then)
ambos/as – both
el gancho – hanger / hook
el (los) pasamanos – handrail(s)

los adjetivos posesivos – possessive adjectives

mi(s) – my	nuestro(s)/a(s) – our
tu(s) – your	vuestro(s)/a(s) – your
su(s) – his / her	su(s) – their
– your (Ud.)	– your (Uds.)

los complementos directos – direct-object
                                  pronouns
lo – it (*masculino*)
la – it (*femenino*)
los – them (*masculino*) (*masculino* y *femenino*)
las – them (*femenino*)

Unidad 10 – el cuerpo humano y las enfermedades

las partes del cuerpo – parts of the body
la boca – mouth
el brazo – arm
la cabeza – head
la cara – face
el cuello – neck
el cuerpo – body
el dedo – finger
los dientes – teeth
la espalda – back
el estómago – stomach
la garganta – throat
el hombro – shoulder
la lengua – tongue
la mano (*femenino*) – hand
la nariz – nose
el oído – inner ear
la oreja – outer ear
el ojo – eye
el pecho – chest
el pelo / el cabello – hair
el pie – foot
el dedo de pie – toe
la pierna – leg
la rodilla – knee
derecho/a – right
izquierdo/a – left

ways to maintain good health
descansar – to rest
dormir (o → ue) – to sleep
hacer ejercicio – to exercise
la salud – health
estar sano/a – to be healthy (people)
ser saludable – to be healthy (food)
las vitaminas – vitamins

preguntas básicas – basic questions
¿Qué te duele? – What hurts (you)?
¿Qué (síntomas) tienes?
   – What (symptoms) do you have?
¿Cómo te sientes? – How do you feel?
¿Qué te pasa? – What's happening (to you)?

las profesiones médicas – medical professions
el / la dentista – dentist
el / la doctor/a / médico/a – doctor
el / la enfermero/a – nurse
el / la farmacéutico/a – pharmacist

to talk about your medical problems
¡Ay! – Ouch! / Ow!
el dolor – pain
doler (o → ue) – to ache / to hurt
la enfermedad – sickness / illness / disease
la fiebre – fever
la gripe / la gripa – flu
la tos – cough
sentir (e → ie) – to feel (used with *nouns*)
Tengo … – I have … / Siento … – I feel …
   dolor de cabeza – a headache
   dolor de estómago – a stomachache
   dolor de garganta – a sore throat
   dolor de muelas – a toothache (molars)
   dolor de oído – an earache
   alergias – allergies
   fiebre – a fever
   gripe – the flu
   mocos – mucous
   resfrío / resfriado – a cold
   tos – a cough
Tengo … – I am …
   ___ años – ___ years old
   hambre – hungry
   sed – thirsty
   calor – hot
   frío – cold
   sueño – sleepy
sentirse (e → ie) – to feel (used with
                    adjectives and *adverbs*)
estar – to be (physical or mental state)
Estoy … – I am … / Me siento … – I feel …
   enfermo/a – sick
   bien – well
   fatal – awful
   horrible – horrible
   resfriado/a – sick (with a cold)
   mal – bad
   (aun) mejor – (even) better
   (aun) peor – (even) worse
   terrible – terrible
así – like this / like that (in this/that way)

las opiniones – opinions
creer (que) – to believe (that)
pensar (e → ie) (que) – to think (that)
que – that (no accent mark)
¿no? – right? (affirmative sentence only)
¿verdad? – right? (affirmative or negative)

to talk about duration
¿Cuánto (tiempo) hace que _____?
    – How long has it been that _____?
Hace tres días que _____.
    – It has been three days that _____.
ahora / ya – now
todavía – still / yet
ya no – not now
ya no más – not any more

what to do when you are sick
la clínica – clinic / doctor's office
la enfermería – nurse's office
el hospital – hospital
la farmacia – pharmacy
hacer una cita – to make an appointment
llamar – to call
    hacer una llamada – to make a call
    marcar – to dial (a phone number)
    oprimir – to press (a button)
    colgar (o → ue) – to hang up (the phone)
    descolgar (o → ue) – to pick up (the phone)
    contestar – to answer
visitar – to visit
deber – to ought (should)
quedarse – to stay / to remain
lastimarse – to get hurt / to hurt oneself
soplarse la nariz – to blow one's nose
mejorarse – to get better
empeorarse – to get worse
tomar – to take / to drink
    la pastilla / la píldora – pill
    la medicina – medicine
    el agua (*femenino*) – water

otras palabras y expresiones útiles
Lo siento. – I am sorry. / I feel (bad for)
           what you are going through.
para + *infinitivo* – in order *to* _____
sólo / solamente / nomás – only (*adverb*)
único/a – only (*adjective*)
    la única cita – the only appointment
cada – each / every
también – also
tampoco – either / neither
pero – but
porque – because
por eso – that's why
mucho – a lot / much (*adverb*)
más – more / else (¿Qué más? – What else?)
si – if / whether (no accent mark)

Unidad 11 – la ciudad

los lugares – places
la avenida – avenue
el banco – bank
la biblioteca – library
la calle – street
el cine – movie theater
la cuadra / la manzana – (city) block
la dulcería – candy shop
la esquina – corner
la estación – station
    de policía – police station
    de tren – train station
el estadio – stadium
la farmacia – pharmacy
el hotel – hotel
la iglesia – church
la librería – bookstore
la mezquita – mosque
el monumento – monument
la oficina de correos – post office
la parada de autobús – bus stop
el parque – park
la plaza – plaza
el restaurante – restaurant
la sinagoga – synagogue
el supermercado (súper) – supermarket
el teatro – theater
el templo – temple
la tienda – store / shop
el zoológico (zoo) – zoo
el zócalo / la plaza mayor – town square

las actividades
abrir – to open
    estar abierto/a – to be open
cerrar (e → ie) – to close
    estar cerrado/a – to be closed
sacar un libro – to check out a book
devolver (o → ue) un libro – to return a book
buscar – to look for
encontrar (o → ue) – to find
ir a pasear – to go for a walk
llegar (a) – to arrive (at) / to get (to)
recoger – to pick up
trabajar / chambear – to work
vender – to sell
la comunidad – community
el partido de + *sport* – _____ game
la película (peli) – movie
la obra de teatro – (theatrical) play

las compras – shopping
la bolsa – bag
la caja – box / cash register
el / la cajero/a – cashier / bank teller
el / la cliente/a – customer / client
los comestibles / los abarrotes – groceries
el / la consumidor/a – consumer
consumir – to consume
el consumismo – consumerism
el champú, *pl.* los champúes – shampoo(s)
el cepillo – brush
el cepillo de dientes – toothbrush
el desodorante – deodorant
el dulce – candy
el hilo dental – dental floss
el jabón – soap
la marca – brand
la pasta dentífrica/dental – toothpaste
el peine – comb
el regalo – gift

el dinero – money
el salario / el sueldo – salary
ganar – to earn
gastar – to spend
ahorrar – to save
el cajero automático – ATM
el NIP (número de identificación personal) – PIN
la cuenta – account
    corriente / de cheques – checking account
    de ahorros – savings account
retirar / sacar – to withdraw / to take out
depositar – to deposit
cobrar – to charge
el cargo adicional – additional charge
la comisión – commission / fee
el cambio – change
el recibo / el comprobante – receipt (of purchase)
el saldo / el balance (de cuenta) – (account) balance
el costo – cost
costar (o → ue) – to cost

el transporte – transportation
a pie – on foot
en + *vehicle* – by _____
tomar / coger (un taxi) – to take / to catch (a cab)
el autobús (bus) – bus
el metro – subway
el taxi – taxi(cab)
el tren – train

el correo – mail
la carta – letter
el correo electrónico – email
enviar (i → í) / mandar – to send
la estampilla / el timbre / el sello – stamp
el paquete – package
recibir – to receive
el sobre – envelope
la tarjeta de cumpleaños – birthday card
la (tarjeta) postal – postcard

las direcciones – directions
a – to / away
¿a cuántas cuadras de _____?
   – how many blocks (away) from _____?
a cinco cuadras (de __) – 5 blocks away (from __)
al lado (de) – next to / to the side (of)
el lado – side
cerca (de) – near / close (to)
lejos (de) – far away (from)
arriba – up / above
abajo – down / below
a la vuelta – around the corner
adelante – ahead
atrás – back
detrás (de) – behind
enfrente (de) – across (from) / in front (of)
delante (de) – ahead (of) / in front (of)
entre – between / among
dobla a la izquierda – turn left
      a la derecha – turn right
sigue derecho – go straight
para / hacia – toward
quedar – to be located
¿Me puede(s) decir en dónde queda _____?
   – Can you tell me where _____ is located?
¿Me puede(s) decir cómo llegar a _____?
   – Can you tell me how to get to _____?

la rutina – routine
a menudo – often
a veces – sometimes
(casi) siempre – (almost) always
(casi) nunca – (almost) never
de vez en cuando – from time to time
frecuentemente – frequently
constantemente – constantly
normalmente – normally
generalmente – generally
en general / por lo general – in general
muchas veces – many times
pocas veces – not very often
raras veces / rara vez – rarely

past activities
hacer: (yo) hice – I did
      (tú) hiciste – you did
ir: (yo) fui – I went
   (tú) fuiste – you went
ver: (yo) vi – I saw
    (tú) viste – you saw
siguiente – following
   al día siguiente – the following day
   a la semana siguiente – the following week
anterior – previous
   la noche anterior – the previous night
anoche – last night
anteayer / antier – the day before yesterday
anteanoche – the night before last
ayer – yesterday
una vez – once / one time
dos veces – twice / two times
la última vez (que) – the last time (that)
la única vez (que) – the only time (that)
pasado/a – last / past
   el lunes pasado – last Monday
   la semana pasada – last week
   el fin de semana pasado – last weekend
hace + *tiempo* – _____ ago
   hace 3 años – 3 years ago
luego / más tarde – later
antes (de) – before
después (de) / luego (de) – after / afterward(s)
tarde – late
temprano – early
pronto – soon

otras palabras y frases útiles
¿Qué onda? – What's up?
¿Qué hay (de nuevo)? – What's new?
   Nada en especial. / No mucho. – Not much.
para – for (intended recipient)
para + *infinitivo* – in order *to* _____
empujar – to push
jalar / halar – to pull
crear – to create
el producto – product
los bienes – goods
los servicios – services
cambiar – to change / to exchange
la opción, *pl.* las opciones – option(s)
quizá(s) / a lo mejor – maybe
la capital – capital (of a city, state, country)

Unidad 12 (parte 1) – la vida escolar

las materias / las asignaturas – subjects
el alemán – German
el álgebra (*femenino*) – algebra
el arte (*masc.*), *pl.* las artes (*fem.*) – art, (the) arts
la banda – band
la biología – biology
el cálculo – calculus
el chino – Chinese
las ciencias – science(s)
el coro – choir
la clase de _____ – _____ class
la educación física – physical education
el español – Spanish
la física – physics
el francés – French
la geografía – geography
la geometría – geometry
la historia – history
el inglés – English
el idioma (*masculino*) / la lengua – language
el japonés – Japanese
la literatura – literature
    la novela – novel
las matemáticas – math
la música – music
la orquesta – orchestra
la química – chemistry
la tecnología – technology
difícil – difficult / hard
fácil – easy
la tarea – homework / task

los materiales escolares – school supplies
la agenda – daily planner
el armario / el casillero / el lóquer – locker
la bandera – flag
el borrador – eraser
la calculadora – calculator
la computadora / el ordenador – computer
el cuaderno – notebook
el diccionario – dictionary
la engrapadora / la grapadora – stapler
el escritorio – desk
el horario – schedule
el lápiz, *pl.* los lápices – pencil(s)
el libro – book
el mapa (*masculino*) – map
el marcador – marker
    de borrado seco – dry-erase marker
la mochila – backpack
el papel – paper

el pizarrón – whiteboard
la pluma / el bolígrafo – pen
el proyector – projector
el pupitre – student desk
el reloj – clock / watch
el (los) sacapuntas – pencil sharpener(s)
la silla – chair
el (los) sujetapapeles – paper clip(s)
la transparencia – transparency

las actividades extracurriculares
el anuario – yearbook
el club, *pl.* los clubs – club(s)
cuidar niños – to babysit
el equipo – team / equipment
el / la miembro (de) – member (of)
participar – to participate
el periódico – (the) newspaper
practicar deportes – to play sports
la reunión – meeting
tocar un instrumento – to play an instrument
trabajar como voluntario/a – to volunteer
el / la tutor/a – tutor

las personas – people / persons
el / la asistente/a – assistant / aide
el / la compañero/a de clase – classmate
el / la consejero/a – counselor
el / la director/a – principal
el / la enfermero/a – nurse
el / la estudiante – student
el / la maestro/a / docente – teacher
el / la secretario/a – secretary
la Sra., la Srta., el Sr. – Mrs., Miss, Mr.

los lugares – places
el ala (*femenino*), *pl.* las alas – wing(s)
el auditorio – auditorium
la biblioteca – library
la cafetería – cafeteria
el edificio – building
el escenario – stage
el gimnasio – gymnasium (gym)
el laboratorio – laboratory
la oficina – office
    de asistencia – attendance office
el piso – floor
el salón de clase / el aula (*femenino*) – classroom
el suelo – ground
el teatro – theater
la universidad (uni) – (the) university / college

¿Cuándo?

temprano – early
a tiempo – on time
tarde – late
antes (de) – before
después (de) – after / afterwards
durante – during
el período / el periodo – period (of time)
el bloque – block
el cuarto – quarter
el semestre – semester
el año – year
escolar – school (*adjective*)
pasado/a – last / past
próximo/a – next
anterior – previous
siguiente – following
empezar (e → ie) – to start / to begin
terminar – to end / to finish
en/por la mañana – in the morning
en/por la tarde – in the afternoon
en/por la noche – at night

la hora – time (of day) / hour

¿A qué hora _____? – At what time _____?
  A la una, a las dos, etc. – At one o'clock, etc.
    y cuarto – quarter past the hour
    y media – half past the hour
  A la una (y) cuarenta y cinco – At 1:45
  A las cuatro (y) quince – At 4:15
de la mañana – in the morning
de la tarde – in the afternoon
de la noche – at night
en punto – on the dot
primero/a (1º / 1ª) – first (1st)
  el primer cuarto (*masculino, singular*)
segundo/a (2º / 2ª) – second (2nd)
tercero/a (3º / 3ª) – third (3rd)
  el tercer cuarto (*masculino, singular*)
cuarto/a (4º / 4ª) – fourth (4th)
quinto/a (5º / 5ª) – fifth (5th)
sexto/a (6º / 6ª) – sixth (6th)
séptimo/a (7º / 7ª) – seventh (7th)
octavo/a (8º / 8ª) – eighth (8th)
noveno/a (9º / 9ª) – ninth (9th)
décimo/a (10º / 10ª) – tenth (10th)
último/a – last / final
el minuto – minute
el segundo – second
el momento – moment
el rato – a small amount of time (a bit)
  Te veo al rato. – I'll see you in a bit.

las acciones

aprender – to learn
conocer (c → zc) – to know (personally)
contestar / responder – to answer
devolver (o → ue) – to return (an item)
enseñar – to teach
entregar – to turn in / to hand in
escribir – to write
estudiar – to study
hablar – to speak / to talk
hacer (una presentación) – to do (a presentation)
hacer una pregunta – to ask a question
hacer fila / hacer cola – to line up / to form a line
jugar (u → ue) – to play
leer – to read
llegar – to arrive
necesitar – to need
repartir – to pass out / to hand out / to distribute
saber (yo sé) – to know (information, facts)
sacar buenas notas – to get good grades
sacar malas notas – to get bad grades
sacar una (foto)copia – to make a (photo)copy
salir (de) – to leave / to go out (from)
tomar/presentar un examen – to take a test
tomar apuntes / sacar apuntes – to take notes
traer – to bring
usar – to use
se permite + *infinitivo* – _____ing is permitted
se prohíbe + *infinitivo* – _____ing is prohibited

otras palabras útiles

la actividad – activity
el capítulo – chapter
la composición – composition
la copia (maestra) – (master) copy
el ejercicio – exercise
el ensayo – essay
la escritura – writing
el examen / la prueba – test / quiz
el informe / el reportaje – report
la lección – lesson
la lectura – reading
la página – page
el párrafo – paragraph
la pregunta – question
el problema (*masculino*) – problem
el proyecto – project
requerir (e → ie) (e → i) – to require
el requisito – requirement
la respuesta – answer / response
la rúbrica / la directriz – rubric
la unidad – unit

Unidad 12 (parte 2) – la vida profesional

los títulos profesionales – professional titles	el campo – field
el / la abogado/a – lawyer / attorney	el derecho – law
el / la arquitecto/a – architect	la arquitectura – architecture
el / la médico/a – medical doctor	la medicina – medicine
el / la pediatra – pediatrician	la pediatría – pediatrics
el / la gineco-obstetra – OB/GYN	la ginecología-la obstetricia – too long ☺
el / la cirujano/a – surgeon	la cirugía – surgery
el / la anestesiólogo/a – anesthesiologist	la anestesia – anesthesia
el / la oftalmólogo/a – ophthalmologist	la oftalmología – ophthalmology
el / la optometrista – optometrist	la optometría – optometry
el / la ortodoncista – orthodontist	la ortodoncia – orthodontia
el / la dentista / odontólogo/a – dentist	la odontología – dentistry
el / la quiropráctico/a – chiropractor	la quiropráctica – chiropractic
el / la terapeuta / terapista – therapist	la terapia – therapy
el / la masajista – massage therapist	el masaje – massage
el / la nutricionista / dietista – nutritionist / dietitian	la nutrición – nutrition
el / la enfermero/a – nurse	la enfermería – nursing
el / la veterinario/a – veterinarian	la veterinaria – veterinary medicine
el / la psiquiatra – psychiatrist	la psiquiatría – psychiatry
el / la psicólogo/a – psychologist	la psicología – psychology
el / la consejero/a – counselor / advisor	la consejería – counseling
de finanzas – financial advisor	de finanzas – financial counseling
el / la científico/a – scientist	las ciencias – science(s)
el / la antropólogo/a – anthropologist	la antropología – anthropology
el / la biólogo/a – biologist	la biología – biology
el / la bioquímico/a – biochemist	la bioquímica – biochemistry
el / la químico/a – chemist	la química – chemistry
el / la farmacéutico/a / farmaceuta – pharmacist	la farmacología – pharmacology
el / la físico/a – physicist	la física – physics
el / la arqueólogo/a – archeologist	la arqueología – archeology
el / la gerente/a – manager	la gestión – management
el / la supervisor/a – supervisor	la supervisión – supervision
el / la jefe/a – boss	la jefatura / el liderazgo – leadership
el / la dueño/a – owner	la propiedad – ownership / property
el / la secretario/a – secretary	la secretaría – secretariat
el / la recepcionista – receptionist	la recepción – reception
el / la asistente/a – assistant	la asistencia – assistance
de oficina – office assistant	
médico/a – medical assistant	
el / la administrador/a – administrator	la administración – administration
el / la ingeniero/a – engineer	la ingeniería – engineering
eléctrico/a – electrical engineer	eléctrica – electrical engineering
mecánico/a – mechanical engineer	mecánica – mechanical engineering
el / la matemático/a – mathematician	las matemáticas – mathematics
el / la estadístico/a – statistician	la estadística – statistics
el / la actuario/a de seguros – actuary	el análisis de riesgos – risk analysis
el / la economista – economist	la economía – economy
el / la contador/a – accountant	la contabilidad – accounting
el / la analista – analyst	el análisis – analysis
el / la programador/a – programmer	la programación – programming

el / la investigador/a – investigator

el / la policía (poli) – police officer

el / la detective – detective
    privado/a – private detective

el / la diseñador/a – designer
    gráfico/a – graphic designer
    (de) web – web (www.) designer

el / la desarrollador/a – developer
    de aplicaciones – app developer
    de software – software developer

el / la técnico/a – technician

el / la informático/a – computer expert

el / la tecnólogo/a – tech expert
    en sistemas (de información) – IT tech

el / la traductor/a – translator (written)

el / la intérprete – interpreter (verbal)

el / la lingüista – linguist

el / la artista – artist

el / la músico/a – musician

el actor / la actriz – actor / actress

el / la cantante – singer

el / la cantautor/a – singer-songwriter

el / la escritor/a – writer

el / la autor/a – author

el / la poeta – poet

el / la pintor/a – painter

el / la modelo – model

el / la periodista – journalist

el / la plomero/a – plumber

el / la contratista – contractor

el / la electricista – electrician

el / la mecánico/a – mechanic
    de automóviles (autos) – auto mechanic

el / la jardinero/a – gardener / landscaper

el / la conserje – janitor / custodian

el / la obrero/a – laborer (usually manual)

el / la trabajador/a – worker (any)

el / la empleado/a – employee

el / la especialista – specialist

el / la cajero/a – cashier / bank teller

el / la emprendedor/a – entrepreneur

el / la mesero/a – waiter / waitress

el / la cocinero/a – cook / chef

el / la experto/a / perito/a – expert

el / la agente – agent

el / la empresario/a – business man/woman

el / la vendedor/a – salesperson

el / la estético/a – esthetician / beautician

el / la peluquero/a – barber / hairdresser

el departamento de _____ – _____ department
    recursos humanos – human resources dept.
    servicio al cliente – customer service dept.

---

la investigación – research / investigation

la policía (poli) – (the) police / policing

las investigaciones reservadas – investigation

el diseño – design
    gráfico – graphic design
    (de) web – web design

el desarrollo – development
    de aplicaciones – app development
    de software – software development

la informática / la computación – computing

la tecnología – technology
    en sistemas (de información) – IT

la traducción – translation (written)

la interpretación – interpretation (verbal)

la lingüística – linguistics

el arte (*masc.*), *pl.* las artes (*fem.*) – art, (the) arts

la música – music

el cine (cinema), el teatro, la televisión, etc.

la música – music

la escritura – writing

la literatura – literature

la poesía – poetry

la pintura – painting

la moda – fashion

el periodismo – journalism

la plomería – plumbing

la contratación – contracting

la electricidad – electricity

la mecánica – mechanics
    de automóviles (autos) – auto mechanics

la jardinería – gardening / landscaping

la limpieza – cleaning

la obra / la labor – labor

el trabajo / la chamba – work / job

el empleo – employment

la especialidad – specialty

la caja – cash register

(trabajar) por cuenta propia – self-employed

el servicio – service

la gastronomía – gastronomy

la pericia – expertise

la agencia – agency

los negocios – business

las ventas – sales

la estética – esthetics / beauty

la peluquería – hairdressing

el personal – personnel

otras personas y organizaciones – other people and organizations

el / la cliente/a – client / customer
el / la oficial – official
el club rotario – rotary club
la ONG (organización no gubernamental) – NGO (non-governmental organization)
sin fines de lucro – not-for-profit / non-profit
la empresa – business / company
la sociedad anónima (S. A.) – corporation (Inc.)
el gobierno – (the) government
    federal – federal
    estatal – state
    municipal – city / municipal

el / la colega – colleague
el / la socio/a – associate / partner
trabajar como voluntario/a – to volunteer

rentable – profitable
la compañía – large company

gubernamental – governmental
el país – (the) country
el estado – (the) state
la ciudad – (the) city
el condado – (the) county

los materiales de oficina – office supplies

la agenda – daily planner
el bloc de notas – notepad
el borrador – eraser
la calculadora – calculator
la cinta adhesiva – adhesive tape
la computadora / el ordenador – computer
el cuaderno – notebook
el documento – document
la engrapadora / la grapadora – stapler
el escritorio – desk
la fotocopiadora – photocopier
el horario – schedule
la impresora – printer
el lápiz, *pl.* los lápices – pencil(s)
el maletín, *pl.* los maletines – briefcase(s)
la máquina de fax – fax machine
el marcador – marker
el pizarrón – whiteboard
la pluma / el bolígrafo – pen
el proyector – projector
el reloj – clock / watch
el (los) sacapuntas – pencil sharpener(s)
la silla – chair
el (los) sujetapapeles – paper clip(s)
la transparencia – transparency

los idiomas más comunes

el alemán – German
el árabe – Arabic
el bengalí – Bengali
el chino – Chinese
    el mandarín – Mandarin
    el cantonés – Cantonese
el español – Spanish
el francés – French
el hindi – Hindi
el inglés – English
el italiano – Italian
el japonés – Japanese
el portugués – Portuguese
el ruso – Russian
la lengua de signos/señas – sign language
el lenguaje corporal – body language

otras palabras y frases útiles

dedicarse (a) – to dedicate oneself (to)
¿A qué te dedicas? – What do you do for work?
    Me dedico a la ingeniería. / Soy ingeniera.
(la) oferta y (la) demanda – supply and demand
el salón de _____ – _____ room
    descanso – break room
    conferencias – conference room
renunciar (a) – to quit (a job)
tomar una decisión – to make a decision
el currículum / la hoja de vida – résumé / CV
la entrevista – interview
las prestaciones – employment benefits
la base de datos – database
el cubículo – cubicle
el tiempo / el plazo – time
el puesto / la plaza – position
    de tiempo completo – full-time position
    de tiempo parcial – part-time position
¡Gusto en verte! – Nice to see you!

la hora – time (of day) / hour

¿A qué hora _____? – At what time _____?
    A la una, a las dos, etc. – At one o'clock, etc.
        y cuarto – quarter past the hour
        y media – half past the hour
    A la una (y) cuarenta y cinco – At 1:45
    A las cuatro (y) quince – At 4:15
de la mañana – in the morning
de la tarde – in the afternoon
de la noche – at night

Unidad 13 – la rutina diaria

la rutina diaria – daily routine
acostarse (o → ue) – to lie down
afeitarse / rasurarse (las piernas) – to shave
almorzar (o → ue) – to eat lunch
amarrarse los zapatos – to tie one's shoes
bañarse – to take a bath
cenar – to eat dinner
cepillarse (el pelo, los dientes) – to brush
desayunar – to eat breakfast
el despertador – alarm clock
despertarse (e → ie) – to wake up
    estar despierto/a – to be awake
dormir (o → ue) (o → u) – to sleep
    roncar – to snore
dormirse (o → ue) (o → u) – to fall asleep
    estar dormido/a – to be asleep
ducharse – to shower
la higiene – hygiene
irse (de) / marcharse (de) – to leave (from)
lavarse (la cara, las manos, los dientes)
    – to wash one's _____
levantarse – to get up
maquillarse – to put on makeup
    desmaquillarse – to take off one's makeup
peinarse (el pelo) – to comb
prepararse / alistarse (para) – to get ready (for)
regresar – to return
salir (de) – to leave / to go out (from)
secarse (el pelo, el cuerpo) – to dry one's _____
soler (o → ue) + *inf.* – to be in the habit of _*ing*
vestirse (e → i) (e → i) (de) – to get dressed
    desvestirse – to get undressed

la música – music
la banda – band
tocar – to play (an instrument)
la canción – song
cantar – to sing
el coro – choir / chorus
la orquesta – orchestra
el instrumento musical – musical instrument
    el clarinete – clarinet
    el contrabajo – upright bass / double bass
    la flauta – flute
    el piano – piano
    el saxofón – saxophone
    el tambor – drum
        la batería – drums (drum kit)
    la trompeta – trumpet
    el violín – violin

las actividades extracurriculares
participar (en) – to participate (in)
el anuario – yearbook
las artes marciales – martial arts
el club, *pl.* los clubs – club(s)
el consejo estudiantil – student council
cuidar niños – to babysit
los deportes – sports
    el atletismo – track and field
    el béisbol – baseball
    el hockey – hockey
    el sófbol – softball
    el fútbol – soccer
    el fútbol americano – football
    el básquetbol – basketball
    el voleibol – volleyball
    la natación – swimming
    el golf – golf
entrenar – to train
el equipo (de _____) – (_____) team
jugar (u → ue) – to play (a sport, a game)
levantar pesas – to lift weights
montar en bicicleta (bici) – to ride a bicycle
nadar – to swim
practicar – to practice
el periódico (de la escuela) – newspaper
repartir – to pass out / to hand out
ser miembro (de) – to be a member (of)
trabajar como voluntario/a – to volunteer
el / la tutor/a – tutor
agarrar / coger – to grab

la hora – time (of day) / hour
¿A qué hora? – At what time?
a las siete (y) cincuenta – At 7:50
al diez para las ocho – At 7:50
a las ocho menos diez – At 7:50
a eso de las ocho – at about 8:00
alrededor de las ocho – at around 8:00
como a las ocho – like at 8:00
y media – :30
y cuarto – :15
menos cuarto – 15 minutes to the hour
antes de + *infinitivo* – before _____*ing*
después de + *infinitivo* – after _____*ing*
durante – during
mientras – while
el momento – moment
a la vez / al mismo tiempo – at the same time

palabras de acción habitual (el presente)
(casi) siempre – (almost) always
(casi) nunca – (almost) never
(casi) todos los días – (almost) every day
(casi) todo el tiempo – (almost) all the time
a veces – sometimes
muchas veces – many times
a menudo – often
de vez en cuando – from time to time
constantemente – constantly
normalmente – normally
usualmente – usually
frecuentemente – frequently
generalmente – generally
por lo general – in general / generally
en general – in general
los lunes – (on) Mondays
los fines de semana – (on) the weekends
cada sábado – each Saturday / every Saturday
cada día – each day / every day

palabras claves que indican el pretérito
anoche – last night
anteayer / antier – the day before yesterday
anteanoche – the night before last
ayer – yesterday
siguiente – following
   al día siguiente – the following day
   a la semana siguiente – the following week
anterior – previous
   la noche anterior – the previous night
una vez – once / one time
dos veces – twice / two times
la última vez (que) – the last time (that)
la única vez (que) – the only time (that)
hace + *tiempo* – _____ ago
   hace 3 semanas – 3 weeks ago
   hace 4 años – 4 years ago
pasado/a – last / past
   el miércoles pasado – last Wednesday
   la semana pasada – last week
   el fin de semana pasado – last weekend
luego / más tarde – later
antes (de) – before
después (de) / luego (de) – after / afterward(s)
tarde – late
temprano – early
pronto – soon

otras palabras y expresiones útiles
tener que ver (con) – to have to do (with)
depender (de) – to depend (on)
   depende del día – depends on the day
estar de buen humor – to be in a good mood
estar de mal humor – to be in a bad mood
pero – but
porque – because
   Llegué tarde porque salí de casa tarde.
como – since / given that (to start a sentence)
   Como salí de casa tarde, llegué tarde.
mismo/a – same
por lo menos – at least
con – with
sin – without
sin + *infinitivo* – without _____ ing
el secador – hair dryer
la toalla – towel
final – final
el final – (the) end
al final – at the end

Unidad 14 – la ropa

las prendas de vestir – articles of clothing
el abrigo – coat
la bata – bathrobe
la blusa – blouse
la bolsa – purse / bag
las botas – boots
la bufanda – scarf
el calcetín, *pl.* los calcetines – sock(s)
la camisa – shirt
la camiseta – T-shirt
la cartera – wallet
el chaleco – vest
    salvavidas – life vest / life jacket
la chamarra / la chaqueta – jacket
las chanclas / las sandalias – sandals
el cinturón / el cinto – belt
    la hebilla – buckle
la corbata – tie / necktie
el esmoquin – tuxedo
la falda – skirt
la gorra / la cachucha – hat (with visor) / ball cap
el gorro – hat (without visor)
los guantes – gloves
los jeans – jeans (pronounced as in English)
la joyería – jewelry / jewelry store
    el anillo – ring
    el arete / el pendiente – earring
    el brazalete / la pulsera – bracelet
    el collar – necklace
las manoplas – mittens
los mocasines – dress shoes / loafers
los pantalones – pants
    los (pantalones) cortos – shorts
    deportivos – sweatpants / athletic pants
las pantuflas – slippers
el pañuelo – handkerchief
el pijama / la piyama – pajamas
la ropa – clothing / clothes
el saco – sports jacket (suit jacket)
el sombrero – hat (with full brim)
la (camisa) sudadera – sweatshirt
el suéter – sweater
    de cuello alto – turtle-neck sweater
el traje – suit
el traje de baño / el bañador – bathing suit
el vestido – dress
los zapatos – shoes
    de tacón alto – high-heel shoes
los (zapatos de) tenis – tennis shoes

las partes de la ropa
el bolsillo – pocket
el botón – button
la capucha – hood
el cierre – zipper
la costura – seam
el cuello – collar
la manga (corta, larga) – (short, long) sleeve

las descripciones
apretado/a / ajustado/a – tight
cómodo/a – comfortable
corto/a – short
elegante – elegant / fancy / formal
flojo/a / suelto/a – baggy / loose
incómodo/a – uncomfortable
largo/a – long
sencillo/a – simple / casual / every-day
estar de moda – to be in fashion/style
llevar / portar – to carry
llevar (puesto/a) – to wear (clarifies ambiguity)
ponerse – to put on (oneself)
probarse (o → ue) – to try on (oneself)
quitarse – to take off (oneself)
usar – to use / to wear (a specific size)
verse – to look (as in, "How do I look?")
vestirse (e → i) (e → i) (de) – to get dressed

los comparativos – comparatives
más + *adjetivo* + que – more _____ than
menos + *adjetivo* + que – less _____ than
mejor que – better than
peor que – worse than
tan + *adjetivo* + como – as _____ as

sizes
el número (de zapatos) – size (in numbers)
la etiqueta – tag / label
la talla – size (official size from a tag)
    extra grande (XG) – extra large
    grande (G) – large
    mediana (M) – medium
    chica (C) – small
    extra chica (XC) – extra small
    unitalla – one size fits all
el tamaño – size (general – house, cat, etc.)
grande – large
mediano/a – medium
pequeño/a – small

fabrics, patterns, colors
la tela / el tejido – fabric
el algodón – cotton
el cuero / la piel – leather / hide
la lana – wool
la lona – canvas
la mezclilla – denim
el nilón – nylon
la pana – corduroy
el plástico – plastic
el poliéster – polyester
el rayón – rayon
la seda – silk
sintético/a – synthetic
el diseño / el patrón – design / pattern
de cuadros – checkered / plaid
de rayas – striped
floreado/a – floral / flowery
liso/a – straight / smooth / plain
¿De qué es _____? – What is _____ made of?
   Es de _____. – It's made of _____.
¿De qué color es _____? – What color is _____?
   La camisa es morada claro. (*claro* modifies *color*)
   La camisa es de un color morado oscuro.

de compras
el / la cajero/a – cashier
el / la vendedor/a – salesperson
el catálogo – catalog
el producto – product
desear – to desire / to want
buscar – to look for
encontrar (o → ue) – to find
escoger – to choose
costar (o → ue) – to cost
comprar – to buy / to purchase
vender – to sell
pagar – to pay (for)
devolver (o → ue) – to return (an item)
el cheque – check
(el dinero en) efectivo – cash (money)
la tarjeta de crédito (débito) – credit (debit) card
barato/a (una ganga) – cheap (a bargain)
caro/a (un robo) – expensive (a ripoff)
nuevo/a – new
de segunda mano (usado/a) – second-hand (used)
la tienda de segunda mano – second-hand store
la liquidación – clearance / liquidation
estar en liquidación – to be on clearance
la tienda de descuentos – discount store
el descuento / la rebaja – sale
estar de descuento/rebaja – to be on sale

la tienda de ropa – clothing store
la zapatería – shoe store
para mí, ti, ella, nosotros – for me, you, her, us
por 30 dólares – for 30 dollars
el / la costurero/a – seamster / seamstress
el / la sastre/a – tailor (mainly for men's clothing)
sin compromiso – without any commitment (to buy)

los adjetivos demostrativos – demonstrative adj.
este (*masc.*) / esta (*fem.*) / esto (*neutro*) – this
estos / estas – these
ese / esa / eso – that (nearer than *aquel*)
esos / esas – those
aquel / aquella / aquello – that (farther than *ese*)
aquellos / aquellas – those

el clima (*masculino*) / el tiempo – the weather
hace (mucho) calor – it's (really) hot
hace (mucho) frío – it's (really) cold
hace (mucho) viento – it's (really) windy
hace (mucho) sol – it's (really) sunny
hace (muy) buen tiempo – it's (very) nice out
está (muy) nublado – it's (very) cloudy
llover (o → ue) (la lluvia) – to rain
nevar (e → ie) (la nieve) – to snow
lloviznar (la llovizna) – to drizzle
granizar (el granizo) – to hail
la tormenta – storm

otras palabras y expresiones útiles
parecer (c → zc) – to seem (like)
¿Qué te parece? – What do you think (of it)?
   Me parece bien. – It seems fine.
   Me parece flojo/a. – It seems loose.
quedar – to fit
¿Cómo te queda? – How does it fit you?
   Me queda bien. – It fits fine.
   Me queda un poco flojo/a. – It fits a little loose.
el cesto de la ropa sucia – dirty-clothes hamper
el piso / el suelo – floor / ground
la fiesta / la pachanga / el reventón – party / blowout
colgar (o → ue) – to hang (up)
guardar – to put away / to keep
otro/a – other / another
¡Qué + *adjetivo*! – How _____!
alguien – someone
nadie – no one
      – anyone (in a negative sentence)
todo el mundo – everyone
por todas partes – everywhere
la parte superior – the top (part)
la parte inferior – the bottom (part)

Unidad 15 – la alimentación y los restaurantes

los alimentos y las bebidas – food and drinks

el aceite de oliva – olive oil
el aderezo – salad dressing (thick)
el agua embotellada – bottled water
el agua purificada – purified water
el aliño – salad dressing (vinegar, oil)
el arroz – rice
la avena – oats
el (la) azúcar – sugar
el bistec – steak
la carne de res – beef
el cerdo / el puerco – pork / pig
el chile – spicy pepper (sauce)
el chorizo – a type of spicy sausage
la crema – sour cream / whipped cream
la ensalada (de) – salad
las especias – spices
el frijol (pinto, negro) – (pinto, black) bean
la fruta – fruit
el helado / la nieve – ice cream
el hielo – ice
el huevo – egg
el jugo / el zumo – juice
la leche – milk
el licuado / el batido – smoothie
el marisco – shellfish
la paleta – popsicle
el pastel / la torta / la tarta – cake
el pescado – fish (prepared)
el pollo – chicken
el postre – dessert
el maíz / el elote – corn
el pan – bread
la papa / la patata – potato
la papita – potato chip
el pimiento – (bell) pepper
el queso (rallado) – (shredded) cheese
el refresco / la soda / la gaseosa – soft drink
la sal y la pimienta – salt and (black) pepper
la salchicha – sausage / hot dog
la salsa (picante) – (hot) sauce
la sazón, *pl.* las sazones – seasoning(s)
la sopa / el caldo (de) – soup / broth
la tapa / el antojito – finger food
el tocino – bacon
la tortilla de harina – flour tortilla
la tortilla de maíz – corn tortilla
la tortilla dorada – taco shell
la tortilla española (de patatas) – like a quiche
el totopo – tortilla chip
el trigo – wheat

las descripciones y las acciones

algo – something
asqueroso/a – disgusting / gross
    ¡Qué asco! / ¡Guácala! – Yuck!
beber / tomar – to drink
bravo/a – very spicy (hot)
bueno/a – good
caliente – hot (temperature)
chupar – to suck
crujiente / crispi – crunchy / crispy
delicioso/a / rico/a – delicious
dulce – sweet
engullir – to gobble down / to gulp down
eructar – to burp
escupir – to spit
estar – to be (based on your experience)
frío/a – cold
grasoso/a – fatty
    la grasa – fat / grease
incluir (y) – to include
lamer / lamber – to lick
malo/a – bad
masticar – to chew
merendar (e → ie) – to snack at midday
    la merienda – afternoon snack
mismo/a – same
morder (o → ue) – to bite
    la mordida / el mordisco – bite
oler (o → hue) – to smell
    huele(n) (a) – smell(s) (like)
el olor (a) – smell (of)
el pedazo / el trozo – piece / chunk
picante / picoso/a – spicy (medium)
el plato (principal) – (main) dish
probar (o → ue) – to taste / to try
la ración / la porción – portion / side
saborear – to taste / to savor
sabe(n) (a) – taste(s) (like)
sabroso/a / bueno/a – tasty
salado/a – salty
satisfacer (conjugates like *hacer*) – to satisfy
satisfecho/a / lleno/a – satisfied / full
soso/a / insípido/a – bland
ser – to be (characteristics)
tener (mucha) hambre – to be (really) hungry
    estar hambriento/a – to be hungry
tener (mucha) sed – to be (really) thirsty
    estar sediento/a – to be thirsty
tibio/a – warm
tragar(se) – to swallow
vomitar – to vomit

la preparación – preparation

afilado/a / filoso/a – sharp (blade)
agregar / añadir – to add
asado/a – broiled / grilled / rotisserie
casero/a – homemade
cocinado/a / cocido/a – cooked
cocinar / cocer (o → ue) (c → z) – to cook
con – with
congelado/a – frozen
congelar – to freeze
cortar – to cut
crudo/a – raw
la cucharada – teaspoonful
descongelar – to thaw
echar – to throw on, in, or out
enlatado/a – canned
faltar – to be missing
freír (e → í) (e →) – to fry
fresco/a – fresh
frito/a – fried
fundido/a – melted
hecho/a a mano – made by hand
al horno – baked
hornear – to bake
la lata – can
lavar – to wash
molido/a – ground (up)
la olla – pot
a la parrilla – grilled / barbequed
picar / triturar – to chop (up) / to dice
poner a fuego lento – to let simmer
preparar – to prepare
puntiagudo/a – sharp (point / tip)
quemado/a – burnt / burned
quemar – to burn
relleno/a – stuffed
revuelto/a – scrambled
el (la) sartén – frying pan / skillet
sazonar – to season
sin – without

el tiempo y el espacio (las preposiciones)

alrededor (de) – around
antes (de) – before
debajo (de) – below / underneath
detrás (de) – behind
en – in / on / at
encima (de) / sobre – on top (of)
enfrente (de) / delante (de) – in front (of)
entre – between / among
en seguida – next / immediately following
luego (de) / después (de) – after / afterward(s)

el restaurante – restaurant

a la carta – a la carte (by itself)
el aperitivo / el entremés – appetizer
la caja para llevar – to-go box / doggy bag
los cubiertos – silverware
    la cuchara – spoon
    el cuchillo – knife
    el tenedor – fork
la cuenta – (the) bill / (the) check
dar (yo doy) – to give
derramar – to spill out / to spill over
la especialidad de la casa – house special
llevar – to carry / to take (from here to there)
llevarse – to take with (oneself)
el mantel – tablecloth
el / la mesero/a – server (waiter / waitress)
    el / la camarero/a – server (waiter / waitress)
el menú / la carta – menu
el mostrador – counter
pasar (la sal) – to pass (the salt)
pagar (por) – to pay (for) / to pay for
pagar $30 por ____ – to pay $30 for ____
para llevar – to-go / for carry-out
pedir (e → i) (e → i) – to order / to request
por favor – please
el platillo – saucer
el plato del día – special of the day
el popote / la paja / el pitillo – straw
la propina – tip / gratuity
la servilleta – napkin
servir (e → i) (e → i) – to serve
sobrar – to be too much
las sobras – leftovers
el tamaño – size
la taza – cup
el tazón – bowl
traer – to bring (from there to here)
los trastes / los platos – dishes
el vaso – glass
verter (e → ie) – to pour / to spill

otras palabras y expresiones útiles

Se me hace agua la boca. – It makes my mouth water.
Es para chuparse los dedos. – It's finger-licking good.
Se me antoja(n) _____. – I'm in the mood for _____.
Me apetece(n) ___. – ___ sound(s) appetizing to me.
abrir el apetito – to whet one's appetite
¿Qué hay de comer? – What is there to eat?
¿Qué hay de postre? – What's for dessert?
una mesa para 4 – a table for 4
Yo quisiera ___ / Me gustaría ___ – I would like ___
¿Me pudiera traer ____? – Could you bring me ____?

Unidad 16 – los deportes, los juegos y las diversiones

los deportes – sports

el atletismo – track and field
el básquetbol / el baloncesto – basketball
el béisbol – baseball
el billar – billiards / pool
el boliche – bowling
el ciclismo – cycling
el clavadismo – diving
el cross – cross country
el fútbol (sóquer) – soccer
el fútbol americano – (American) football
la gimnasia – gymnastics
el golf – golf
el hockey – hockey (pronounced as in English)
el lacrosse – lacrosse
la lucha libre – wrestling
la natación – swimming
las porras / la animación – cheerleading
el ráquetbol – racquetball
el rugby – rugby
el sófbol – softball
el voleibol – volleyball

las acciones

anotar un punto/tanto – to score a point
atrapar / cachar – to catch
batear – to bat
calentarse (e → ie) – to warm up / to get warmed up
    el calentamiento – warm-up
competir (e → i) (e → i) – to compete
correr – to run
derrapar – to slide
entrenar – to train / to practice
esquiar (i → í) – to ski
estirarse (los músculos) – to stretch (one's muscles)
    el estiramiento – stretching
hacer clavados – to dive
jugar (u → ue) – to play (sports)
lanzar – to throw / to pitch
levantar pesas – to lift weights
luchar – to fight / to struggle / to wrestle
meter un gol, cesto – to score a goal, basket
montar en bicicleta – to ride a bicycle
nadar – to swim
patear – to kick
patinar sobre hielo, ruedas – to ice, roller skate
pegar / golpear / dar – to hit
practicar – to practice / to play (sports)
sacar la pelota – to serve the ball
saltar / brincar – to jump
tirar – to shoot (basketball, soccer, etc.) / to throw

el equipo – equipment

el balón, *pl.* los balones – (big, inflatable) ball(s)
el bate – bat
la bola (de boliche, de billar) – ball (solid)
la cancha / el campo – court / field
el casco – helmet
el disco de hockey – hockey puck
el esquí, *pl.* los esquíes – ski(s)
el guante (de béisbol) – (baseball) glove
el palo (de golf, de hockey, etc.) – club / stick
el patín, *pl.* los patines – skate(s)
la pelota (de tenis) – (tennis) ball
las pesas – weights
la piscina (pisci) / la alberca – swimming pool
la pista – (race) track / (skating, hockey) rink
la portería – goal (soccer, hockey, etc.)
los protectores – pads
la raqueta (de tenis) – (tennis) racket
la red – net
el tablero – board (diving, chess, etc.)
el uniforme – uniform
los zapatos con clavos / los tacos – cleats

la liga – league

el campeón / la campeona – champion
el campeonato / la final – championship / (the) finals
la competencia – meet / competition
contra – against
la derrota – defeat / loss
derrotar / vencer (c → z) – to defeat
empatar – to tie
el empate – tie
el error – error
ganar – to win / to earn
mundial – world (*adjective*)
el mundo – world
el partido – game / match
el penalti – penalty
perder (e → ie) – to lose
premiar – to award
el premio – prize / award
retar / desafiar (i → í) – to challenge
el reto / el desafío – challenge
la rivalidad – rivalry
la temporada – (sports) season
    la postemporada – postseason / playoffs
el torneo – tournament
el triunfo – triumph
triunfar – to triumph
el trofeo – trophy
la victoria – victory / win

los juegos y las diversiones – fun and games
apostar (o → ue) – to bet
la apuesta – bet
la diversión – fun (*noun*)
(jugar a) el ajedrez – chess
(jugar a) las damas – checkers
(jugar a) las cartas – cards
(jugar a) el juego de mesa – board game
el desfile – parade
la exposición (expo) (de arte) – (art) exhibit
(hacer) un crucigrama (*masc.*) – crossword puzzle
(hacer) un pícnic – picnic
(hacer) un rompecabezas – puzzle
tocar un instrumento – to play an instrument
la obra de teatro – (theatrical) play
ensayar – to rehearse / to try out (for something)
la fiesta de disfraces – costume party
el disfraz, *pl.* los disfraces – costume(s)
la música clásica – classical music
la música rock – rock music
el concierto – concert
(la música) en vivo / en directo – live (music)
el disco compacto / el cidí – compact disc / CD
el archivo de mp3 – mp3 file
el video/vídeo musical – music video
aburrirse – to get bored
divertirse (e → ie) (e → i) – to have fun
pasarlo bien, mal – to have a good, bad time

las personas
el / la árbitro/a – referee / umpire
el / la atleta – athlete
el / la ciclista – cyclist
el / la clavadista – diver
el / la entrenador/a – coach / trainer
el / la fan / hincha / aficionado/a – fan
el / la jugador/a – player
el / la miembro (de) – member (of)
el / la nadador/a – swimmer
el / la porrista / animador/a – cheerleader
el equipo – team

las descripciones
alegre / feliz – happy
chévere / chido/a – cool / sweet / awesome
divertido/a – fun (*adjective*)
estupendo/a – stupendous
genial – cool / brilliant
lento/a – slow
lentamente / despacio – slowly
rápido/a – fast / quick
rápidamente – quickly
lo máximo / la leche – the best/coolest thing

los números ordinales – ordinal numbers
primero/a (1º / 1ª) – first (1st)
    el primer cuarto (*masculino, singular*)
segundo/a (2º / 2ª) – second (2nd)
tercero/a (3º / 3ª) – third (3rd)
    el tercer cuarto (*masculino, singular*)
cuarto/a (4º / 4ª) – fourth (4th)
quinto/a (5º / 5ª) – fifth (5th)
sexto/a (6º / 6ª) – sixth (6th)
séptimo/a (7º / 7ª) – seventh (7th)
octavo/a (8º / 8ª) – eighth (8th)
noveno/a (9º / 9ª) – ninth (9th)
décimo/a (10º / 10ª) – tenth (10th)
último/a – last / final

non-action verbs in the preterite
poder: (yo) pude – I succeeded / managed to
    no pude – I failed to
querer: (yo) quise – I wanted / attempted to
    no quise – I didn't want / I refused to
saber: (yo) supe – I found out
    no supe – I didn't find out
tener: (yo) tuve – I got / received
    no tuve – I didn't get / receive
    (yo) tuve que – I had (was forced) to
    no tuve que – I didn't end up having to

otras palabras y expresiones útiles
Deséame suerte. – Wish me luck.
¡Buena suerte! – Good luck!
¡Qué horror! – How awful! / How terrible!
¡Qué desastre! – What a disaster!
¡Qué bueno/bien! – Good! / Great!
Ándale (pues). – Get to it (then).
¡Ánimo! – Come on! (encouragement) / Cheer up!
¡Échale ganas! – Give it all you got! / Do your best!
al fin de cuentas … – when it was all over …
de todas formas – anyway / anyhow
    de todos modos – anyway / anyhow
    de todas maneras – anyway / anyhow
Te toca a ti. – It's your turn.
Le toca a Mario. – It's Mario's turn.
digo – I mean (self correction)
tener que ver (con) – to have to do (with)
¿Cómo te va? – How is it going for you?
    (Todo) me va bien. – (Everything) is going well for me.
¿Cómo te fue? – How did it go for you?
    (Todo) me fue bien. – It (all) went well for me.
bastante – quite / rather (*adverb*), enough (*adjective*)
¡Basta (ya)! – That's enough (already)! / Stop it!
tener tiempo de + *infinitivo* – to have time *to* _____
para + *infinitivo* – in order *to* _____

Unidad 17 – la niñez y la juventud

las descripciones
el niño / el chamaco – boy / child
la niña / la chamaca – girl / child
el / la vecino/a – neighbor
amable – kind / nice
antipático/a – mean
artístico/a – artistic
atrevido/a – daring
callado/a – quiet / not talkative
chistoso/a – funny
codo/a / tacaño/a – cheap / stingy
consentido/a – spoiled
deportista – athletic
desobediente – disobedient
(bien) educado/a – well mannered
egoísta – selfish
flojo/a / perezoso/a – lazy
generoso/a – generous
impaciente – impatient
joven – young
maleducado/a – rude
(hermano) mayor – older (brother)
(hermana) menor – younger (sister)
molesto/a / molestoso/a – annoying
obediente – obedient
paciente – patient
prudente – cautious / careful
simpático/a – nice
sociable – sociable
tímido/a – timid / shy
travieso/a – mischievous
viejo/a – old
demasiado + *adjetivo* – too _____
demasiado/a – too much
la cualidad – quality / characteristic

adonde van los niños
la biblioteca – library
la dulcería – candy store
la librería – book store
el parque – park
asistir (a) – to attend
la guardería infantil – daycare
el preescolar – preschool
el kínder – kindergarten
la escuela primaria – elementary school
la escuela secundaria – middle school
la escuela preparatoria – high school
    (school nomenclature varies by country)

el equipo del patio de recreo
el recreo / el receso – recess
el patio de recreo – playground
el cajón de arena – sandbox
el carrusel – merry-go-round
el columpio – swing
el sube y baja – see-saw / teeter-totter
el tobogán – slide

los juguetes – toys
el animal de peluche – stuffed animal
    el oso de peluche – teddy bear
el bloque – block
el camión – truck
el dinosaurio – dinosaur
el escondite / las escondidas – hide and seek
el juego – game
la muñeca – doll
el muñeco – action figure
el robot, *pl.* los robots – robot(s)
el tren (de juguete) – (toy) train
el regalo – gift / present

las mascotas – pets
el animal – animal
el burro – donkey
el caballo – horse
la cabra – goat
el cangrejo – crab
el cerdo / el cochino – pig
la cobaya / el cuy (cui) – guinea pig
la gallina – hen
el gallo – rooster
el gato – cat
el hámster – hamster
el hurón – ferret
la lagartija – (small) lizard
la llama – llama
la oveja – sheep
el pájaro – bird
el pavo – turkey
el pavo real – peacock
el perro – dog
el pez, *pl.* los peces – fish
el ratón – mouse
la serpiente – snake
la tortuga – turtle
la vaca – cow
la correa – leash

what you used to do (el imperfecto)

ser: (yo) era – I used to be
ir: (tú) ibas – you used to go
ver: (él) veía – he used to see/watch
acompañar – to accompany / to go with
aprender – to learn
bromear (con) – to joke / to kid (around) (with)
caminar – to walk
cantar – to sing
canturrear – to sing softly / to hum
chillar – to scream / to cry
colarse (o → ue) / colearse – to cut in line
la colección – collection
coleccionar – to collect
compartir (con) – to share (with)
el comportamiento – behavior
comportarse / portarse – to behave (oneself)
conocer (c → zc) – to know (personally)
                 – to be familiar with (a place, etc.)
correr – to run
crecer (c → zc) – to grow (up)
decir (yo digo) (e → i) – to say / to tell
desobedecer (c → zc) – to disobey
dibujar – to draw
enojarse (con / de) – to get angry (with, at / from)
escribir – to write
estudiar – to study
extrañar / echar de menos – to miss
fingir – to pretend
gritar – to yell / to shout
hablar en voz alta – to speak out loud / aloud
hablar en voz baja – to speak quietly
hacer un berrinche – to throw a fit/tantrum
jugar (u → ue) – to play
leer – to read
llorar – to cry
    la lágrima – tear
molestar / fastidiar – to annoy / to bother
montar en triciclo – to ride a tricycle
mentir (e → ie) (e → i) – to lie
la mentira – lie
murmurar – to mutter
obedecer (c → zc) – to obey
olvidar – to forget
pelear(se) (con) – to fight (with)
practicar – to practice
quejarse (de) – to complain (about)
la realidad – reality
recordar (o → ue) – to remember
recordar + *infinitivo* – to remember _____ing
recordar (a) – to remind (of)
refunfuñar – to grumble
saber – to know (information, facts)

saber + *infinitivo* – to know how to _____
saltar / brincar (la cuerda/soga) – to jump (rope)
soportar / aguantar – to put up with / to tolerate
susurrar – to whisper
tararear – to hum
tener (e → ie) – to have
la verdad – (the) truth
vivir – to live

la frecuencia de la acción habitual
(el presente o el imperfecto)

a menudo / muchas veces – often
a veces – sometimes
raras veces / rara vez – rarely
cada – each / every
nunca / jamás – never
                 – ever (in a negative sentence)
nunca jamás – never ever
(casi) siempre – (almost) always
cuando – when
de pequeño/a / de niño/a – as a kid / as a child
de vez en cuando – from time to time
constantemente – constantly
frecuentemente – frequently
típicamente – typically
generalmente – generally
normalmente – normally
(casi) todos los días – (almost) every day
todos los viernes – every Friday

otras palabras y expresiones útiles

castigar – to punish
regañar – to scold / to reprimand
hay – there is / there are
había – there was / there were
diferente / distinto/a – different / distinct
mismo/a – same
igual (que) – the same (as)
pero – but
por eso – that's why / for that
porque – because
más + *adjetivo* + que – more _____ than
menos + *adjetivo* + que – less _____ than
tan + *adjetivo* + como – as _____ as
de (posesión) – of (there is no apostrophe)
    el gato de mi mamá – my mom's cat
alguno/a(s) – some
    algún – some (before *singular, masculine noun*)
ninguno/a – none (effectively no *plural* form)
            – any (in a negative sentence)
    ningún – no (before *singular, masculine noun*)
            – any (in a negative sentence)
unos / unas – some

Unidad 18 – la familia y las celebraciones

los familiares – family members
el abuelo – grandfather
el abuelito – grandpa
la abuela – grandmother
la abuelita – grandma
el bisabuelo – great grandfather
la bisabuela – great grandmother
el tatarabuelo – great great grandfather
la tatarabuela – great great grandmother
el cuñado – brother-in-law
la cuñada – sister-in-law
el esposo – husband / spouse
la esposa – wife / spouse
el hermano – brother
la hermana – sister
el hermanastro – stepbrother
la hermanastra – stepsister
el medio hermano – half brother (*medio* is *adv.*)
la medio hermana – half sister (*medio* is *adverb*)
el hijo – son / child
la hija – daughter / child
el nieto – grandson / grandchild
la nieta – granddaughter / grandchild
el padre – father
el papá – dad
el papi – daddy
la madre – mother
la mamá – mom
la mami – mommy
el padrastro – stepfather / stepdad
la madrastra – stepmother / stepmom
el / la pariente/a – relative
el / la primo/a – cousin
el sobrino – nephew
la sobrina – niece
el suegro – father-in-law
la suegra – mother-in-law
el tío – uncle
la tía – aunt
el novio – boyfriend / groom
la novia – girlfriend / bride
el yerno – son-in-law
la nuera – daughter-in-law
el parentesco – family relationship / kinship
el / la gemelo/a – identical twin
el / la mellizo/a / cuate/a – fraternal twin
el / la antepasado/a / el ancestro – ancestor
estar casado/a (con) – to be married (to)
estar divorciado/a (de) – to be divorced
estar separado/a (de) – to be separated

estar soltero/a – to be single
estar muerto/a – to be dead
estar vivo/a – to be alive

las celebraciones
invitar – to invite
la invitación – invitation
la reunión (familiar) – meeting / family reunion
la tradición – tradition
la costumbre – custom
la celebración – celebration
celebrar – to celebrate
felicitar – to congratulate
¡Felicidades / Felicitaciones! – Congratulations!
la boda – wedding
casarse (con) – to get married (to)
el aniversario (de boda) – (wedding) anniversary
la fiesta de sorpresa – surprise party
la fiesta de cumpleaños – birthday party
el (los) cumpleaños (cumple) – birthday(s)
cumplir ____ años – to turn ____ years old
el nacimiento – birth
nacer (c → zc) – to be born
el funeral – funeral
morir(se) (o → ue) (o → u) – to die
el pastel – cake
la vela – candle
encender (e → ie) – to turn on / to light
apagar – to turn off / to extinguish
regalar – to give (as a gift)
dar – to give
charlar / platicar / hablar – to chat / to talk
cantar – to sing
bailar – to dance
el baile – dance
la graduación – graduation
graduarse – to graduate
el globo – balloon
el festival – festival
la feria – fair
explicar – to explain
decir (yo digo) (e → i) – to say / to tell
pedir (e → i) – to ask for / to request
servir (e → i) – to serve
el dulce – candy / sweet
empezar / comenzar (e → ie) – to start / to begin
terminar / acabar – to finish / to end
divertirse (e → ie) (e → i) – to have fun
aburrirse – to get bored
el / la aguafiestas – party pooper / wet blanket

pasarlo bien, mal – to have a good, bad time
decorar – to decorate
tomar / beber – to drink
comer – to eat
comprar – to buy
la flor – flower
la tarjeta (de cumpleaños) – (birthday) card
preguntar – to ask (a question)
tener lugar / ser – to take place
ir + a + *infinitivo* – to be going *to* _____

los días feriados
el día feriado / el día festivo – holiday
el día de boda, fiesta, etc. – wedding day, etc.
el Año Nuevo – New Year's Day
el Día de los Enamorados – Valentine's Day
el Día de la Madre – Mother's Day
el Día del Padre – Father's Day
el Día de la Independencia – Independence Day
los fuegos artificiales – fireworks
el Día de las Brujas – Halloween
el Día de (Acción de) Gracias – Thanksgiving
el pavo / el guajolote – turkey
el Hanukkah – Hanukkah
la Nochebuena – Christmas Eve
la Navidad – Christmas
la Nochevieja – New Year's Eve
el _2_ de _abril_ del _1984_ – April 2, 1984

las bebidas alcohólicas (el alcohol)
el aguardiente – spirit (general)
la cerveza / la chela – beer
el champán / la champaña – champagne
la ginebra – gin
el jerez – sherry
el ron – rum
el tequila (*masculino*) – tequila
el vino (blanco, tinto) – (white, red) wine
el (la) vodka – vodka
la resaca / la cruda – hangover

para saludar y/o despedirse
abrazar – to hug
besar – to kiss
conocer (c → zc) – to know personally
                 – to be familiar with
                 – to meet
dar la mano – to shake hands
decir hola – to say hello
saludar – to greet
saludar con la mano – to wave
decir adiós – to say goodbye
despedirse (e → i) (de) – to say goodbye (to)

otras palabras y expresiones útiles
adorar – to adore
odiar – to hate
el odio – hate
amar – to love
el amor – love
reconocer (c → zc) – to recognize
el reconocimiento – recognition
encontrar (o → ue) / hallar – to find
buscar – to look for
gustar – to please / to be pleasing
el gusto – pleasure / (sense of) taste
faltar – to be missing / to be absent
quedar – to remain / to be remaining
llevar – to wear / to take / to carry
mientras – while
la gente – people
¿A qué edad …? – At what age …?
a los _____ años – at _____ years old
darse cuenta (de) – to realize
de nuevo / otra vez – again
especial – special
ver (yo veo) – to see / to watch
hecho/a a mano – made by hand
saber (yo sé) – to know (information, facts)
estar de acuerdo – to be in agreement
tener razón – to be right
el desastre – disaster
el éxito – success
¡No me digas! – You don't say. / No way!
el uno al otro – each other / one another

los pronombres de complemento reflexivo

me – myself	nos – ourselves
te – yourself	os – yourselves
se – himself / herself	se – themselves
yourself	yourselves

los pronombres de complemento indirecto

me – me	nos – us
te – you	os – you
le – him / her / you	les – them / you

los pronombres de complemento directo

me – me	nos – us
te – you	os – you
lo / la – him / her / you	los / las – them / you
it (thing)	them (things)

los adjetivos posesivos

mi(s) – my	nuestro/a(s) – our
tu(s) – your	vuestro/a(s) – your
su(s) – his / her / your	su(s) – their / your

Unidad 19 – de viaje

planear / planificar – to plan
viajar – to travel
el viaje – trip
la agencia de viajes – travel agency
el / la viajero/a – traveler
el país – country
ahorrar – to save (money or time)
gastar – to spend
vender – to sell
comprar – to buy
el boleto – ticket
    de ida y vuelta – roundtrip ticket
    sólo de ida – one-way ticket
el itinerario – itinerary
el horario – schedule
conseguir (e → i) – to get (physically) / to obtain
traer (allí → aquí) / llevar (aquí → allí) – to bring
la credencial / el carnet – form of identification
el pasaporte – passport
la guía turística – travel guide (book)
el lujo – luxury
la necesidad – necessity
el equipaje – luggage / baggage
la mochila – backpack
la maleta – suitcase
hacer la maleta / empacar – to pack
recomendar (e → ie) – to recommend
la recomendación – recommendation
reservar – to reserve
la reservación – reservation
la habitación simple – single room (one bed)
la habitación doble – double room (two beds)
sencillo/a / simple – simple
la ropa – clothing
los anteojos / las gafas / los lentes – glasses

el aeropuerto – airport
salir / partir – to leave / to depart
la salida – departure / exit
llegar – to arrive
la llegada – arrival
facturar (el equipaje) – to check (luggage)
recoger (el equipaje) – to pick up / to claim
la recogida de equipaje – baggage claim
pasar por – to go through / to pass by
el control de seguridad – security checkpoint
la aduana – customs
el / la aduanero/a – customs agent
mostrar (o → ue) – to show
el (la) terminal – terminal

el vuelo – flight
con destino a – with destination to / departing to
procedente de – originating in / arriving from
la escala – stop / layover
la demora – delay
esperar – to wait (for)
la aerolínea – airline

el avión – airplane
el / la pasajero/a – passenger
el / la piloto/a – pilot
el / la auxiliar de vuelo – flight attendant
despegar – to take off
aterrizar – to land
la salida de emergencia – emergency exit
el asiento – seat
sentarse (e → ie) – to sit (down)
el pasillo – aisle
la ventanilla – window (of a vehicle)
el cinturón de seguridad – seat belt / safety belt
abrocharse – to buckle (oneself) up
desabrocharse – to unbuckle (oneself)
la emergencia – emergency
el incendio – fire
en caso de – in case of
poner música – to put on music
los audífonos / los auriculares – headphones
el (la) radio – radio
encender (e → ie) / prender – to turn on
apagar – to turn off
el ventilador – fan
la luz, *pl.* las luces – light(s)
el / la turista – tourist

el dinero – money
la lana / la plata / la feria – money (slang: "dough")
el dinero en efectivo – cash
la moneda – coin / monetary unit
    cara o cruz (varies by country) – heads or tails
el billete – bill (money) / ticket
la cartera / el billetero – wallet / billfold
barato/a – cheap / inexpensive
caro/a / costoso/a – expensive
cambiar – to change / to exchange
la casa de cambio – currency-exchange place
la tasa de cambio – exchange rate
la tarjeta de crédito – credit card
la tarjeta de débito – debit card
el cheque de viajero – traveler's check
regatear – to haggle / to bargain

hacer una excursión – to go on an outing
la oficina de turismo – tourist office
el / la guía – guide (person)
la jornada – day's journey / day trip
el pueblo – town / indigenous peoples (as a group)
el / la indígena – indigenous (native) person
el mercado – market
la artesanía – handicraft / workmanship
el / la artesano/a – artisan
hecho/a a mano – made by hand
la joyería – jewelry / jewelry store
el recuerdo – souvenir / memory
incluir (y) – to include
disfrutar (de) – to enjoy
la naturaleza – nature
continuar (u → ú) – to continue
explorar – to explore
experimentar – to experience / to experiment
con toda confianza – with confidence (don't be shy)
tener confianza (en) – to be confident (in)
tener curiosidad (sobre) – to be curious (about)
tener cuidado (de / con) – to be careful (of / with)
tener miedo (a / de) – to be afraid (of)
suficiente / bastante – sufficient / enough
la llave – key
el llavero – keychain
el (reloj) despertador – alarm (clock)
regresar / volver (o → ue) – to return
el metro – subway
el autobús / el bus – bus (inter-city travel)
el camión – small bus (inner-city travel)
el (taxi) colectivo – minivan-style taxi
compartir (con) – to share (with)
colocar / poner – to put / to place / to set

la posesión
propio/a – own
el mío / la mía
   los míos / las mías – mine
el tuyo / la tuya
   los tuyos / las tuyas – yours
el suyo / la suya
   los suyos / las suyas – his / hers / yours
el nuestro / la nuestra
   los nuestros / las nuestras – ours
el vuestro / la vuestra
   los vuestros / las vuestras – yours (Spain)
el suyo / la suya
   los suyos / las suyas – theirs / yours (*pl.*)
cuyo/a – whose (gender based on possession)
   Ej. la persona cuyo carro …
      la persona cuya cartera …
      la persona cuyos amigos …
      la persona cuyas cosas …

el futuro / el porvenir – the future
antes de + *infinitivo* – before _____ing
después de + *infinitivo* – after _____ing
al + *infinitivo* – upon _____ing
ir a + *infinitivo* – to be going *to* _____
tener ganas de + *infinitivo* – to want *to* _____
querer + *infinitivo* – to want *to* _____
pensar + *infinitivo* – to plan *to* _____
preferir + *inf.* – to prefer *to* _____
tener que + *inf.* – to have *to* ___ (person specific)
hay que + *inf.* – to have *to* ____ / one must ____
necesitar + *infinitivo* – to need *to* _____
poder + *infinitivo* – to be able *to* _____
intentar + *infinitivo* – to try *to* _____
deber + *inf.* – to ought *to* (should / must) _____
a partir de (ayer, las 8:00) – as of (yesterday, 8:00)
de ahora en adelante – from now on

otras palabras y expresiones útiles
para + *infinitivo* – in order *to* _____
ya – already / now
apenas – barely / just now (time)
ni modo – oh well
ni siquiera – not even
¡(Mucho) ojo! – Pay (close) attention!
¡Aguas! – Watch out! / Look out!
¡Cuidado! – Careful!
¡Buen viaje! – Have a good trip!

los mandatos (el imperativo) (tú) – commands
gastar → gasta(lo) – spend (it)
   → <u>no</u> (lo) gastes – don't spend (it)
prender → prende(la) – turn (it) on
   → <u>no</u> (la) prendas – don't turn (it) on
compartir → comparte(melo) – share (it with me)
   → <u>no</u> (se lo) compartas – don't share (it
                              with him / her / them)

los mandatos irregulars (tú)
salir → sal – leave
   → no salgas – don't leave
traer → trae – bring
   → no traigas – don't bring
hacer → haz – do
   → no hagas – don't do
tener → ten – have
   → no tengas – don't have
poner → pon – put
   → no pongas – don't put
ir → ve – go
   → no vayas – don't go
ver → ve – look
   → no veas – don't look

Unidad 20 – las características

las cualidades – qualities (personality traits)

activo/a – active
alegre / feliz – happy
amigable – friendly
apasionado/a – passionate
capaz – capable
caprichoso/a – capricious / fickle
cariñoso/a – affectionate
celoso/a / envidioso/a – jealous / envious
compasivo/a – compassionate
complicado/a – complicated
comprensivo/a – understanding
confiable – trustworthy
considerado/a – considerate
coqueto/a – flirtatious
emocional – emotional
enojón / enojona – one who gets angry a lot
estúpido/a / tonto/a / bobo/a – stupid / dumb
exigente – demanding
franco/a – frank / straightforward
generoso/a – generous
gritón / gritona – one who yells a lot
hábil – skilled / skillful
humilde – humble / from a poor background
idealista – idealist / idealistic
imbécil / idiota – imbecile / idiot(ic)
impulsivo/a – impulsive
incomprensivo/a – not understanding
incapaz – incapable
ingenuo/a – naïve
íntimo/a – close / intimate
leal – loyal
mentiroso/a – liar
metiche / entremetido/a – nosey
modesto/a – modest
muy / bien – very
necio/a – foolish
optimista – optimist / optimistic
orgulloso/a – proud / prideful
perfeccionista – perfectionist
pesimista – pessimist / pessimistic
quejón / quejona – one who complains a lot
reservado/a – reserved
responsable – responsible
sensato/a – sensible
sensible – sensitive
sentimental – sentimental
sincero/a – sincere
talentoso/a – talented
tranquilo/a / quieto/a – calm / tranquil
vanidoso/a – vain

cómo nos relacionamos con otras personas

abusar (de) – to abuse
la actitud – attitude
admirar – to admire
el / la amigo/a / cuate/a – friend
la amistad – friendship / friend
apoyar – to support
burlarse (de) – to make fun (of)
el / la compañero/a – companion / mate
compartir (con) – to share (with)
comprometerse (con / a) – to commit (to)
el conflicto – conflict
caer (bien, mal) – (like *gustar*, but as a friend)
coquetear / flirtear – to flirt
confiar (i → í) (en) – to trust (in) / to confide (in)
el consejo – advice
dar consejo / aconsejar – to give advice
dejar de + *infinitivo* – to quit _____ing
los / las demás – the rest / the others
la discusión – discussion / argument
discutir – to discuss / to argue
enojarse / enfadarse (con) – to get angry (with)
entender (e → ie) / comprender – to understand
explicar – to explain
gozar (de) / disfrutar (de) – to enjoy
hacer caso (a) – to listen (to) / to mind / to obey
    No me hagas caso. – Never mind.
influir (y) (en / sobre) – to influence
intentar / tratar de + *infinitivo* – to try *to* _____
invitar – to invite
jurar – to swear (to promise)
llevarse (bien, mal) (con) – to get along (with)
el malentendido – misunderstanding
mantener (e → ie) – to maintain / to keep
obligar (a) – to compel / to obligate
el problema (*masculino*) / la bronca – problem
prometer – to promise
quejarse (de) – to complain (about)
rajarse – to back down / to back out
reírse (e → í) (e →) (de) – to laugh (at)
relacionarse (con) – to relate (with)
rendirse (e → i) / darse por vencido/a – to give up
resolver (o → ue) – to resolve / to solve
respetar – to respect
seguir (e → i) – to continue / to follow
seguir / continuar + -*ando*, -*iendo* – to keep ___ing
el sentido de humor – sense of humor
    tener un buen sentido … – to have a good …
surgir – to arise
tener en común (con) – to have in common (with)
visitar – to visit

los buenos modales – good manners

a sus (tus) órdenes – at your service
    a la orden – at your service
    para servir(le / te) – at your service
adelante – go ahead (of me)
agradecer (c → zc) – to thank
la bondad – kindness
    tener la bondad de + *inf.* – to be so kind as to ___
con permiso – excuse me (to pass by someone)
contar (o → ue) (con) – to count (on)
dar las gracias – to give thanks
    ¡Mil gracias! – Thank you so much!
de nada – you're welcome (it was nothing)
    por nada – it was nothing
    con mucho gusto – my pleasure
    (no hay) de qué – don't mention it
    no hay por qué – don't mention it
el gesto – (hand) gesture
perdón – excuse me (to ask for forgiveness)
    ¡Mil disculpas! – I'm so sorry! / Pardon me!
perdonar / disculpar – to pardon / to forgive
por favor – please
prestar – to lend / to loan
tomar prestado/a – to borrow

actividades en las que puedes participar

el asilo para ancianos – assisted-living home
el / la ayudante/a / asistente/a – helper / assistant
el club, *pl.* los clubs – club(s)
    el club rotario – rotary club
dar clases particulares – to give private lessons
el grupo – group
el individuo – individual (regardless of gender or sex)
individual – individual (*adjective*)
inscribirse / enrolarse (en) – to sign up / to enroll
el manicomio – insane asylum / mental hospital
el orfanatorio / el orfanato – orphanage
la redacción – writing
redactar – to write
tomar una clase – to take a class
trabajar como voluntario/a – to volunteer

los superlativos – superlatives

el / la más (+ *adjetivo*) – *the* most _____ (-est) *one*
    lo más (+ *adjetivo*) – *the* most _____ (-est) *thing*
el / la menos (+ *adjetivo*) – *the* least _____ *one*
    lo menos (+ *adjetivo*) – *the* least _____ *thing*
el / la mejor – *the* best *one*
    lo mejor – *the* best *thing*
el / la peor – *the* worst *one*
    lo peor – *the* worst *thing*
el que / *la* que – *the one* that
    lo que – what / *the thing* that

the many ways "to become"

convertirse (en) – often magical or fantastical
hacerse – often through effort
ponerse – often used with emotions
    Se puso triste. – She got (became) sad.
transformarse (en) – magical or through effort
llegar a ser – often used with professions
    Llegué a ser maestro. – I became a teacher.
volverse – often a mental transformation
    Se volvieron locos. – They went crazy.

otras palabras y expresiones útiles

abarcar – to encompass
además (de) – in addition (to) / besides
apropiado/a – appropriate
aunque – although / even though
averiguar – to check / to find out
la cantidad – quantity
a causa de + *sustantivo* – because of + *noun*
a causa de que + *verbo* – because + *verb*
acerca de / sobre – about
el / la ciudadano/a – citizen
consistir (en) / constar (de) – to consist (of)
contra – against
darse cuenta (de) – to realize
debido a – due to
decepcionar / defraudar / desilusionar – to disappoint
desperdiciar / malgastar – to waste
enterarse (de) – to find out (about)
la imagen – image
imaginar(se) – to imagine
inapropiado/a – inappropriate
el instinto – instinct
máximo/a – maximum
mínimo/a – minimum
    lo más mínimo – the slightest / bare minimum
mudarse – to move / to change residences
obtener / adquirir (i → ie) – to obtain / to acquire
personal – personal
sin embargo – nevertheless / however
tanto/a – so much
tanto/a como – as much as
tantos/as – so many
tantos/as como – as many as
valer (yo valgo) – to be worth
el valor – value / worth
valorar – to value
el talento – talent
la habilidad – ability
la destreza – skill (usually manual)
el don – (natural) gift
silbar / chiflar – to whistle
chasquear los dedos – to snap (one's fingers)

Unidad 21 – donde vivimos

la ciudad – the city
el apartamento / el departamento – apartment
el atasco – traffic jam
el / la ciclista – cyclist
la contaminación (del aire) – (air) pollution
la fuente – fountain / source
el peatón / la peatona – pedestrian
el (los) rascacielos – skyscraper(s)
las rejas – bars (on a window)
el tráfico – traffic
el transporte público – public transportation
urbano/a – urban (pertaining to the city)

el campo – the country
el aire libre – fresh air / open air
cultivar – to farm / to cultivate
el deber – duty / chore
el (los) espantapájaros – scarecrow(s)
la finca – country residence
el granero – barn
el / la granjero/a – farmer
la granja – farm
la naturaleza – nature
el paisaje – countryside / landscape
rural – rural (pertaining to the country)
el terreno – plot of land
el / la vaquero/a – cowboy / cowgirl

las zonas residenciales de las afueras – suburbs
el cerco / la cerca – fence
el farol – street light
el jardín – yard / garden
el tope / el policía acostado – speed bump
el transporte particular – private transportation
el / la vecino/a – neighbor
el vecindario / el barrio – neighborhood

las ventajas y desventajas de los tres
abundante – abundant / plentiful
afortunado/a – fortunate
    la fortuna – fortune
aislado/a – isolated
aislar (i → í) – to isolate
al alcance de la mano – within reach / accessible
alcanzar – to reach
aprovechar – to take advantage of (good)
    aprovecharse (de) algo, alguien – (selfishly)
amplio/a – ample / enough
animado/a – lively
animarse – to cheer up / to liven up

apurarse / apresurarse – to hurry / to rush
el asalto – assault
atar – to tie up / to tie down
bello/a / hermoso/a – beautiful
el beneficio – benefit
la calma – calm / calmness
caminar – to walk
comparar – to compare
la comunidad – community
contribuir (y) – to contribute
conveniente – suitable / convenient
convenir (e → ie) – to suit
el crimen – crime (serious, usually murder)
cruzar – to cross
decidir – to decide
dejar – to leave (behind)
dejar de + *infinitivo* – to quit _____ing
dejar / permitir – to let / to allow / to permit
la delincuencia – delincuency (generic crime)
el / la delincuente – delinquent / criminal
desatar – to unleash / to let loose
la desesperación – desperation / despair
desesperado/a – desperate
desesperar(se) – to despair / to panic
diario/a – daily (*adjective*)
a diario / diariamente – daily (*adverb*)
diferente / distinto/a – different / distinct
la diferencia – difference
la desventaja – disadvantage
la distancia (a) – distance (to)
la diversidad – diversity
desanimarse – to get discouraged
las drogas – drugs
escaparse – to escape
escuchar – to listen to
el espacio – space
estar en contacto (con) – to be in contact (with)
fenomenal – phenomenal
la gente – people
grave – serious / grave
el / la habitante – inhabitant
hay – there is / there are (*present*)
había – there was / there were (*imperfect*)
el homicidio – homicide
ideal – ideal
los impuestos – taxes
intentar + *inf.* / pretender + *inf.* – to try *to* _____
loco/a – crazy
el ladrón / la ladrona – thief / burglar / robber
lamentar – to regret

la libertad (de) – (the) freedom (to)
leve – mild / slight
lindo/a – nice / cute / pretty
lleno/a (de gente) – full (of people)
maravilloso/a – marvelous / wonderful
matar – to kill
merecer(se) (c → zc) – to deserve
mudarse – to move / to change residences
ofrecer (c → zc) – to offer
oír (yo oigo) (y) – to hear
la oportunidad – opportunity
el (la) chance – chance / opportunity
parecer (c → zc) que – to seem that
el peligro – danger
peligroso/a – dangerous
pisar – to walk on / to tread on / to set foot on
la población – population
por un lado … – on (the) one hand …
por otro lado … – on the other hand …
puro/a – pure / sheer
el racismo – racism
racista – racist
rápido/a – fast / quick
robar – to steal / to rob
el robo – robbery
el ruido – noise
sano/a – healthy
seguro/a – safe
semejante / similar / parecido/a – similar
la semejanza – similarity
severo/a – severe
sin embargo / no obstante – nevertheless
situado/a – situated
la sociedad – society
sublime – sublime
la suerte – luck
suertudo/a – lucky
tardar (en) – to take (time) (to)
la tranquilidad – tranquility / calmness
tranquilizar / calmar – to calm
tratar bien, mal – to treat well, badly
la ubicación – location
ubicar / localizar – to locate
ubicarse (estar ubicado/a) – to be located
la ventaja – advantage
vale la pena – it's worth it / it's worth the trouble
vivir – to live
la vida – life
    social – social life
    nocturna – night life
la violencia – violence
visitar – to visit
las viviendas / el alojamiento – housing

por donde andamos
la acera / la banqueta – sidewalk
el atajo – shortcut
la autopista / la carretera – highway
la avenida – avenue
la calle – street
el camino – path / walkway
el cruce – crosswalk / intersection
la encrucijada / la intersección – intersection
el peaje – toll
el puente – bridge
la ruta – route
el sendero / la vereda – trail / path
dar una vuelta – to go around / to take a walk
dar media vuelta – to turn around
dar marcha atrás – to back up / to reverse
manejar / conducir (c → zc) – to drive
andar / pasear – to go (around, about) / to walk

las señales de tránsito – traffic signals
ALTO / PARE / STOP – STOP
CEDA EL PASO – YIELD
SENTIDO ÚNICO – ONE WAY
NO ESTACIONAR – NO PARKING
VELOCIDAD MÁXIMA – SPEED LIMIT
NO ADELANTAR – NO PASSING
el semáforo – traffic light
incorporarse (a) – to merge (with)

otras palabras y expresiones útiles
el origen – origin
todavía / aún – still / yet
ya – already / now
así – like this / like that (in this/that way)
así que … – (and) so …
fuera – out
fuera de – outside of / out of / beyond
    fuera de control – out of control
    fuera de servicio – out of order (not working)
afuera – outside
dentro – in
dentro de – within
adentro – inside
cualquier – any (before *singular noun*)
    cualquier cosa – anything
cualesquier – any (before *plural noun*)
cualquiera – any one
cualesquiera – any ones
¿Y qué? – So what?
de todos los tiempos – of all time
en absoluto – at all (in a negative sentence)
con respecto a / respecto de – with respect to
en relación con / con relación a – in relation to

Unidad 22 – el entretenimiento

cómo vemos la televisión y las películas
alquilar / rentar – to rent
la audiencia – audience
la antena – antenna
cambiar – to change
el canal – channel
devolver (o → ue) – to return (an item)
el dividí / el DVD – DVD
filmar – to film
grabar – to record
el público – (the) public / (the) audience
la televisión por cable – cable TV
la televisión por satélite – satellite TV
ver – to see / to watch
mirar – to watch / to look at

la televisión, las películas y su influencia
absurdo/a – absurd
aburrido/a – boring (ser)
　　　　　 – bored (estar)
acerca de / sobre – about
el actor – actor
la actriz, *pl.* las actrices – actress(es)
afectar – to affect
analizar – to analyze
anunciar – to announce
el anuncio – announcement
argüir (y) – to debate / to argue
el argumento – argument / stance on a subject
ayudar (a) – to help (to)
bostezar – to yawn
la calidad – quality
　　de alta calidad – high quality
　　de baja calidad – low quality
chillar – to scream
chistoso/a / gracioso/a – funny
el cine (cinema) – cinema / movie theater
comprobar (o → ue) – to prove
el comentario – commentary / comment
comentar – to comment
el comercial – commercial
conmover (o → ue) – to move (emotionally)
conmovedor/a – (emotionally) moving
controlar – to control
criticar – to critique / to criticize
crítico/a – critic / critical
la crítica – critique / criticism
dañoso/a / dañino/a – harmful
dar – to give
de acción – action
de ciencia ficción – science fiction

de comedia – comedy
de fantasía – fantasy
deportivo/a – sports
de terror – horror / scary
demasiado/a – too much
el derecho (a) – (the) right (to)
la discusión – discussion / argument
la desnudez – nudity
desnudo/a / encuerado/a – nude / naked
los dibujos animados – cartoons
doblado/a – dubbed (into another language)
el documental – documentary
el drama (*masculino*) – drama
el efecto – effect
emocionarse – to get excited
emocionado/a – excited
emocionante – exciting
enfocarse (en) – to focus (on)
enseñar – to teach / to show
entretener(se) (e → ie) – to entertain (oneself)
entretenido/a – entertaining (ser)
　　　　　　 – entertained (estar)
el entretenimiento – entertainment
la entrevista – interview
entrevistar – to interview
el episodio – episode
equivocarse – to be wrong / to make a mistake
la escena – scene
el estilo – style
evaluar (u → ú) – to evaluate
exagerado/a – exaggerated
exagerar – to exaggerate
extranjero/a – foreign
extraño/a / raro/a – weird
fascinante – fascinating
fascinar – to fascinate
fijarse (en) – to take notice (of) / to fixate (on)
la furia – fury
hacer / causar / ocasionar – to make / to cause
hacer daño / causar daño / ocasionar daño – to harm
importar – to matter / to be important
la imagen – image
la influencia – influence
influenciar / influir (y) (en / sobre) – to influence
el infomercial – infomercial
la información – information
informativo/a – informative
inmediato/a – immediate
inmediatamente / de inmediato – immediately
interpretar – to interpret
interesante – interesting

interesar – to interest
la ira – wrath / rage
llorar – to cry
el / la locutor/a – speaker
manipular – to manipulate
mediocre – mediocre
el miedo – fear
negativo/a – negative
notar – to note / to take note of
las noticias – (the) news
opinar – to be of an opinion / to have an opinion
la opinión – opinion
la película (peli) / el filme – movie / film
el pensamiento – thought
pensar (e → ie) – to think
la percepción – perception
el personaje – character (in a movie, show, etc.)
la pesadilla – nightmare
policiaco/a / policíaco/a – police / detective
por eso – for that / that's why / therefore
positivo/a – positive
preocuparse (de) – to worry (oneself) (about)
prestar/poner atención (a) – to pay attention (to)
profundo/a / hondo/a – profound / deep
   poco profundo/a – shallow
el programa (*masculino*) – show / program
prohibir (i → í) – to prohibit
el pronóstico de tiempo – weather forecast
el pudor – modesty (often sexual or body shame)
el punto de vista – point of view
reír(se) (e → í) (e →) (de) – to laugh (at)
el reportaje – (news) report
reportar – to report
el / la reportero/a – reporter
representar – to represent
ridículo/a – ridiculous
la risa – laughter
la rabia – rage / anger
el romance – romance
romántico/a – romantic
el secreto – secret
la secuela – sequel
según – according to
la serie – series
el significado – meaning
sin supervisión – without supervision
la sociedad – society
soñar (o → ue) (con) – to dream (about)
   el sueño – dream
los subtítulos – subtitles
tal como, *pl.* tales como – such as
la telenovela – soap opera
la temporada – season (of a TV series)

tener razón – to be right
el tipo / la clase – type / class
el tráiler / el corto / el avance – trailer
tras – after
   uno/a tras otro/a – one after the other
tratarse (de) – to be about
la vergüenza – embarrassment / shame / disgrace
vergonzoso/a – embarrassing / shameful / disgraceful
violento/a – violent

para hablar de la hora
a las 19:30 horas – at 19:30 hours
a eso de las 20:00 horas – at about 8:00 PM
desde – from
durar – to last
en estreno – debut / premier / for the first time
estrenarse / salir – to debut / to come out
en punto – on the dot
hasta – until
recientemente – recently
es la 1:00 pasada – it's past 1:00
son las 3:00 pasadas – it's past 3:00
pasada la 1:00 – after 1:00
pasadas las 10:00 – after 10:00

la censura – censor / censorship
censurar – to censor
la clasificación – rating / classification
clasificar – to rate / to classify
apto/a para toda la familia – suitable for the
                              whole family
prohibido/a para menores – minors prohibited
se recomienda discreción – viewer discretion
                              advised
estar a favor (de) – to be in favor (of)
estar en contra (de) – to be against
apaciguar / pacificar – to appease / to pacify

otros medios de comunicación
a través de / por medio de – through / by way of
el (la) internet / la red – (the) internet
el periódico / el diario – newspaper
el (la) radio – radio
la revista – magazine

el imperfecto progresivo
estar + *gerundio* (-*ing* form) – to be _____*ing*
   ¿Qué estabas haciendo? – What were you doing?
   Estaba levantando pesas. – I was lifting weights.
cuando – when
mientras – while (at the same time)
mientras que – whereas (used for contrast)

Unidad 23 – el medioambiente y la naturaleza

el medioambiente – (the) environment
el (la) mar / el océano – sea / ocean
la ola – wave
la orilla – shore / shoreline
la costa – coast
la marea – tide
la corriente – current
la deriva – drift
a la deriva – adrift
el delfín, *pl.* los delfines – dolphin(s)
el pulpo – octopus
el calamar – squid
la almeja – clam
el mejillón, *pl.* los mejillones – mussel(s)
la ostra – oyster
la concha – shell
la ballena – whale
la ballena asesina / la orca – killer whale
el cachalote – sperm whale
el león marino, *pl.* los leones marinos – sea lion(s)
la morsa – walrus
la foca – seal
el tiburón, *pl.* los tiburones – shark(s)
la langosta – lobster
el cangrejo – crab
el arrecife – reef
el coral – coral
las algas – algae / seaweed
el río – river
el cauce – riverbed
el (la) margen, *pl.* los márgenes – river bank(s)
la trucha – trout
el salmón, *pl.* los salmones – salmon
el riachuelo – brook / stream
el arroyo – creek
el lago – lake
la charca – pond
el pantano – swamp / marsh
el cocodrilo – crocodile
el caimán, *pl.* los caimanes – alligator(s)
el lagarto – lizard
la lagartija – small lizard
la serpiente / la culebra – snake
el reptil – reptile
el anfibio – amphibian
la rana – frog
el renacuajo – tadpole
el sapo – toad
el árbol – tree
la rama – branch

la corteza (de árbol) – (tree) bark
el bosque – forest
la selva tropical – tropical rainforest
frondoso/a – thick with leaves, branches, trees
la planta – plant
la hoja – leaf
el tallo – stem / stalk
el pétalo – petal
la raíz, *pl.* las raíces – root(s)
fructuoso/a – fruitful / successful
infructuoso/a – fruitless / unsuccessful
dar fruto(s) – to bear fruit / to be successful
fértil – fertile
estéril – barren
la semilla – seed
sembrar (e → ie) – to sow / to plant seeds / to seed
la siembra – planting / sowing
cosechar – to harvest / to reap
la cosecha – harvest
el (los) oasis – oasis (oases)
el espejismo – mirage
la isla – island
el paraíso – paradise
el archipiélago – archipelago
el / la depredador/a – predator
la presa – prey
el mamífero – mammal
el puerco espín – porcupine
el castor – beaver
el mapache – raccoon
el zorrillo / la mofeta – skunk
el glotón, *pl.* los glotones – wolverine(s)
el tejón, *pl.* los tejones – badger(s)
feroz – ferocious
la ardilla – squirrel
el zorro – fox
el lobo – wolf
el coyote – coyote
la nutria – otter
el elefante – elephant
la jirafa – giraffe
el rinoceronte – rhinoceros
el hipopótamo – hippopotamus
el puma (*masculino*) – mountain lion / cougar
el tigre – tiger
el león, *pl.* los leones – lion(s)
el jaguar – jaguar
el leopardo – leopard
el guepardo – cheetah
la pantera – panther

la hiena – hyena
el avestruz, *pl.* los avestruces – ostrich(es)
veloz – fast / quick / fleet / speedy
el canguro – kangaroo
el ornitorrinco – (duckbilled) platypus
el bisonte – bison
el alce – elk / moose
el venado / el ciervo – deer
el oso (pardo, polar) – (brown, polar) bear
el cerdo / el cochino / el guarro – pig
la bestia de carga – beast of burden
el buey – ox
el ave (*femenino*) / el pájaro – bird
la rapaz, *pl.* las rapaces – raptor(s)
el búho / la lechuza – owl
el águila (*femenino*), *pl.* las águilas – eagle(s)
el halcón, *pl.* los halcones – hawk(s) / falcon(s)
el cóndor, *pl.* los cóndores – condor(s)
el (los) albatros – albatross(es)
la gaviota – seagull
el pingüino – penguin
el pelícano – pelican
el tucán, *pl.* los tucanes – toucan(s)
la cigüeña – stork
el colibrí, *pl.* los colibríes – hummingbird(s)
el pájaro carpintero – woodpecker
el ganso – goose
el pato – duck
el insecto – insect
el escarabajo – beetle
la hormiga – ant
el (los) ciempiés – centipede(s)
el (los) milpiés – millipede(s)
la mariposa – butterfly
la libélula – dragonfly
la luciérnaga – firefly / lightning bug
el arácnido – arachnid
la araña – spider
el alacrán / el escorpión – scorpion
la manada – small pack (wolves), herd, flock, etc.
el ganado – livestock (cattle, bison, etc.)
la bandada – flock (birds), school (fish), etc.
el rebaño – large flock (sheep), etc.
terrestre – terrestrial (pertaining to land)
marítimo/a – maritime (pertaining to the sea)
las placas tectónicas – tectonic plates
la atmósfera / la atmosfera – atmosphere
la capa de ozono – ozone layer
el iceberg, *pl.* los icebergs – iceberg(s)
el glaciar – glacier
amarillento/a / amarilloso/a – yellowish
azulado/a / azuloso/a – bluish
verdoso/a – greenish

verde azulado – bluish green
incoloro/a – colorless
el olor (a) – smell (of)
inodoro/a – odorless
apestar – to stink
el metano – methane
el oxígeno – oxygen
el hidrógeno – hydrogen
el nitrógeno – nitrogen
el dióxido de carbono – carbon dioxide
advertir (e → ie) (e → i) – to warn
la advertencia – warning
atreverse a + *infinitivo* – to dare *to* _____
los animales salvajes – wild animals
las plantas silvestres – wild plants
el cacto / el (los) cactus – cactus (cacti / cactuses)
psicodélico/a – psychedelic
el hongo – mushroom
el peyote – peyote
venenoso/a – poisonous / venemous
envenenar – to poison
el fuego – fire
la fogata – campfire
la leña – firewood / lumber
el palo – stick
ligero/a – light-weight
pesado/a – heavy
mojado/a – wet
seco/a – dry
contaminado/a – polluted / contaminated
romper – to break / to tear
esperar – to hope (for)
suplicar / rogar (o → ue) – to plead / to beg
conservar – to conserve
prometer – to promise
la promesa – promise
olvidar – to forget
perder (e → ie) – to lose
perdido/a – lost
el amanecer / el alba (*femenino*) – dawn
el anochecer – nightfall
la puesta del sol / el atardecer – sunset
las tinieblas / la oscuridad – darkness
la luz, *pl.* las luces – light(s)
el crepúsculo – twilight
el silencio – silence
el sonido – noise
el parque nacional – national park
la colina – hill
el valle – valley
la montaña – mountain
el prado / la pradera / la llanura / la vega
    – (the) plains / meadow / prairie / lowlands

la sombra – shadow / shade
peligroso/a – dangerous
en peligro de extinción – endangered
extinto/a – extinct
en cautiverio – captive / in captivity
hundir – to sink
proteger – to protect
escoger – to choose
el hoyo / el agujero / el hueco – hole
la grieta – crack
la cueva / la caverna – cave / cavern
el murciélago – bat
reciclar – to recycle
el reciclaje / el reciclamiento – recycling
reciclable – recyclable
la meta – goal
establecer (c → zc) – to establish / to set
lograr – to achieve / to accomplish
lograr + *infinitivo* / conseguir (e → i) + *infinitivo*
    – to manage *to* _____ / to succeed at _____*ing*
tener sentido – to make sense
callar – to (make) quiet (down)
al azar – randomly / at random
el líder / la lideresa – leader
el liderazgo – leadership
echar un vistazo (a) – to take a look (at)
tomar medidas – to take measures
descartar – to discard / to throw out
desechable – disposable
despreciar – to disregard / to discount / to despise
menospreciar – to undervalue / to think nothing of
apreciar – to appreciate / to think highly of
hurgar – to rummage
el recordatorio – reminder
acudir (a) – to show up (to)
obstinado/a / terco/a – obstinate / stubborn
la avaricia / la codicia – greed
avaricioso/a / codicioso/a – greedy
egoísta – selfish
privilegiado/a – privileged
priorizar – to prioritize
la excusa / el pretexto – excuse
feo/a – ugly
bello/a / hermoso/a – beautiful
embellecer (c → zc) – to make beautiful
florecer (c → zc) – to flourish / to bloom
entristecer (c → zc) / agüitar – to sadden
agobiar / abrumar – to overwhelm
cansar / agotar – to exhaust
desgastarse / deteriorarse – to wear/waste away
el volcán, *pl.* los volcanes – volcano(s)
erupcionar – to erupt
la ceniza – ash

tumbar – to knock over / to knock down
derribar / demoler (o → ue) – to demolish
arruinar – to ruin
arrasar / destruir (y) – to raze / to destroy
talar – to cut down
el desastre (natural) – (natural) disaster
el tornado – tornado
el huracán, *pl.* los huracanes – hurricane(s)
la inundación – flood
inundar – to flood
la avalancha – avalanche
el deslave – mudslide / landslide
escaso/a – scarce
la escasez – scarcity / shortage
la sequía – drought
el recurso (natural) – (natural) resource
el oro (dorado/a) – gold (golden)
la plata (plateado/a) – silver
el cobre – copper
el mineral – mineral
el gas natural – natural gas
el petróleo – oil / petroleum
el calentamiento global – global warming
el cambio climático – climate change
el clima (*masculino*) – climate / weather
la meteorología – meteorology
la consecuencia – consequence
las repercusiones – repercussions
la superficie – surface
la certidumbre – certainty
la incertidumbre – uncertainty
la muchedumbre – masses (of people, etc.)
el / la hipócrita – hypocrite
la hipocresía – hypocrisy
pasmado/a / boquiabierto/a – aghast / stunned
intimidar – to intimidate
intimidante – intimidating
bajo – under / underneath
a la intemperie / al aire libre – out in the open
los detalles / los pormenores – details

otras expresiones útiles
estar a punto de + *infinitivo* – to be about *to* _____
tener en mente / en cuenta – to keep in mind
tomar en cuenta – to take into account
haber de / tener que – to have *to* _____
    Ej. He de hacerlo. / Tengo que hacerlo.
ser tiempo de + *infinitivo* – to be time *to* _____
    Ej. Es tiempo de buscar otro trabajo.
ser hora de + *infinitivo* – to be time (of day) *to* ___
    Ej. Era hora de cenar.
cada vez más – more and more
una y otra vez – over and over (again)

Unidad 24 – los misterios, los fenómenos y los complots

la religión y las creencias – religion and beliefs
afirmar – to affirm
el alma (*femenino*), *pl.* las almas – soul(s)
el altar – altar
ateo/a – atheist
el chamán / la chamana – shaman
cierto/a / verdadero/a – certain / true
comprobar (o → ue) – to prove
confesar (e → ie) – to confess
la conjetura – conjecture
convencer (c → z) – to convince
creer (en, que) – to believe (in, that)
el culto – cult
el / la curandero/a – healer
el desierto – (the) desert
el dios – god
la diosa – goddess
la duda – doubt
dudar – to doubt
enterrar (e → ie) / sepultar – to bury
la especulación – speculation
especular – to speculate
el espíritu – spirit
falso/a – false
la fe – faith
el homenaje – homage
   rendir (e → i) homenaje – to pay homage
imposible – impossible
investigar – to investigate
negar (e → ie) – to deny
negarse a + *infinitivo* – to refuse *to _____*
la ofrenda – offering
posible – possible
la prueba – test
rezar / orar – to pray
el ritual – ritual
sacrificar – to sacrifice
el sacrificio – sacrifice
la secta – sect
la señal – sign / signal
la sepultura – grave
suponer – to suppose
supuesto/a / dizque – supposed / so-called
el tabú, *pl.* los tabúes – taboo(s)
el / la testigo – witness
la tribu – tribe
el tributo – tribute
   pagar tributo – to pay tribute
la tumba / el sepulcro – tomb
el vudú – voodoo

la mitología y la cultura – mythology and culture
acordarse (o → ue) (de) – to remember
aparecer (c → zc) – to appear
la aparición – apparition
construir (y) – to build / to construct
cultural – cultural
desaparecer (c → zc) – to disappear
desconocido/a – unknown
el / la duende/a – goblin / elf
encantado/a – enchanted
enorme – enormous
los escalofríos – (the) chills
la escultura – sculpture
la estatua – statue
la estructura – structure
la evidencia – evidence
existir – to exist
explicable – explainable
extraño/a – weird / strange
extraordinario/a – extraordinary
el fantasma (*masculino*) – ghost
el fenómeno – phenomenon
la figura – figure / shape
el / la gigante/a – giant
gigantesco/a – gigantic
el / la gnomo/a – dwarf / troll / gnome
el hada (*femenino*) – fairy (regardless of gender or sex)
la huella – print / track
inexplicable – unexplainable / inexplicable
legendario/a – legendary
la leyenda – legend
el lugar / el sitio – place / site
el misterio – mystery
misterioso/a – mysterious
el mito – myth
mitológico/a – mythological
el monstruo – monster (regardless of gender or sex)
mover (o → ue) – to move
el / la ogro/a – ogre
el peregrinaje – pilgrimage
el / la peregrino/a – pilgrim / traveler
pertenecer (c → zc) (a) – to pertain / to belong (to)
la piedra – rock / stone
la piel de gallina – goosebumps
la pirámide – pyramid
el rastro – trace
el reporte / la noticia – report / piece of news
rodear – to surround / to circle
la rueda – wheel
la sensación – sensation / feeling

sobrenatural – supernatural
la teoría – theory
teórico/a – theoretical
la travesía – journey / voyage
el Triángulo de las Bermudas – the Bermuda Triangle

las medidas – measurements / measures
calcular – to calculate / to figure
medir (e → i) – to measure
el metro – meter
el centímetro – centimeter
el milímetro – millimeter
el pie – foot (12 inches)
la pulgada – inch
la yarda – yard (3 feet)
estrecho/a / angosto/a – narrow
así de estrecho/a – like this narrow (w/hand gesture)
ancho/a – wide
(así) de ancho/a – (like this wide) in width
la anchura – width
alto/a – tall / high
(así) de alto/a – (like this tall) in height
la altura – height
grande – big / large
la grandeza – greatness / grandeur
así de grande – like this big
pequeño/a / chico/a – small
así de pequeño/a – like this small
largo/a – long
la largura / la longitud – length
(así) de largo/a – (like this long) in length
como – like / as
el diámetro – diameter
pesar – to weigh
la tonelada – ton
la libra – pound
el kilogramo – kilogram

el horóscopo – horoscope
el signo del Zodiaco – Zodiac sign
Aries – Aries
Tauro – Taurus
Géminis – Gemini
Cáncer – Cancer
Leo – Leo
Virgo – Virgo
Libra – Libra
Escorpio – Scorpio
Sagitario – Sagittarius
Capricornio – Capricorn
Acuario – Aquarius
Piscis – Pisces
predecir (e → i) – to predict

el universo – (the) universe
la galaxia – galaxy
la Vía Láctea – (The) Milky Way
el sistema solar (*masculino*) – solar system
el sol – (the) sun
el planeta (*masculino*) – planet
   Mercurio – Mercury
   Venus – Venus
   Tierra – Earth
   Marte – Mars
   Júpiter – Jupiter
   Saturno – Saturn
   Urano – Uranus
   Neptuno – Neptune
   Plutón – Pluto
la luna (llena, nueva) – (full, new) moon
la estrella – star
la estrella fugaz – shooting star
el cometa (*masculino*) – comet
el asteroide – asteroid
el meteorito – meteorite
el eclipse (lunar, solar) – (lunar, solar) eclipse
el rayo – ray
la aurora boreal – aurora borealis (northern lights)
la aurora austral – aurora australis (southern lights)
el solsticio – solstice
el equinoccio – equinox
emitir – to emit
iluminar / alumbrar – to illuminate / to light
brillar / resplandecer (c → zc) – to shine / to glow
terrestre – terrestrial / of Earth
extraterrestre – extraterrestrial / alien
el / la marciano/a – Martian
el ovni (objeto volador no identificado) – UFO
la nave espacial – spaceship
volar (o → ue) – to fly
el / la astronauta – astronaut
vaciar (i → í) – to empty
vacío/a – empty

otras palabras y expresiones útiles
a pesar de (que) – in spite of (the fact that)
aunque – although / even though
el complot – plot / conspiracy
conspirar – to conspire / to plot
de la nada – out of nowhere
de repente – suddenly / all of a sudden
en medio de la nada – in the middle of nowhere
entonces / pues – so / well / then / therefore
estar convencido/a (de) – to be convinced (of)
estar seguro/a (de) – to be sure (of)
que yo sepa – that I know of / as far as I know
todo con medida – everything in moderation

Unidad 25 – el cuerpo humano y la medicina

la anatomía – anatomy
el abdomen – abdomen
las amígdalas – tonsils
el apéndice (vermicular) – appendix
el antebrazo – forearm
la arteria – artery
la articulación, *pl.* las articulaciones – joint(s)
la axila / el sobaco – underarm / armpit
la barbilla – chin
el bazo – spleen
la boca – mouth
    bucal – mouth (*adjective*)
el brazo – arm
la cabeza – head
la cadera – hip
la cara / el rostro – face
el cartílago – cartilage
la ceja – eyebrow
la célula – cell
el cerebro / el seso – brain
    los sesos – brains
el cérvix / el cuello uterino – cervix
la cintura – waist
el codo – elbow
el colon – colon
la columna vertebral / espina dorsal – spinal column
el corazón – heart
la costilla – rib
el cuello – neck
el cuerpo – body
    corporal – body (*adjective*)
el dedo – finger
    el meñique – pinky
    el dedo anular – ring finger
    el dedo mayor / el dedo corazón – middle finger
    el dedo índice – index finger
    el pulgar – thumb
el dedo de pie – toe
    el dedo gordo – big toe
el diente / la muela – tooth / molar
las encías – gums
la entrepierna – inner thigh
el (la) enzima – enzyme
el esmalte – enamel
el esófago – esophagus
la espalda – back
el esqueleto – skeleton
el estómago – stomach
    estomacal – stomach (*adjective*)
    los jugos gástricos – gastric juices
la frente – forehead

las fosas nasales – nostrils
el ganglio/nódulo linfático – lymph node
la garganta – throat
los genitales – genitals
la glándula (suprarrenal) – (adrenal) gland
el glóbulo (blanco, rojo) – (white, red) blood cell
el hígado – liver
el hombro – shoulder
el hueso – bone
la ingle – groin
el intestino / la tripa – intestine
    las tripas – guts
el labio – lip
la lengua – tongue
el ligamento – ligament
la mandíbula – jaw
la mano (*femenino*) – hand
la médula – (bone) marrow
la mejilla / el cachete – cheek
la muñeca – wrist
el músculo – muscle
el muslo – thigh
las nalgas – buttocks
la nariz, *pl.* las narices – nose(s)
el nervio – nerve
el nudillo – knuckle
el oído – inner ear
el ojo – eye
el ombligo – navel / belly button
la oreja – outer ear
el órgano – organ
la palma – palm
el páncreas – pancreas
la panza / la barriga / el vientre – belly
la pantorrilla (los gemelos) – calf (calf muscles)
el párpado – eyelid
el pecho – chest
el pelo / el cabello – hair
el pene – penis
la pestaña – eyelash
    pestañear / parpadear – to blink
el pezón, *pl.* los pezones – nipple(s)
el pie – foot
la piel – skin
la pierna – leg
el pubis – pubic region
el pulmón, *pl.* los pulmones – lung(s)
la retina – retina
el riñón, *pl.* los riñones – kidney(s)
la rodilla – knee
la sangre – blood

el seno / la mama – breast
el talón, *pl.* los talones – heel(s)
el tejido – tissue
el tendón, *pl.* los tendones – tendon(s)
el testículo – testicle
el tobillo – ankle
el torso – torso
la uña – fingernail / toenail
el útero / la matriz – uterus / womb
la vagina – vagina
el vaso sanguíneo – blood vessel
la vejiga – bladder
la vena – vein
la vesícula biliar – gall bladder
la vulva – vulva

las descripciones
alto/a – tall
la altura / la estatura – height / stature
   de estatura mediana – medium height
   de gran altura – of great stature (tall)
bajo/a / chaparro/a – short
de piel blanca (blanco/a) – white
de piel negra (negro/a) – black
de piel oscura / morena (moreno/a) – dark-skinned
de tercera edad – senior
   edad avanzada – advanced age
delgado/a – thin
demacrado/a / emaciado/a – emaciated
demacrarse – to waste away
estar de/en buena forma – to be in good shape
flaco/a – skinny
gordo/a – fat
obeso/a – obese
indigente – indigent
diestro/a – righthanded
zurdo/a – lefthanded
rubio/a – blonde
pelirrojo/a – redhead
moreno/a – brunette
de pelo castaño/moreno – brown-haired
de pelo canoso – gray-haired
las canas – gray hairs
menor de edad – minor (underage)
sano/a – healthy / in good health
medir (e → ie) (e → i) – to measure
   ¿Cuánto mide el paciente?
   El paciente mide 175 centímetros.
la libra – pound (lb.)
subir de peso / ganar peso – to gain weight
   subir de peso 5 libras / ganar 5 libras
bajar de peso / perder peso – to lose weight
   bajar de peso 10 libras / perder 10 libras

pesar – to weigh
   La paciente pesa 145 libras.
   La asistenta médica pesó al paciente.
¿Qué tan + *adjetivo*? – How _____?
¿Qué tan obeso es? – How obese is he?
¿Cuán + *adjetivo*? – How _____?
¿Cuán delgado es? – How thin is he?
tener sobrepeso – to be overweight
la orientación sexual – sexual orientation
   bisexual – bisexual
   gay (pronounced "*guey*") – gay
   heterosexual – heterosexual
   homosexual – homosexual
   lesbiano/a / lésbico/a – lesbian
   transexual – transgender

los problemas y las enfermedades
el aborto espontáneo – miscarriage
el abuso – abuse (usually sexual)
la adicción / las adicciones – addiction(s)
   ser adicto/a (a) – to be addicted (to)
las agruras / la acidez estomacal – heartburn
el alcohol – alcohol
el / la alcohólico/a – alcoholic
el alcoholismo – alcoholism
la alergia – allergy
   ser alérgico/a (a) – to be allergic (to)
los altibajos – highs and lows / ups and downs
   los bajos – lows (mood, energy, etc.)
   los altos – highs (mood, energy, etc.)
la amigdalitis – tonsillitis
la ampolla – blister
la ansiedad – anxiety
la apendicitis – appendicitis
la arruga – wrinkle
la artritis (reumatoide) – (rheumatoid) arthritis
el asma (*femenino*) – asthma
el autismo – autism
la bacteria / el germen – bacteria / germ
bacteriano/a – bacterial
balbucear / tartamudear – to stutter / to stammer
benigno/a – benign
caerse (yo me caigo) – to fall accidentally
la caída – fall
el calambre – cramp
el callo – callus
el cáncer (metastásico) – (metastatic) cancer
canceroso/a – cancerous
el cancerígeno / el carcinógeno – carcinogen
cardiaco/a / cardíaco/a – cardiac
la(s) caries dentaria(s) – dental cavity (cavities)
la ceguera – blindness
ciego/a – blind

la cicatriz, *pl.* las cicatrices – scar(s)
la cirrosis – cirrhosis
el coágulo / el cuajarón sanguíneo – blood clot
el colesterol alto/elevado – high cholesterol
colorrectal – colorectal
el coma (*masculino*) – coma
    caer en coma – to fall into a coma
las complicaciones – complications
concebir (e → i) – to conceive
la concepción – conception
la conjuntivitis – conjunctivitis
la conmoción cerebral – concussion
(estar) constipado/a – to have a stuffy nose
contagiarse (de) / contraer – to contract
contagioso/a – contagious
las contracciones – contractions
la crisis – attack / fit
    alérgica – allergy attack
    asmática – asthma attack
    cerebral / convulsiva – seizure
    epiléptica – epileptic fit / seizure
dar positivo por _____ – to test positive for _____
la demencia – dementia
la depresión – depression
deprimente – depressing
deprimido/a – depressed
deprimir – to depress
el derrame cerebral / el infarto cerebral – stroke
desangrar – to bleed out
el desencadenante – trigger
la deshidratación – dehydration
deshidratado/a – dehydrated
desmayarse – to pass out / to faint
la diabetes – diabetes
la(s) diagnosis – diagnosis (diagnoses)
la diarrea – diarrhea
el dolor (agudo) – (sharp) pain
la drogadicción – drug addiction
    ser drogadicto/a – to be a drug addict
drogado/a – drugged
ebrio/a / borracho/a / tomado/a – intoxicated / drunk
el efecto secundario – side effect
embarazada – pregnant
el embarazo – pregnancy
    ectópico – ectopic pregnancy
embarazarse (de) – to get pregnant (with)
enfermarse – to get sick
la enfermedad / la afección – illness / disease
la enfermedad transmitida sexualmente – STD
el entumecimiento – numbness
entumecido/a – numb
entumirse – to fall asleep (body part)
envenenarse – to be poisoned

la espinilla / el grano – pimple / zit
la esquizofrenia – schizophrenia
el estornudo – sneeze
estornudar – to sneeze
estreñido/a – constipated
el estreñimiento – constipation
estreñirse (e → i) – to become constipated
el factor – factor
la flema – phlegm
el fuego – cold sore (herpes sore)
fumar – to smoke
    el cigarro / el cigarrillo – cigarette
    el puro – cigar
    la nicotina – nicotine
    el tabaco – tobacco
la gastritis – gastritis
la gingivitis – gingivitis
el hematoma (*masculino*) / el moretón – bruise
    el ojo morado – black eye
la hemorragia – hemorrhage
la hemorroide – hemorrhoid
la hepatitis – hepatitis
la herida – wound
herir (e → ie) (e → i) – to wound
el herpes – herpes
el hipo – (the) hiccups
hincharse – to become swollen / to swell (up)
la hinchazón – swelling
el hormigueo – tingling sensation
el infarto / el ataque al corazón – heart attack
la infección – infection
infectar – to infect
la inflamación – inflammation
la intoxicación alimentaria – food poisoning
intoxicado/a – (food) poisoned
el latido irregular del corazón – irregular heartbeat
latir – to beat (heart)
la llaga – sore
lastimar(se) – to hurt (oneself) / to get hurt
la lesión – injury
lesionar(se) – to injure (oneself)
el lunar – mole
maligno/a – malignant
la mancha – stain
manchar – to stain
la migraña / la jaqueca – migraine
mortal – mortal / fatal / deadly
el mal aliento – bad breath
el maltrato – mistreatment (usually physical abuse)
marearse – to get motion (sea) sick
el mareo – motion (sea) sickness
las náuseas – nausea
la neumonía / la pulmonía – pneumonia

el nivel – level
    los niveles altos – high levels
        de triglicéridos – high triglyceride levels
        de azúcar en la sangre – high blood sugar
ovular – to ovulate
la ovulación – ovulation
el parásito – parasite
el parto – childbirth / delivery
la presión de sangre – blood pressure
    la alta presión de sangre / la hipertensión
    la baja presión de sangre / la hipotensión
el pus – pus
quebrarse (e → ie) – to break (one's ____)
el quiste – cyst
la retinopatía – retinopathy
resbalar(se) – to slip accidentally
el riesgo – risk
    estar a riesgo (de) – to be at risk (of)
romperse – to break (one's ____) / to tear (one's ____)
roto/a – broken / torn
las ronchas – hives
salir (bien, mal) – to come/turn out (well, badly)
el salpullido / el sarpullido – rash
sangrar (el sangrado) – to bleed (bleeding – *noun*)
la sensación (de ardor) – (burning) sensation
el SIDA (síndrome de inmunodeficiencia adquirida) – AIDS
el síntoma (*masculino*) – symptom
el síndrome – syndrome
el SMSL (síndrome de la muerte súbita del lactante) – SIDS
la(s) sobredosis – overdose(s)
la somnolencia / la soñolencia – drowsiness
sordo/a (sordomudo/a) – deaf (deaf-mute)
súbito/a / repentino/a – sudden
sufrir (de) / padecer (c → zc) – to suffer (from)
el TEPT (trastorno de estrés postraumático) – PTSD
torcerse (o → ue) – to twist / to sprain (one's ____)
toser – to cough
el trastorno – disorder
el trauma (*masculino*) – trauma
la tuberculosis – tuberculosis
el tumor – tumor
la úlcera – ulcer
la varicela – chickenpox
la verruga – wart
el VIH (virus de la inmunodeficiencia humana) – HIV
    ser seropositivo/a – to be HIV positive
el VPH (virus del papiloma humano) – HPV
la violación – rape / violation
violar – to rape / to violate
el (los) virus – virus(es)
viral – viral
vomitar (los vómitos) – to vomit (vomiting – *noun*)
el vómito – vomit

preguntas básicas (tú)
¿Cómo te sientes? – How do you feel?
¿Cómo te encuentras? – How do you feel?
¿Qué te pasa? – What's going on (for you)?
¿Qué pasó? – What happened?
¿Qué te duele? – What hurts (you)?
¿Qué tienes? – What (symptoms) do you have?
¿Cómo te va? – How is it going (for you)?
¿Qué tal? – How are things?
¿Con qué frecuencia? – How often?

respuestas básicas
¡Ay! – Ouch! / Ow!
(a mí) me duele _____ – my _____ hurts
tener dolor de _____ – to have a _____ ache
tener / sentir (with *nouns*)
    calor – to be hot
    frío – to be cold
    fiebre / calentura – to have a fever
    gripe / gripa – to have the flu
    resfrío / resfriado – to have a cold
    tos – to have a cough
    problemas para + *inf.* – problems with ____ing
    dificultades para + *infinitivo* – difficulty ____ing
sentirse / encontrarse (with *adjectives* or *adverbs*)
    fatal – awful
    horrible / terrible – horrible / terrible
    resfriado/a – to have a cold
    (aun) mejor – (even) better
    (aun) peor – (even) worse
casi no – not really

la duración
¿Cuánto tiempo hace que tienes fiebre?
    – How long have you had a fever?
Hace dos días que tengo fiebre.
    – I have had a fever for two days.
Tengo fiebre desde hace dos días.
    – I have had a fever for two days.
He tenido fiebre por dos días.
    – I have had a fever for two days.
¿Cuánto tiempo hacía que tenías fiebre?
    – How long had you had a fever?
Hacía dos días que tenía fiebre.
    – I had had a fever for two days.
Tenía fiebre desde hacía dos días.
    – I had had a fever for two days.
Había tenido fiebre por dos días.
    – I had had a fever for two days.
por – for (duration of time)
todavía (no) – still / (not) yet
ya – already / now
ya no – not any more

para mejorarse o prevenir una enfermedad

el aborto – abortion
el agua oxigenada – hydrogen peroxide
el agua salada – salt water
la aguja – needle
la alternativa – alternative
amamantar / dar pecho – to breastfeed
el (los) análisis – analysis (analyses)
   de semen – semen analysis
la anestesia – anesthesia
anormal – abnormal
el antibiótico – antibiotic
el anticonceptivo – contraceptive
   el condón / el preservativo – condom
   "cuidar" (a la mujer) – (the) "pull-out" method
   el DIU (dispositivo intrauterino) – IUD
   el implante – implant
   la abstinencia (abstenerse) – abstinence
el antídoto – antidote
el antihistamínico – antihistamine
el aparato – piece of equipment / device
aplicar(se) / poner(se) – to apply / to put on (oneself)
el asilo para ancianos – retirement home
ayunar – to fast
   en ayunas – without breakfast / fasting
la báscula – scale (for weight)
la biopsia – biopsy
el catéter – catheter
el cepillo de dientes – toothbrush
cepillarse/lavarse los dientes – to brush one's teeth
la (operación) cesárea – cesarean section
chequear / checar – to check (to examine)
el chequeo – check (exam)
circuncidar – to circumcise
la circuncisión – circumcision
la cita / la consulta – appointment / consultation
la cirugía (plástica / estética) – (plastic) surgery
la clínica – clinic
la colonoscopia / la colonoscopía – colonoscopy
concertar (e → ie) – to arrange / to put together
concertar/hacer una cita – to make an appointment
el cuidado de (la) salud – healthcare
el cuidado paliativo – palliative care
el cuidado primario – primary care
cuidar(se) – to take care of (oneself)
la cura – (the) cure
curar – to cure
dar a luz (a) / aliviarse – to give birth (to)
dejar de + *infinitivo* – to quit _____ing
descansar – to rest
la diálisis – dialysis
la dieta – diet
   estar (ponerse) a dieta – to be (to go) on a diet

las grasas – fats
las proteínas – proteins
los carbohidratos – carbohydrates
digerir (e → ie) (e → i) – to digest
la digestión – digestion
el dispositivo – device
dormir (o → ue) (o → u) – to sleep
la(s) dosis – dose(s)
el empaste – (dental) filling
encasar (un hueso) – to set (a bone)
la epidural / la ráquea / la raquídea – epidural
el examen médico – medical exam
el (examen) físico – physical (exam)
examinar – to examine
el expediente / el historial clínico – medical chart
extirpar – to remove (surgically)
estéril – sterile
esterilizar – to sterilize
el estetoscopio – stethoscope
la farmacia / la droguería / la botica – pharmacy
los fármacos / las drogas – pharmaceuticals / drugs
el fluoruro – fluoride
la(s) gasa(s) – gauze
el glucómetro – glucometer
la gota – drop (of liquid) / gout
el hospital – hospital
el hábito – habit
   los hábitos alimenticios – eating habits
hacer gárgaras – to gargle
hacer preguntas – to ask questions
el hilo dental – dental floss
   usar el hilo dental – to floss
el inhalador (de rescate) – (rescue) inhaler
la histerectomía – hysterectomy
la incisión – incision
el IMC (índice de masa corporal) – BMI
intramuscular – intramuscular
intravenoso/a – intravenous
la inyección – injection
inyectar – to inject
el jarabe – (cough) syrup
la jeringa – syringe
el laboratorio – laboratory
la lactancia – lactation
la ligadura de trompas – tubal ligation
la mamografía – mammography / mammogram
el manicomio – mental hospital
mandar (a alguien a) – to send (someone to)
mandar (a) + *infinitivo* – to tell someone *to* _____
el medicamento – medication
   de mostrador – over-the-counter medication
la medicina / la droga – medicine / drug
mejorarse – to get better

el masaje – massage
monitorizar / monitorear – to monitor
la muestra – sample
    de orina – urine sample
    de heces / de materia fecal – stool sample
la pasta dental / la pasta dentífrica – toothpaste
la pastilla / la píldora / la tableta – pill / tablet
pinchar – to poke (with a needle) / to inject
la puntada / el punto de sutura – stitch
la operación – operation
operar – to operate
el orden (en orden) – order (in order / in place)
la orden – order (what was requested) / request
ordenar – to order / to request
prevenir (e → ie) – to prevent
priorizar – to prioritize
probar (o → ue) – to test
el procedimiento – procedure
proceder – to proceed
la prueba – test
    de sangre – blood test
quedarse en la cama – to stay in bed
la quimioterapia – chemotherapy
el quirófano – operating room (OR)
quirúrgico/a – surgical
la recuperación – recovery
recuperarse – to recover
la radiografía / los rayos equis – X-ray
la radioterapia – radiation therapy
la rehabilitación – rehabilitation
rehabilitar(se) – to rehabilitate (oneself)
la receta / la prescripción – prescription
el repuesto / el recambio – refill
respirar (inhalar, exhalar) – to breathe
resucitar – to resuscitate
el resultado – result
revivir – to revive / to relive
sacar sangre – to draw blood
la sala de emergencia – emergency room (ER/ED)
la sala de espera – waiting room
la sala de recuperación – recovery room
sanar(se) – to heal / to get better
el seguro / la aseguranza (médico/a) – insurance
el sexo (seguro) – (safe) sex
el seguimiento – follow-up
los signos vitales – vital signs
el sistema inmunológico – immune system
    "las defensas" – defenses
sobrio/a – sober
la sobriedad – sobriety
someterse (a) – to undergo / to subject oneself (to)
sonarse (o → ue) la nariz – to blow one's nose
la sonda – probe

el suero medicinal – IV fluids
suturar – to suture / to stitch
la temperatura – temperature
la terapia (del habla) – (speech) therapy
el termómetro – thermometer
la tira – strip
la tirita / la curita – adhesive bandage (Band Aid)
tomar – to take (by mouth) / to drink
tomar – to take (temperature, blood pressure, etc.)
tomar una decisión – to make a decision
el trasplante – transplant
el ultrasonido – ultrasound
la vasectomía – vasectomy
la vacuna – vaccine
vacunar (contra) – to vaccinate (against)
la venda – bandage
la venda adhesiva / la curita – adhesive bandage
vendar – to bandage
el yeso / la escayola – (plaster) cast

las posturas corporales y las expresiones faciales
acostarse (o → ue) – to lie down
acuclillarse – to squat down / to crouch down
    estar en cuclillas – to be crouching
asentir (e → ie) (e → i) con la cabeza – to nod
acurrucarse – to curl up / to snuggle up
agacharse – to duck down / to bend over
alzar / levantar (la cabeza) – to lift (one's head)
arrodillarse – to kneel down / to get on one's knees
bajar (la cabeza) – to lower (one's head)
boca abajo – upside down / face down
    prono/a – prone
boca arriba – right-side up / face up
    supino/a – supine
estar cabizbajo/a – to have one's head down (due
    to sadness, worry, embarrassment, dejection)
encogerse de hombros – to shrug one's shoulders
empinarse – to lean over / to bend over
erguirse (e → i) – to stand/sit up straight
    estar erguido/a – to be upright
fruncir el ceño – to frown
guiñar un ojo – to wink
hacer una mueca – to make a face
    la mueca – (funny) face / facial expression
levantarse – to get up
negar (e → ie) con la cabeza – to shake one's head no
ponerse de pie / pararse – to stand up
    estar de pie / estar parado/a – to be standing
    estar de puntillas – to be on one's tippy-toes
señalar con el dedo / apuntar – to point
sentarse (e → i) – to sit down / to sit up
    estar sentado/a – to be seated / to be sitting
sonreír (e → í) (e →) – to smile

los ejercicios y los estiramientos

hacer – to do
    (los) abdominales – situps / crunches
    (las) dominadas – pullups
    (las) lagartijas / (las) flexiones – pushups
    (los) marineros – jumping jacks
    (las) sentadillas – squats
levantar pesas – to lift weights
montar en bicicleta – to ride a bicycle
nadar – to swim
caminar – to walk
    salir a caminar / ir a pasear – to go for a walk
estirarse – to stretch
saltar / brincar – to jump / to bounce
manejar (el estrés, etc.) – to manage (stress, etc.)

los títulos profesionales

el / la anestesiólogo/a – anesthesiologist
el / la asistente/a médico/a – medical assistant (MA)
el / la asociado/a médico/a – physician assistant (PA)
el / la cardiólogo/a – cardiologist
el / la consejero/a – counselor / advisor
el / la cirujano/a – surgeon
    ortopédico/a – orthopedic surgeon
el / la dentista – dentist
el / la dermatólogo/a – dermatologist
el / la dietista / nutricionista – dietitian / nutritionist
el / la encargado/a – (the) person in charge
el / la enfermero/a (practicante/a) – nurse (practitioner)
el / la especialista (en) – specialist (in)
el / la farmacéutico/a / farmaceuta – pharmacist
el / la gastroenterólogo/a – gastroenterologist
el / la gineco-obstetra – OB/GYN
    el / la ginecólogo/a – gynecologist
    el / la obstetra – obstetrician
el / la intérprete – interpreter (verbal)
el / la masajista – massage therapist
el / la médico/a – medical doctor (MD)
el / la neumólogo/a – pulmonologist
el / la neurólogo/a – neurologist
el / la optometrista – optometrist
el / la oncólogo/a – oncologist
el / la ortodoncista – orthodontist
el / la ortopedista – orthopedist
el / la pediatra – pediatrician
el / la proveedor/a – provider
el / la psicólogo/a – psychologist
el / la psiquiatra – psychiatrist
el / la quiropráctico/a – chiropractor
el / la radiólogo/a – radiologist
el / la terapeuta / terapista – therapist
el / la traductor/a – translator (written)
el / la urólogo/a – urologist

otras palabras y expresiones útiles

lo antes posible / tan pronto (como sea) posible /
    lo más pronto posible / cuanto antes
    – as soon as possible
como mucho – at (the) most
como pronto – at the earliest
como tarde / a más tardar – at the latest
bilingüe – bilingual
trilingüe – trilingual
cuatrilingüe – quadrilingual
multilingüe – multilingual
tutear / tratar a alguien de "tú" – to speak to
    someone as "tú"
ustedear / tratar a alguien de "Ud." – to speak to
    someone as "usted"
de parte de (de mi parte) – on behalf of
la razón de (la cita) – (the) reason for (the appt.)
de hecho – in fact / actually
actualmente – currently
actualizar – to update
disponible – available
la disponibilidad – availability
el testamento vital – living will
la voluntad anticipada – advance directives
estar atento/a a la llamada – to be on call
confidencial – confidential
la confidencialidad – confidentiality
consentir (e → ie) (e → i) – to consent
el consentimiento – consent
lamentar – to regret
lamentablemente – regrettably
¿A ver? – Let me see?
A ver … – Let's see …
o sea / es decir – that is to say (clarification)
mejor dicho / más bien – rather (slight correction)
evidentemente – evidently
efectivamente – effectively
aparentemente / por lo visto – apparently
¿A nombre de quién? – Under what name?
a nombre de _____ – under (name)
el milagro – miracle
bendecir (e → i) – to bless
bendito/a – blessed
la bendición – blessing
maldecir (e → i) – to curse
maldito/a – cursed / damned
la maldición – curse
el formulario / la forma – form
    llenar – to fill out
    la casilla – check box
    la marca de verificación/visto – checkmark
    firmar – to sign (one's name)
el costado – side (of the body or any solid object)

Unidad 26 – la vida doméstica

las viviendas / el alojamiento – housing

el apartamento / el departamento – apartment
la casa – house
la casa de remolque – mobile home
el parque de remolques – mobile home park
el condominio – condominium
la hipoteca – mortgage
el hogar – home / hearth
alojar / hospedar – to host / to put (someone) up
alojarse / hospedarse / quedarse (en) – to stay (at)
el / la huésped/a – guest (overnight)
el / la invitado/a – guest (for the day)
recibir / acoger – to welcome (to one's home)
estar/ser bienvenido/a – to be welcome
dar la bienvenida – to welcome
la (cordial / cálida) acogida – (warm) welcome
acogedor/a – welcoming

la vivienda – dwelling

el balcón – balcony
el (cuarto de) baño / el servicio – bathroom
el camino particular – driveway
la casa (de ____ pisos) – (____ story) house
la cocina – kitchen
el comedor – dining room
el cuarto (de huéspedes) – (guest) room
el desván / el ático / el altillo / el entretecho – attic
el dormitorio / la habitación / la recámara / la alcoba
    – bedroom
la entrada – entryway / entrance
la(s) escalera(s) – stairs / staircase
    escaleras abajo – downstairs
    escaleras arriba – upstairs
el estudio – studio / study
el frente – (the) front
el fondo – (the) bottom / (the) back / background
el garaje / la cochera – garage / carport
el jardín – yard
el lavadero – laundry room
la pared / el muro – wall
el patio – patio
el (primer) piso – (first) floor
    de madera – wood floor (wooden)
    de azulejo – tile floor
el porche – porch
el portal – entryway / front door
la sala / el living – living room
la sala de estar – family room
el sótano – basement
el suelo – ground / floor (not numbered)
el taller – workshop

el techo / el cielo – ceiling
el tejado / el techo – roof
la ventana – window

las cosas de la casa o del jardín

la alfombra – carpet
la almohada – (bed) pillow
el árbol – tree
    el arce – maple tree
    el manzano – apple tree
    el naranjo – orange tree
    el olmo – elm tree
    el peral – pear tree
    el pino – pine tree
    el roble – oak tree
el arbusto – bush
    el rosal – rosebush
el banco / la banca – bench
la bañera / la tina – bathtub
la cama / el lecho – bed
el cartel / el póster, *pl.* los pósters – poster(s)
el cerco / la cerca – fence
el césped / el sacate (zacate) – lawn
la chimenea – fireplace / chimney
los cobertores – (the) covers
la cobija / la manta – blanket
la colcha / el cubrecama(s) – comforter / bedspread
el colchón – mattress
el cojín – throw pillow / couch cushion
la cómoda – dresser
la cortina – curtain
las cosas – things / stuff
el cuadro – picture (usually framed)
la ducha – shower
el electrodoméstico – electrical appliance
el escritorio – desk
el espejo – mirror
el estéreo – stereo
    la bocina / el parlante / el altavoz – speaker
el estante – shelf / bookcase
la estantería – bookcase / shelving
la estufa – stove
el fregadero – kitchen sink
el guardarropa / el clóset / el armario – closet
el horno (de microondas) – (microwave) oven
el huerto – garden
el inodoro / el retrete / la taza – toilet (bowl)
la lámpara – lamp
el lavabo / el (los) lavamanos – bathroom sink(s)
la lavadora – washing machine
el (los) lavaplatos – dishwasher(s)

la llave / el grifo – faucet
el mantel – tablecloth
la mecedora – rocking chair
la mesa – table
el mostrador – counter / countertop
el mueble – piece of furniture
la plancha – iron
la plomería – plumbing
la puerta – door
    la bisagra – hinge
    el dintel – doorway / doorjamb
    el picaporte – doorknocker / door handle
    el pomo – doorknob
    la manija / la manilla – door handle
    la cadena – chain
    la cerradura – lock
    entreabierto/a – halfway open
    abierto/a de par en par – wide open
el refrigerador (refri) / el frigorífico / la nevera
   – refrigerator (fridge)
el reloj – clock / watch
la repisa – mantelpiece / windowsill / shelf
    el alféizar / la alfeiza – ledge / windowsill
la sábana – bed sheet
el (los) salvamanteles – placemat(s) / coaster(s)
la secadora – (clothes) dryer
la silla – chair
el sillón, *pl.* los sillones – arm chair(s)
el sofá (*masculino*) – couch / sofa
el tapete – rug
el televisor – TV set
hacer juego con – to go with / to match

las herramientas y la ferretería
los alicates – plyers
la arandela – washer
el azadón – hoe
la cinta (adhesiva) – (sticky / adhesive) tape
el clavo – nail
el contenedor / el recipiente – container
el (los) cortacésped – lawnmower(s)
el cubo / el balde – bucket / pail
el destapador de inodoros / el amigo – toilet plunger
el destornillador – screwdriver
la escoba – broom
la ferretería – hardware / hardware store
el flexómetro / la cinta métrica – tape measure
la fregona / el trapeador – mop
la herramienta – tool
el rastrillo – rake
la lima – file
la llave – key
la llave inglesa – wrench
la manguera – (garden) hose

el martillo – hammer
la pala – shovel
el papel de lija – sandpaper
la tachuela – tack / pushpin
las tijeras – scissors
el tornillo – screw / bolt
la tuerca – nut

las descripciones
antiguo/a – antique / old
áspero/a – rough (surface)
bastante – quite / rather (*adverb*)
bastante / suficiente – enough (*adjective*)
blando/a / suave – soft
confortable / cómodo/a – comfortable
cuadrado/a – square
de cuero – (made of) leather
de madera – wooden / (made of) wood
de metal – (made of) metal
de tela – (made of) cloth
de mala calidad / chafa – low quality
de buena calidad – high quality
duro/a – hard
incómodo/a – uncomfortable
limpio/a – clean
liso/a – smooth (surface)
mugriento/a / sucio/a – filthy / dirty
    la mugre / la suciedad – filth / dirtiness
ovalado/a – oval (shaped)
plano/a – flat (surface)
redondo/a – round
delantero/a – front
trasero/a – back

los quehaceres y otras acciones
abrir la llave/el agua – to turn on the water
abrir la puerta con llave – to unlock the door
alimentar / dar de comer – to feed
apretar (e → ie) – to tighten / to squeeze
arar – to plow
arreglar – to tidy up / to fix
barrer – to sweep
cerrar la llave/el agua – to turn off the water
cerrar la puerta con llave – to lock the door
cocinar / cocer (o → ue) (c → z) – to cook
coser – to sew
colgar (o → ue) – to hang (up)
cortar (el césped) – to cut / to mow (the lawn)
criar (i → í) niños – to raise kids
el deber doméstico – domestic duty
doblar / plegar (e → ie) – to fold
desempolvar – to dust
empapar – to soak
excavar – to dig

fregar (e → ie) / trapear – to mop
fregar – to scrub
guardar – to put away / to keep
hacer la cama – to make the bed
lavar – to wash
lijar – to sand
limar – to file (down)
limpiar – to clean (up)
martillar / clavar – to hammer
mojar – to wet
mover con pala – to shovel
pasar la aspiradora / aspirar – to vacuum
pasar un trapo – to wipe (with a rag)
planchar – to iron
poner / colocar – to put / to place / to set
preparar – to prepare
pulir – to polish
el quehacer (de la casa) – (household) chore
quitar – to clear off / to remove (from surface)
rastrillar (las hojas) – to rake (the leaves)
recoger – to pick up / to straighten up
regar (e → ie) – to water
reparar – to repair / to fix
rociar (i → í) – to spray
sacar – to take out / to remove (from within)
sacudir – to shake
secar – to dry
soler (o → ue) + *inf.* – to be in the habit of ____*ing*
tejer – to knit
tender (e → ie) – to lay out / to stretch out
tender a + *infinitivo* – to tend *to* _____
tocar/llamar a la puerta – to knock on the door
la fuerza – strength
la debilidad – weakness
el punto débil – weakness / weak point
el punto fuerte – strength / strong point

el coche / el carro / el auto – car / automobile

la motocicleta (moto) – motorcycle
el / la motociclista / motorista – motorcyclist / biker
el monovolumen – minivan
el camión – truck (general)
la troca – pickup (truck)
el / la conductor/a – driver
conducir (c → zc) / manejar – to drive
el volante – steering wheel
arrancar el carro – to start the car
el arranque – ignition
la batería – (car) battery
el salpicadero – dashboard
la guantera – glovebox
el (los) parabrisas – windshield(s)
el (los) limpiaparabrisas – windshield wiper(s)

el foco – headlight
el asiento – seat
el respaldo – backrest
la cajuela / el maletero – trunk
la defensa / el (los) parachoques – bumper(s)
el motor – engine
la transmisión – transmission
el espejo retrovisor – rearview mirror
 el ángulo muerto – blind spot
el intermitente / la flecha – blinker
la velocidad – speed / gear
la palanca – gearshift
el pedal – pedal
 el acelerador – accelerator / gas pedal
 el freno – brake
 el embrague – clutch
el velocímetro – speedometer
la llanta – tire
la rueda – wheel
el escape – exhaust pipe / tailpipe
la gasolina – gasoline
el gasóleo – diesel fuel
el tanque / el depósito – gas tank
el aceite / el óleo (de motor) – (motor) oil
adelantar – to go ahead (of) / to pass
estacionar / parquear / aparcar – to park
 el estacionamiento / el aparcamiento – parking lot
descomponerse / estropearse – to break down
la grúa – tow truck / crane
remolcar – to tow
atropellar – to run over
estallar / explotar – to explode
chocar / estrellarse (con / contra) – to crash (into)

otras palabras y expresiones útiles
el ama de casa (*femenino*) – homemaker / housewife
bajar – to go down / to lower
subir – to go up / to raise
abajo – below / down
arriba – above / up
el chisme – gossip
chismear – to gossip
el / la chismoso/a – one who gossips
el / la criado/a – housekeeper / nanny
de otra manera – otherwise
hay – there is / there are
había – there was / there were
hay que + *infinitivo* – one has *to* _____
había que + *infinitivo* – one had *to* _____
haber de + *infinitivo* – to have *to* _____
 Hubo de hacerlo. – He had to do it.
¿Qué hay (de nuevo)? – What's new?
¿Qué hubo(le)? – What's new?

Unidad 27 – las ciencias y la tecnología

la física – physics
la astrofísica – astrophysics
    la astronomía – astronomy
    el espacio exterior – outer space
    el agujero negro – black hole
    la rotación – rotation
    rotar – to rotate
    girar – to spin / to turn
    alrededor (de) / en torno (a) – around
    la órbita – orbit
    el eje – axis
    la trayectoria – trajectory
físico/a – physical
la masa – mass
la velocidad – velocity / speed
acelerar – to accelerate
la aceleración – acceleration
la gravedad – gravity
la fuerza de gravedad – gravitational force
el momento – momentum
la inercia – inertia
el volumen – volume
la capacidad – capacity
la magnitud – magnitude
el campo – field
electromagnético/a – electromagnetic
magnético/a – magnetic
el magnetismo – magnetism
el imán – magnet
la acción – action
la reacción nuclear – nuclear reaction
térmico/a – thermal
atómico/a – atomic
el átomo – atom
    el electrón – electron
    el protón – proton
    el neutrón – neutron
el ion – ion
la carga – charge
eléctrico/a – electrical
negativo/a – negative
positivo/a – positive
neutro/a – neutral
la partícula – particle
el núcleo – nucleus
la fusión nuclear – nuclear fusion
la fisión nuclear – nuclear fission
radioactivo/a / radiactivo/a – radioactive
la energía – energy
potencial – potential
cinético/a – kinetic

la química – chemistry
la bioquímica – biochemistry
    el ADN (ácido desoxirribonucleico) – DNA
    la hormona – hormone
    el metabolismo – metabolism
la materia – matter
el estado – state of being
el sólido (sólido/a) – solid
el líquido (líquido/a) – liquid
el gas (gaseoso/a) – gas (gaseous)
el plasma (*masculino*) – plasma
    plasmático/a – plasmatic / plasma
la reacción química – chemical reaction
el enlace químico – chemical bond
    el enlace covalente – covalent bond
    el enlace iónico – ionic bond
el químico (químico/a) – chemical
la molécula – molecule
el elemento – element
el compuesto (compuesto/a) – compound
la tabla periódica de los elementos – periodic table
                           of elements

la biología – biology
la microbiología – microbiology
la taxonomía – taxonomy
agrupar – to group (together)
el dominio – domain
    el reino – kingdom
    el filo / la división – phylum
    la clase – class
    el orden – order
    la familia – family
    el género – genus
    la especie – species
la nomenclatura – nomenclature
    binomial – binomial nomenclature
la evolución – evolution
evolucionar – to evolve
la filogenia – phylogeny
adaptarse (a) – to adapt (to)
la mutación – mutation
mutante – mutant
complejo/a – complex
el ser (vivo, humano) – (living, human) being
el organismo – organism
el gen – gene
la genética – genetics
genético/a – genetic
sobrevivir (a) – to survive
la sobrevivencia / la supervivencia – survival
el / la sobreviviente / superviviente – survivor

la electricidad – electricity

el amperio – ampere
la corriente – current
    eléctrica – electrical current
    alterna – alternating current (AC)
    continua – direct current (DC)
el circuito – circuit
el corto circuito – short circuit
la potencia / el potencial – power
el voltaje – voltage
el voltio – volt
el vataje – wattage
el vatio – watt

la tecnología – technology

el telescopio – telescope
el microscopio – microscope
los (anteojos) prismáticos – binoculars
la lupa – magnifying glass
el alcoholímetro – breathalyzer
el altímetro – altimeter
el velocímetro – speedometer
la máquina – machine
el (teléfono) celular (celu) / el móvil – cell / mobile
la tableta / la tablet – tablet
la informática / la computación – computing
la base de datos – database
los datos – data
la computadora (compu) / el ordenador – computer
la fuente de alimentación – power supply
iniciar – to start / to boot up (app, computer, etc.)
reiniciar – to restart / to reboot
el procesador – processor
el hardware – hardware
el disco duro – hard drive
la memoria – memory
el equipo – (computer) equipment
el estuche / la funda – (carrying, protective) case
el router – router
el módem – modem
el software – software
la pantalla (táctil) – (touch) screen
el teclado (táctil) – (touch) keyboard
la tecla – key (of a keyboard)
la impresora – printer
imprimir – to print
el ratón (táctil) – mouse (touch pad)
el micrófono – microphone
electrónico/a – electronic
el alambre – wire
inalámbrico/a – wireless
el tomacorriente – surge protector
la clavija – power plug

el enchufe – power outlet
enchufar – to plug in
el cable – cable / cord
    de extensión – extension cord
la pila – battery
el cargador – charger
cargar – to charge / to load
sobrecargar – to overload
avanzado/a – advanced
avanzar – to advance
el avance / el adelanto – advancement
progresar – to progress
el progreso – progress
obsoleto/a – obsolete
el paso – step
la etapa – stage (of a process)
la pauta – guideline
la manera / la forma – (the) way
la posibilidad – possibility
el proceso – process
procesar – to process
actual / corriente – current (time)
actualmente – currently
hoy en día – nowadays
reciente – recent
recién / recientemente – recently
últimamente – lately
la iluminación – lighting / illumination
la calefacción – heating
el aire acondicionado – air conditioning
central – central
la temperatura ambiente – room temperature
la novedad – novelty
el transformador – transformer
el fusible – fuse
el interruptor – light switch / power switch
el conductor – conductor
la bombilla – lightbulb
el adaptador – adapter
la conexión – connection
conectar – to connect
convertir (e → ie) (e → i) (en) – to convert (to)
descubrir – to discover / to uncover
el descubrimiento – discovery
inventar – to invent
la invención / el invento – invention
ocupar – to occupy
el modelo – model / template
sonar (o → ue) (a) – to sound (like) / to ring
caber (yo quepo) – to fit (inside)
técnico/a – technical
el programa (*masculino*) – program
programar – to program / to schedule

los medios de comunicación social – social media

la red social – social network
la red – network / (the) internet / (the) net
el (la) internet – (the) internet / (the) web
el dominio – domain
la plataforma – platform
el sitio web – website
la página web – web page
en línea – online
hacer clic (izquierdo, derecho) – to (left, right) click
arrastrar – to drag
guardar – to save
cortar, copiar, pegar – to cut, to copy, to paste
surfear / navegar – to surf / to navigate
el buscador – search engine
buscar – to search (for)
la búsqueda / la busca – search
en busca/búsqueda de – in search of
la aplicación / la app – application / app
googlear – to google
el foro / el fórum – forum
el chat – chat (digital)
chatear – to chat (digitally)
el texto – text
textear – to text
mandar / enviar (i → í) – to send
el correo electrónico – email
el / la remitente – sender
el / la destinatario/a – recipient
la bandeja de entrada – inbox
el mensaje / el recado – message
dejar un recado – to leave a message
tuitear – to tweet
el tuit – tweet
el perfil – profile
la contraseña – password
el nombre de usuario – user name
el / la usuario/a – user
la clave – key / passcode
acceder (a) – to access
el wifi – WiFi
la cobertura – coverage
cubrir – to cover
la captura de pantalla – screenshot
el vínculo / el enlace – link
por defecto – by default
el promedio – average
funcionar – to work / to function
servir (e → i) – to work / to function
servir (de) – to serve (as)
el / la nómada digital – digital nomad
la prensa – (the) press
las noticias – (the) news

otras palabras y expresiones útiles

junto a – next to
junto con – along with
cada cual / cada uno – each one (thing)
cada quien / cada uno – each one (person)
alguno/a que otro/a _____
    – an occasional _____ (here and there)
para colmo – to top it all off
yo, a mi vez (ella, a su vez) – I, in turn (she, in turn)
asimismo / también – also / too
específico/a – specific
de hecho – actually / in fact
a medida que – as
proponer – to propose
la propuesta – proposal
la subvención – (monetary) grant
la patente de invención – patent
el premio – award / prize
el cumplido – compliment
el halago / la alabanza / el elogio – praise / flattery
halagar / alabar / elogiar – to praise / to flatter
agradar / complacer (c → zc) – to please
agradable – pleasant / pleasing
desagradable – unpleasant
favorable – favorable
la mayoría – (the) majority
la minoría – (the) minority
el consenso – consensus
científico/a – scientific
el método – method
observar – to observe
la(s) hipótesis – hypothesis (hypotheses)
el experimento – experiment
el estudio – study
controlar – to control
repetir (e → i) – to repeat
el objetivo – objective
comprobar (o → ue) – to prove
rechazar – to reject
aceptar – to accept
colaborar – to collaborate
confirmar – to confirm
el esfuerzo – effort / endeavor
aumentar – to increase / to raise
disminuir (y) – to decrease / to diminish
la esperanza – hope
ampliar (i → í) / expandir – to broaden / to expand
extender (e → ie) – to extend
adepto/a – adept
inepto/a – inept
el conocimiento – knowledge
la sabiduría – wisdom
sabio/a – wise

Unidad 28 – el crimen, las delincuencias y la justicia

los crímenes y las delincuencias
el crimen – crime (serious crime, like murder)
la delincuencia – delincuency (generic crime)
el delito – crime (less serious than *crimen*)
el / la delincuente – delinquent / criminal
el / la criminal – criminal
la violencia – violence
el terrorismo – terrorism
el / la terrorista – terrorist
robar – to rob / to steal
a mano armada – at gunpoint
el ladrón / la ladrona – thief
disparar / tirar – to shoot
a quemarropa – at point-blank range
golpear / pegar – to hit
a palos – with sticks or clubs (bludgeon)
a puñetazos – by punching / with (his/her) fists
asesinar – to assassinate / to murder
el asesinato – assassination
matar – to kill
la matanza – killing
a puñaladas – by stabbing
apuñalar – to stab
el / la asesino/a – assassin / murderer
el / la sicario/a – hitman / hitwoman
el tiroteo – shootout
la masacre – massacre
el atentado / el ataque – attack
asaltar / atacar – to assault / to attack
lidiar / pelear / luchar – to fight / to struggle
dañar / hacer daño (a) – to damage / to harm
destruir (y) / destrozar – to destroy
recurrir (a) – to resort (to)
la pandilla – gang
el / la pandillero/a – gang member
el / la secuestrador/a – kidnapper
secuestrar / raptar – to kidnap
el secuestro – kidnapping
linchar – to lynch
provocar – to provoke
incitar – to incite
el motín – riot
la huelga – strike
la protesta / la manifestación – protest
acosar – to harass
el acoso (sexual) – (sexual) harassment
hubo (haber) – there was/were (used for events)
había (haber) – there was/were (describes scene)
el narcotráfico – drug trafficking
el / la narcotraficante – drug dealer
la mula / el burro – drug mule

el contrabando – contraband
la cocaína – cocaine
la heroína – heroin
la marihuana / la mota – marijuana / pot
la jerga / el argot – jargon / slang
estafar – to cheat / to swindle
el / la estafador/a – cheater / swindler
chantajear / extorsionar – to blackmail / to extort
el chantaje / la extorsión – blackmail / extortion
sobornar – to bribe
el soborno / la mordida – bribe
el soplón / la soplona – snitch / rat / whistleblower
soplar – to snitch / to rat out / to blow the whistle
el / la cabeza de turco – fall guy
el chivo expiatorio – scapegoat
el / la cómplice – accomplice
denunciar – to turn in / to report / to denounce
la venganza – revenge / retribution
entregarse / rendirse – to turn oneself in / to surrender
el arma (*femenino*), *pl.* las armas – weapon(s)
el arma de fuego – firearm
armar – to arm / to assemble / to put together
la bomba (explosiva) – bomb
explotar / estallar / explosionar – to explode
el explosivo – explosive
hacer explotar / detonar – to set off / to detonate
la navaja / el cuchillo / el arma blanca – knife
la pistola – pistol
la ametralladora – machine gun
el rifle – rifle
la escopeta – shotgun
el casquillo – bullet shell
la bala – bullet
    (el chaleco) antibala – bulletproof (vest)
la guerra – war
la paz – peace

el lugar de los hechos – crime scene
la víctima – victim (regardless of gender or sex)
resultar – to become (injured, wounded, etc.)
herido/a – wounded
ileso/a – uninjured
sano/a y salvo/a – safe and sound
estar a salvo – to be safe
la precaución – precaution
morir (o → ue) (o → u) / fallecer (c → zc) – to die
el / la muerto/a / difunto/a – dead person
el cadáver – dead body
la cuestión de vida o muerte – matter of life or death
el / la paramédico/a – paramedic
los primeros auxilios – first aid

resucitar / revivir / volver a la vida – to resuscitate
la ambulancia – ambulance
las urgencias – (the) emergency room (ER/ED)
investigar – to investigate
el / la detective – detective
la policía (poli) – (the) police / police force
el / la policía (poli) – police officer
arrestar – to arrest
detener (e → ie) – to detain
clandestino/a – undercover
la patrulla – patrol car / squad car
la fuerza de tarea (antidroga) – (anti-drug) task force
perseguir (e → i) – to chase / to pursue
el / la sospechoso/a – suspect
sospechoso/a – suspicious
evitar / evadir – to avoid / to evade
huir (y) – to flee
dirigirse (a) – to head in a direction
dirigir – to direct
esconder(se) / ocultar(se) – to hide (oneself)
cazar – to hunt
la caza – hunt / manhunt
el / la cazador/a de recompensas – bounty hunter
suceder / ocurrir – to happen / to occur
el suceso / el evento / el acontecimiento – event
el suicidio – suicide
suicidarse – to commit suicide
el / la rehén, pl. los / las rehenes – hostage(s)
arriesgar / poner a riesgo (de) – to (put at) risk (of)
correr el riesgo (de) – to run the risk (of)
asombrar – to amaze / to astonish
espantar / asustar – to scare
preocuparse (de) – to worry / to get worried (about)
temer – to fear
el temor / el miedo – fear
rescatar / salvar – to rescue / to save
el rescate – rescue
alarmar – to alarm
entrar en acción / actuar (u → ú) – to act

el sistema de justicia criminal
bajo custodia – in custody
el / la reo/a – defendant / prisoner / accused
enfrentar cargos – to face charges
el derecho (a) – (the) right (to)
legal – legal
ilegal – illegal
justo/a – fair / just
injusto/a – unfair / unjust
la justicia – justice
el / la abogado/a – lawyer / attorney
el / la juez/a, pl. los / las jueces/zas – judge(s)
el jurado – jury

el / la jurado/a – juror
el tribunal – courtroom / court
el juzgado / la corte – courthouse / court
la ley – (the) law
confiscar / decomisar – to confiscate / to seize
la orden de alejamiento – restraining order
el toque de queda – curfew
el hecho – fact
identificar – to identify
el / la testigo – witness
atestiguar / testificar – to testify
la evidencia – evidence
defender (e → ie) – to defend
la autodefensa / la defensa propia – self-defense
ser inocente – to be innocent
ser culpable – to be guilty
la culpa – blame
culpar / acusar – to blame / to accuse
el / la acusado/a – the accused
llegar a un acuerdo – to reach an agreement
el fallo – ruling / judgment
poner en libertad – to release / to set free
librar / liberar – to free
ser libre – to be free (not detained)
la sentencia / la condena – sentence
sentenciar / condenar – to sentence / to condemn
imponer – to impose
la medida – measure / action
meter en la cárcel / encarcelar – to (put in) jail
la cárcel / la prisión – jail / prison
el bote – (the) joint / (the) pen / (the) slammer
la cadena perpetua – life sentence
la pena de muerte – (the) death penalty
el / la prisionero/a / preso/a – prisoner
severo/a – severe
la multa – fine
castigar – to punish
el castigo – punishment
arrepentirse (e → ie) (e → i) (de) – to repent / to regret
reformar(se) – to reform (to become reformed)
superar – to overcome / to surpass
acabar (con) – to end / to put an end (to)
el fracaso / el fallo – failure
fracasar / fallar – to fail
sorprendente – surprising
el tipo – type / kind / kind of person
demandar – to sue / to demand
la demanda – lawsuit / demand
la deuda – debt
contratar – to contract / to hire
el / la (los / las) guardaespaldas – bodyguard(s)
el / la guardia – guard
vigilar – to watch over (something / someone)

Unidad 29 – la política y los asuntos mundiales

el gobierno – (the) government
    federal – (the) federal government
    estatal – (the) state government
el / la gobernador/a – governor
el gabinete – cabinet
gobernar (e → ie) – to govern
gubernamental – governmental
la constitución – constitution
la separación de poderes – separation of powers
la rama – branch
    judicial – judicial branch
    legislativa – legislative branch
    ejecutiva – executive branch
el distrito – district
el congreso – congress
el / la congresista – member of congress
el / la diputado/a / representante – representative
el senado – senate
el / la senador/a – senator
la presidencia – presidency
el / la presidente/a – president
el / la vicepresidente/a – vice president
el / la secretario/a – secretary
    de la Defensa – Secretary of Defense
    del Estado – Secretary of State
    del Tesoro – Secretary of the Treasury
la Primera Dama – First Lady
el / la primer/a ministro/a – prime minister
el parlamento – parliament

la política – politics / policy
el / la político/a – politician / political
el partido (político) – (political) party
el / la aliado/a – ally / allied
el comunismo – communism
comunista – communist
el socialismo – socialism
socialista – socialist
la democracia – democracy
el / la demócrata – democrat
democrático/a – democratic
la república – republic
republicano/a – republican
el fascismo – fascism
fascista – fascist
conservador/a – conservative
liberal – liberal
las elecciones – (the) election / elections
libre – free
corrupto/a – corrupt
la corrupción – corruption

el fraude – fraud
fraudulento/a – fraudulent
la revolución – revolution
revolucionario/a – revolutionary
la protesta / la manifestación – protest
la marcha – march
marchar(se) – to march / to leave
la dictadura – dictatorship
el / la dictador/a – dictator
la tiranía – tyranny
el / la tirano/a – tyrant
tiránico/a – tyrannical
las represalias – reprisal / retaliation
la diplomacia – diplomacy
el / la diplomático/a – diplomat / diplomatic
las Naciones Unidas – (the) United Nations
la Unión Europea – (the) European Union
la OTAN – NATO
la OPEP – OPEC
el tratado de libre comercio – free-trade agreement
la campaña (electoral) – (electoral) campaign
postularse / lanzarse (para) – to run (for) (office)
el / la candidato/a – candidate
la candidatura – candidacy
prometer – to promise
la promesa – promise
implicar – to implicate / to imply
convencer (c → z) – to convince
el debate – debate
debatir – to debate
el / la rival – rival
vencer (c → z) / derrotar – to defeat
elegir (e → i) – to elect / to choose
votar (por) – to vote (for)
el voto – vote / ballot
la urna – ballot box
el / la ciudadano/a – citizen
indocumentado/a – undocumented
la frontera (política) – (political) border
el muro – wall
la inmigración – immigration
la redada – raid
deportar – to deport
la visa / el visado – visa
el asilo político – political asylum
la ley – law
justo/a – fair
la justicia – justice
injusto/a – unfair
la injusticia – injustice
el ambiente / el entorno – environment

la(s) crisis – crisis (crises)
el tornado – tornado
el huracán – hurricane
el deslave – mudslide / landslide
el terremoto / el seísmo / el sismo – earthquake
el maremoto – earthquake at sea
el temblor – tremor
la nevada – snowfall
la inundación – flood
el apagón – blackout
escaso/a – scarce
la escasez – scarcity / shortage
la sequía – drought
la hambruna – famine
morir(se) de hambre – to starve
la tormenta (eléctrica) – (electrical) storm
el relámpago – lightning
el trueno – thunder
el rayo (cayó) – lightning bolt (struck)
el incendio – fire
la Cruz Roja – (the) Red Cross
humanitario/a – humanitarian
voluntario/a – voluntary
el auxilio / el socorro / el amparo – aid / help
¡Auxilio! / ¡Socorro! – Help!
huir (y) – to flee
el / la refugiado/a – refugee
el refugio – refuge / shelter
sin hogar / sin techo – homeless
el / la mendigo/a – beggar
rogar (o → ue) / suplicar / mendigar – to beg
desamparado/a – helpless / uncared-for
abandonar – to abandon
abandonado/a – abandoned
necesitado/a – needy
vulnerable – vulnerable
entrar en pánico / sentir pánico – to panic
el / la huérfano/a – orphan
el orfanato / el orfanatorio – orphanage
anciano/a – elderly
jubilado/a – retired
jubilarse / retirarse – to retire
los servicios sociales – social services
el seguro social – social security
minusválido/a – handicapped
la minusvalía – handicap
discapacitado/a – disabled
la discapacidad – disability
cojo/a – lame (has a limp) / one-legged
manco/a – one-handed (missing a hand)
tuerto/a – one-eyed (missing an eye)
ciego/a – blind
sordo/a (sordomudo/a) – deaf (deaf-mute)
paralizado/a – paralyzed

las fuerzas armadas – (the) armed forces
el ejército – (the) army
la fuerza aérea – (the) air force
la marina de guerra – (the) navy / (the) marines
la guardia nacional – (the) national guard
militar – military (*adjective*)
el / la marinero/a – sailor / marine
el / la soldado – soldier
alistarse / inscribirse (en) – to enlist / to sign up
la inscripción – enlistment / registration
reclutar – to recruit
la conscripción – (the) draft / military service
el rango – rank
el / la sargento – sergeant
el / la general – general
el / la teniente/a – lieutenant
el capitán / la capitana – captain
el / la coronel – colonel
el / la almirante – admiral
el / la comandante – commandant / commander
el regimiento – regiment
las tropas – troops
mandar – to order / to send
la batalla – battle
batallar – to battle
la guerra – war
la carne de cañón – cannon fodder
la metralla – shrapnel
la granada – grenade
la ametralladora – machine gun
el arma (*femenino*) – weapon
    nuclear – nuclear weapon
    biológica – biological weapon
aniquilar – to annihilate
invadir – to invade
apoderarse (de) / ocupar – to take control (of)
saquear – to plunder / to pillage / to loot
el recurso natural – natural resource
el petróleo – oil / petroleum
el diamante – diamond
el platino – platinum
el acero – steel
expandir – to expand
la expansión – expansion
escoltar – to escort / to guard / to protect
el golpe de Estado – coup d'État
impedir (e → i) – to impede
contener (e → ie) – to contain
obtener (e → ie) – to obtain
encontrar (o → ue) / hallar – to find
realizar – to carry out / to realize (a dream)
llevar a cabo – to carry out / to make happen
la consecuencia – consequence
la repercusión – repercussion

la economía – (the) economy
económico/a – economic / economical
la huelga / el paro – strike
el desempleo – unemployment
el empleo – employment
las cifras – numbers / figures / statistics
financiero/a – financial
las finanzas – finances
la bolsa (mercantil / de valores) – (the) stock market
invertir (e → ie) (e → i) – to invest
el presupuesto – budget
los impuestos – taxes
la responsabilidad – responsibility
beneficiar – to benefit
el beneficio – benefit
donar – to donate
juntar fondos – to gather funds
recaudar fondos – to raise funds
aplicar (para) / solicitar – to apply (for)
rico/a – rich
pobre – poor
la pobreza – poverty
garantizar – to guarantee

los países (y nacionalidades) hispanohablantes
Europa (europeo/a)
    España (español/a)
Norteamérica / América del Norte (norteamericano/a)
    Estados Unidos (estadounidense)
    México (mexicano/a)
Centroamérica / América Central (centroamericano/a)
    Costa Rica (costarricense)
    El Salvador (salvadoreño/a)
    Guatemala (guatemalteco/a)
    Honduras (hondureño/a)
    Nicaragua (nicaragüense)
    Panamá (panameño/a)
El Caribe (caribeño/a)
    Cuba (cubano/a)
    La República Dominicana (dominicano/a)
    Puerto Rico (puertorriqueño/a) (estadounidense)
Sudamérica / América del Sur (sudamericano/a)
    Argentina (argentino/a)
    Bolivia (boliviano/a)
    Chile (chileno/a)
    Colombia (colombiano/a)
    Ecuador (ecuatoriano/a)
    Paraguay (paraguayo/a)
    Perú (peruano/a)
    Uruguay (uruguayo/a)
    Venezuela (venezolano/a)
África (africano/a)
    Guinea Ecuatorial (guineano/a)

otras palabras y expresiones útiles
insistir (en) – to insist (on)
mostrar (o → ue) – to show
demostrar (o → ue) – to demonstrate
completar – to complete
cumplir (con) – to comply / to follow through (on)
exigir – to demand
reprimir – to repress / to suppress
prohibir (i → í) – to prohibit
eficaz / efectivo/a – effective
esperar – to hope (for)
esperar (a) – to wait (for)
la expectativa – expectation
unir(se) (a) – to unite (to get together / to join)
reunir(se) (u → ú) (con) – to reunite (to meet up with)
romper / quebrar (e → ie) – to break
aportar / contribuir (y) – to contribute
ofrecer (c → zc) – to offer
admirar – to admire
acabar de + *infinitivo* – to have just _____*ed*
acabar (con) – to end / to stop / to put an end (to)
sino + *sust.* – but rather (used for contrast w/ "*no*")
    no esto, sino eso – not this, but (rather) that
sino que + *verbo* – but rather
sino también – but also (in addition w/ "*no*")
    no sólo esto, sino también eso – not only this …
estar a favor (de) – to be in favor (of)
estar en contra (de) – to be against
los pros y (los) contras – pros and cons
sugerir (e → ie) (e → i) – to suggest (recommend)
valorar – to value
valer (yo valgo) – to be worth
el / la mismísimo/a – the very same
entre sí – among themselves (ellos / ellas)
       – among yourselves (Uds.)
dominar – to dominate / to be fluent in a language
hispanohablante – Spanish-speaking
hispanoparlante – Spanish-speaking
de habla hispana – Spanish-speaking
de habla española – Spanish-speaking
anglohablante – English-speaking
angloparlante – English-speaking
de habla inglesa – English-speaking

expresiones que requieren el subjuntivo
ojalá (que) – hopefully / god (Allah) willing
para que – so that
con el fin de que – so that (with the goal being that)
a menos que – unless
a no ser que – unless
con tal de que – provided that
acaso que – in case
sin que – without

Unidad 30 – los refranes, los modismos y las expresiones idiomáticas

estar entre la espada y la pared – to be stuck between a rock and a hard place

todo va viento en popa – it's smooth sailing

por las buenas o por las malas – come hell or high water / by hook or by crook / one way or another

a fuerzas – no matter what

para lo bueno y para lo malo – for better or for worse

de la sartén al fuego – out of the frying pan and into the fire

tener la sartén por el mango – to have things under control

ir de mal en peor – to go from bad to worse

de pies a cabeza – from head to toe

blanco y negro – black and white

una cuestión de vida o muerte – a matter of life or death

pedir peras al olmo – to ask the impossible

a otro perro con ese hueso – don't piss down my back and tell me it's raining

de tal palo, tal astilla – the apple doesn't fall far from the tree

del dicho al hecho hay un buen trecho – it's easier said than done

dime con quién andas y te diré quién eres – you are who you hang around

allá donde fueres, haz lo que vieres – when in Rome, do as the Romans do

en boca cerrada no entran moscas – loose lips sink ships

tarde o temprano – sooner or later

no hay mal que por bien no venga – every cloud has a silver lining

llover a cántaros – to rain cats and dogs

zapatero, a tus zapatos – mind your own business / let the cobbler stick to his last

cada quien a lo suyo – every man for himself / everyone for themselves

a cada quien lo suyo – to each his own / to each their own

dar la vuelta a la tortilla – to turn the tables

la prueba de fuego – trial by fire

al pie de la letra – by the book / verbatim

echar leña al fuego – to add fuel to the fire

poner el dedo en la llaga – to add insult to injury / to pour salt in the wound

tomarle el pelo a alguien – to pull someone's leg

comerse el coco – to go nuts (crazy) (thinking about something) / to rack one's brain

perder los estribos – to fly off the handle

media naranja – better half (used to describe one's spouse, soul mate, etc.)

dejar a alguien con la palabra en la boca – to cut someone off (when s/he is speaking)

en la punta de la lengua – on the tip of one's tongue

un callejón sin salida – a dead end

una espada de doble filo – a double edged sword

mandar a alguien a freír espárragos – to tell someone to go fly a kite

mi casa es su casa – make yourself at home

como Pedro por su casa – like he owned the place

hogar, dulce hogar – home sweet home

el / la niño/a de mis ojos – the apple of my eye

matar dos pájaros de un solo tiro – to kill two birds with one stone

yo que tú / yo, en tu lugar – if I were you / if I were in your shoes

sano y salvo / sana y salva – safe and sound

a lo largo de (tiempo, muchos años, etc.) – over the course of (time, many years, etc.)

antes muerta que sencilla – I wouldn't be caught dead wearing that.

colorín colorado este cuento se ha acabado – that's all she wrote

un don nadie / una doña nadie – a nobody

otro cero a la izquierda – a good-for-nothing / a nonentity (like another zero left of the decimal 00.1)

un/a fulano/a (de tal) – a so-and-so (a non-specific or theoretical person – "a John" or "a Jane")

un/a sabelotodo – a know-it-all

meter la pata (meter las cuatro) – to put your foot in it (to really put your foot in it)

el mundo es un pañuelo – (it's a) small world

en un dos por tres – in no time / in a flash / in an instant

cada dos por tres – every now and again

dejar plantado/a a alguien – to stand someone up (like for a date)

seguir en pie – to still stand (plans) / to hold up (not fall through – plans) / to still be on (plans)

la edad del pavo – tween years / early teenage years

a paso de tortuga – at a snail's pace

perder el hilo – to lose one's train of thought

¿Cuánto te va a costar el chiste/la broma? – How much is the thing gonna set you back?

(hay que) ver para creer – seeing is believing (you'll have to see it to believe it)

a estas alturas – at this point

por puros golpes de suerte (un golpe de suerte) – by sheer/pure luck (a stroke of luck)

estar hasta la coronilla – to be fed up / to have had it up to here (hand gesture at head level)

manos a la obra – get to work / let's get to work

por si las moscas – just in case

por encima de mi cadáver – over my dead body

pagar los platos rotos – to pay the piper / to clean up one's mess (figuratively)

rendirle cuentas a alguien – to be held accountable to someone

como buscar una aguja en un pajar – like finding a needle in a haystack

hay gato encerrado – there's something they're not telling me / there's something fishy going on

sudar la gota gorda – to sweat bullets

hacer la vista gorda / hacerse de la vista gorda – to turn a blind eye / to look the other way

pasar por alto – to overlook

meterse en camisa de once varas – to stick one's nose where it doesn't belong

caminar por la cuerda floja – to walk a fine line / to walk a tightrope

menos mal que … (indicative verb) – it's just as well that …

trágame tierra – kill me now / just shoot me (when embarrassed or overwhelmed)

que te parta un rayo – damn you / a pox on you (a curse on whomever the object is)

maldita sea – dammit (damn it)

al fin de cuentas / al fin y al cabo – when it's (is/was) all said and done / when it's (is/was) all over

de cabo a rabo – cover to cover (book) / from beginning to end / from start to finish

a espaldas de alguien (a mis espaldas) – behind someone's back (behind my back)

ponerle los cuernos a alguien – to cheat on someone (in a romantic partnership)

cerrar el pico – to shut one's trap

como si fuera poco – as if that weren't enough

costar un huevo – to cost a fortune / to cost an arm and a leg

darle mala (buena) espina a alguien – to give someone a bad (good) feeling

de una vez por todas – once and for all

empezar la casa por el tejado – to put the cart before the horse

en ascuas – on tenterhooks / on pins and needles / on the edge of one's seat

morderse la lengua – to bite one's tongue

poner las cartas sobre la mesa – to put all the cards on the table

salir el tiro por la culata – to backfire

ser pan comido – to be a piece of cake (easy)

tomar a pecho – to take to heart

ir al grano – to get to the point

cortar por lo sano – to cut one's losses

cada ocho días (cada 15 días) – every week (every two weeks)

de mañana en ocho (de este lunes en ocho) – a week from tomorrow (a week from this Monday)

de todo un poco – a little bit of everything

un día de estos – one of these days

a bote pronto – off the cuff

ponerse las pilas – to buckle down

a solas (con) – alone (with – always with someone or something)

el pájaro de mal agüero – bird of ill omen / bearer of bad news

más vale pájaro en mano que cien volando – a bird in the hand is worth two in the bush

más vale tarde que nunca – better late than never

micha y micha – split it 50/50

frente a frente – face-to-face / head-to-head

ser como uña y mugre (uña y carne) – to be like two peas in a pod / to be (as) thick as thieves

agarrado/a con la mano en la masa – caught with his/her hand in the cookie jar

reír a carcajadas – to laugh out loud

echar/tirar la casa por la ventana – to spare no expense

estar a mano / estar en paz – to be even / to be square (no one owes the other anything)

pegar ojo – to get some shut-eye

pasar la noche en vela – to have a sleepless night

a mi mejor saber y entender / a mi leal saber y entender – to the best of my knowledge

los abajo firmantes (afirmamos, expresamos, etc.) – (We) the undersigned (affirm, express, etc.)

que sueñes con los angelitos – sweet dreams

ponerse al tanto – to wise up / to get with it

decir algo sin pelos en la lengua / no tener pelos en la lengua – to not mince words

tener cara de pocos amigos – to scowl

mejor solo que mal acompañado – (it is) better to be alone than in bad company

no saber (entender, hablar) ni papa – to not know (understand, speak) the first thing (about a subject)

no tiene (ni) pies ni cabeza – I can't make heads or tails of it / it doesn't make any sense at all

esparcir la voz – to spread the word

¿En qué quedamos? – Where do we stand? (on a deal, decision, etc.) / Where does that leave us?

¿Qué más da? – What difference does it make? / What does it matter?

na na na y no sé qué / no sé qué y no sé cuánto – I don't know, whatever, blah blah blah

Había una vez … / Érase una vez … – Once upon a time …

se me pegaron las sábanas – "the sheets stuck to me" (a humorous excuse for getting out of bed late)

San Lunes – "Saint Monday" (a fictitious holiday cited as the reason for not going to work on a Monday)

más sabe el diablo por viejo que por diablo – with age comes wisdom

dar en el clavo – to hit the nail on the head

¿Me entiendes, Méndez, o te explico, Federico? – Do I need to explain it to you?

ser para chuparse los dedos – to be finger-licking good

hacerse agua la boca – to make one's mouth water

estar (sentirse) como gallina en corral ajeno – to be (to feel) like a fish out of water

estar como pez en el agua – to be in one's element

pase lo que pase – whatever happens / no matter what happens

perro ladrador, poco mordedor – his bark is worse than his bite

el tiempo es oro – time is money

hacer hincapié – to dig in one's heels / to put one's foot down

andar con pies de plomo – to proceed with caution

echarle una mano a alguien (con algo) – to give someone a hand (with something)

ser de carne y hueso – to be flesh and blood

algo por el estilo – something along those lines

con uñas y dientes – tooth and nail

a cámara lenta – in slow motion

los trabalenguas

Tres tristes tigres se tragan trigo en un trigal.

Ere con ere – guitarra, ere con ere – barril. ¡Qué rápido ruedan las ruedas del ferrocarril!

Pablito clavó un clavito. ¡Qué clavito clavó Pablito!

Pedro Pérez Pereira, pobre pintor portugués, pinta preciosos paisajes para poder partir para París.

Poquito a poquito Paquito empaqueta poquitas copitas en pocos paquetes.

Como poco coco como, poco coco compro.

Pepe Peña pela papa, pica piña, pita un pito, pica piña, pela papa, Pepe Peña.

Me trajo Tajo tres trajes, tres trajes me trajo Tajo.

Parangaricutirimícuaro

un poco de humor grosero

No es lo mismo: "la papaya tapatía" que "tía, tápate la papaya".

No es lo mismo: "los huevos de araña" que "aráñame los huevos".

No es lo mismo: "huele a traste" que "atrás te huele".

No es lo mismo: "el SIDA tiene cura" que "el cura tiene SIDA".

No es lo mismo: "la verdura" que "verla dura".

No es lo mismo: "tengo un hambre atroz" que "tengo un hombre atrás".

No es lo mismo: "tubérculo" que "ver tu culo".

No es lo mismo: "dos tazas de té" que "dos tetazas".

No es lo mismo: "un metro de encaje negro" que "un negro te encaje un metro".

No es lo mismo: "Cenote Dos Ojos" que "¡Ojo, dos senotes!"

Apuntes

Apuntes

Gramática

Unidad 1

Los cognados – Cognates

Definition: related by descent from the same ancestral language – <u>Merriam Webster Collegiate Dictionary</u>. 10th Edition

Identifying *cognates* is one way to effortlessly increase your vocabulary in Spanish.

> *Ej.* calendario, computadora, secretario, actividad, alfabeto, falso, foto, teléfono, etc.

¡Ojo! – Watch out for false cognates!

> *Ej. embarazada* – pregnant, *actual* – current, *librería* – book store, etc.

Los prefijos y sufijos – Prefixes and Suffixes

Identifying *prefixes* is another great way to effortlessly increase your understanding of a word.

> *Ej.* <u>ben</u>dición – blessing (good), <u>mal</u>dición – curse (bad)

Identifying *suffixes* can help you understand the parts of speech of thousands of cognates.

> *Ej.* ción – tion (ac<u>ción</u> – ac<u>tion</u>, celebra<u>ción</u> – celebra<u>tion</u>, condi<u>ción</u> – condi<u>tion</u>)
>
> dad – ty (universi<u>dad</u> – universi<u>ty</u>, habili<u>dad</u> – abili<u>ty</u>, posibili<u>dad</u> – possibili<u>ty</u>)
>
> sía – sy (corte<u>sía</u> – corte<u>sy</u>, fanta<u>sía</u> – fanta<u>sy</u>)
>
> tura – ture (aven<u>tura</u> – adven<u>ture</u>, cul<u>tura</u> – cul<u>ture</u>)

Las frases y palabras útiles – Useful Words and Phrases

- **La gramática – Grammar**

el adjetivo – adjective

el adverbio – adverb

el artículo definido – definite article

> *el, la, los, las – the*

el artículo indefinido – indefinite article

> *un, una – a(n)*
>
> *unos, unas – some*

concordar / la concordancia – to agree / agreement

el complemento (in)directo – (in)direct object

el pronombre – pronoun

el sustantivo / el nombre – noun

el verbo – verb

el género - gender

> masculino – masculine
>
> femenino – feminine

el número - number

> plural – plural
>
> singular – singular

¿ – used to open a question

¡ – used to open an exclamation

por ejemplo (ej.) – for example (e.g.)

La pronunciación – Pronunciation

The subtleties of Spanish pronunciation can only be learned with a finely tuned ear and deliberate, focused practice to break your tongue of its habits. Here are some rough basics to help you in the beginning.

	Examples in English	Ejemplos en español
a, á	(father)	(semana, estás)
e, é	(met)	(en, miércoles)
i, í	(bee)	(mi, día)
o, ó	(hope)	(dos, adiós)
u, ú	(loop, ~~cute~~)	(usted, tú)
ce/ci	(s) / (thanks – Castilian)	(cero, cinco)
ca/co/cu	(k)	(catorce, cómo, cumpleaños)
ch	(chat)	(ocho, noche)
ge/gi	(happy)	(generoso, gimnasio)
ga/go/gu	(go)	(amiga, domingo, gusto)
h	silent (an honor)	(hola, hasta)
j	(happy)	(José, junio)
ll, y	(yawn)	(yo me llamo, hoy)
ñ	(canyon)	(español, señor, año)
que/qui	(k)	(qué, quién)
rr, r (not between vowels)	(prrrrrrrrrr)	(guitarra, gracias, regular, ~~señora~~)
y ("*i griega*")	(ee)	(y tú)
z	(s) / (thanks – Castilian)	(diez, marzo)

¡Ojo! There are 27 letters in Spanish: the 26 English letters and *ñ* (… l, m, n, ñ, o, p, q …).

El énfasis – Emphasis

➢ If a word ends in a vowel, *n* or *s*, the emphasis falls on the second to the last syllable.

➢ If a word ends in any other letter, the emphasis falls on the last syllable.

A written accent mark has three purposes (none of which changes the sound of the vowel):

➢ to mark a deviation from the above two rules.

> *Ej.* están, típica, cómodo

➢ to distinguish it from other single-syllable words.

> *Ej.* sé / se – I know / herself, himself or themselves
> tú / tu – you / your
> sí / si – yes / if
> él / el – he / the
> qué / que – what / that

➢ to signal a question word.

> *Ej.* qué / lo que – what? / what   dónde / donde – where? / where
> cómo / como – how? / as, like   quién / quien – who? / who(m)
> cuál / lo cual – which? / which   por qué – why?
> cuándo / cuando – when? / when   cuánto – how much

Unidad 2

El género – Gender

- **Los sustantivos – Nouns**

All nouns, whether they are animate or inanimate objects, have gender. The gender of a noun referring to a person depends on the sex of the person: masculine for a man/boy, feminine for a woman/girl (with the exception of generic nouns like *person, family, people, victim*, etc.). The gender of a noun that refers to an object other than a person is independent of the noun's characteristics. For example, *la mesa – table*, is feminine, but not because it has feminine characteristics. Many masculine nouns end in *o* and many feminine nouns end in *a*.

> *Ej.* la computadora – computer, el carro – car

Many nouns, however, end in consonants or vowels other than *o* or *a*.

> *Ej.* la pared – wall, el reloj – clock/watch, el coche – car

Definite articles (*el, la, los, las* – the) are used more frequently in Spanish than in English, and with the gender of the noun playing a determining factor in which article is used, nouns should be learned with their corresponding definite article (*el* libro, *la* televisión). By learning the definite article along with the noun, the gender of the noun is easier to identify.

> *Ej. la* – feminine, *el* – masculine

There are a few examples where the article doesn't seem to match the noun, but if you know the correct article, you'll generally know the noun's gender.

> *Ej.* la radio, el mapa, el programa, la foto

- **Los adjetivos – Adjectives**

Adjectives, like nouns, have gender. Adjectives must always agree in gender with the nouns that they modify (note the article). If the noun is masculine, then the adjective is masculine, etc. If the adjective does not end in *o* or *a* then it can modify both masculine and feminine nouns. Notice that, in Spanish, the adjective usually follows the noun it describes, unlike in English.

> *Ej.* el hombre <u>alto</u> – the <u>tall</u> man, la mujer <u>bonita</u> – the <u>beautiful</u> woman
> la silla <u>azul</u> – the <u>blue</u> chair, el carro <u>azul</u> – the <u>blue</u> car
> la foto <u>magnífica</u> – the <u>magnificent</u> photo, la pared <u>blanca</u> – the <u>white</u> wall

El número – Number

Adjectives must also agree in number with the nouns they modify: singular or plural.

> *Ej.* el profesor inteligente (singular), los profesores inteligentes (plural)

To make a noun or an adjective plural, follow these rules. Notice that *el* becomes *los*.

> ➢ If it ends in a vowel, add *s*.
> > *Ej.* el estudiante listo → lo<u>s</u> estudiante<u>s</u> listo<u>s</u>
> ➢ If it ends in a consonant, add *es*.
> > *Ej.* la pared blanca → la<u>s</u> pared<u>es</u> blanca<u>s</u>

¡Ojo! (*Watch out!*) When combining masculine and feminine, the result is masculine, plural.

Los verbos (el presente) – Verbs (present tense)

In English, we rarely have to think about how to conjugate verbs. In fact, if you have never studied a language other than English, you may not even know (by name) what conjugating a verb is. In order to explain verb conjugation, we must first know what an infinitive is. According to Webster, an infinitive is a verb form having the characteristics of both verb and noun. In English, it is usually used with the word *to*: *to walk*, *to swim*, etc. According to yours truly, it is the most basic and root form of a verb. To conjugate a verb is to change the infinitive so that the resulting form agrees with the subject.

> *Ej.* I walk. You walk. She walks. I swim. You swim. She swims.

In Spanish, each subject (1st person, singular; 1st person, plural; 2nd person, singular; 2nd person, plural; 3rd person, singular; and 3rd person, plural), in most tenses, has a unique verb conjugation. This is best illustrated with the following charts.

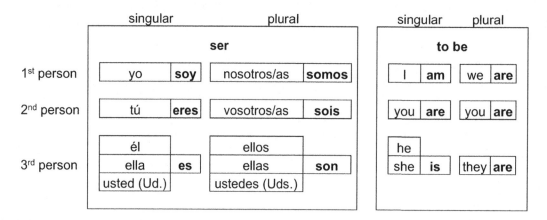

¡Ojo! Usted and *ustedes* are 2nd person, formal, but they are conjugated as 3rd person.

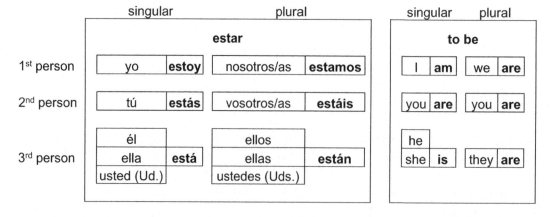

¡Ojo! The *vosotros* form is used primarily in Spain. In Latin America, *ustedes* serves as both the familiar and formal forms of *you, plural*.

Ser vs. estar

The verbs *ser* and *estar* both mean "to be." They each have specific uses and are not interchangeable. You have already seen both of these verbs in context.

> *Ej. ¿De dónde eres? Soy de Colorado.*
> *¿Cómo estás? Estoy bien, gracias.*

Take a look at some of the uses of each of these verbs.

- **Use *ser:***

  - to describe origin. (<u>Soy</u> de Nevada.)

  - to describe time, days, dates, etc. (<u>Son</u> las 8:00 de la mañana.)

  - to describe physical characteristics. (El carro <u>es</u> verde. – The car is green.)

  - to describe character traits. (Eduardo <u>es</u> inteligente.)

- **Use *estar*:**

  - to describe location. (<u>Estamos</u> en Colorado. – We are in Colorado.)

  - to describe mental and emotional states. (<u>Estoy</u> triste. – I am sad.)

  - to describe physical states of being. (La comida <u>está</u> caliente. – The food is hot.)

Both *ser* and *estar* are used with adjectives to describe people and objects but they each have their distinct uses; they are not interchangeable.

Notice that the adjectives agree in both gender and number with the nouns they modify.

> *Ej.* Somos aburridos. – We are boring. (character trait)
> Estamos aburridos. – We are bored. (mental state)
>
> Soy listo. – I am clever/witty. (character trait)
> Estoy listo. – I am ready. (mental state)
>
> Soy preparada. – I am educated. (character trait)
> Estoy preparada. – I am prepared. (mental/physical state)
>
> Eres bonita. – You are pretty. (character trait)
> Estás bonita. – You look pretty. (physical state)
>
> Ellas son alegres. – They are happy people. (character trait)
> Ellas están alegres. – They are feeling happy. (mental state)
>
> El café es caliente. – Coffee is a hot drink. (physical characteristic)
> El café está frío. – The coffee is cold. (physical state)

Los verbos (el presente) – Verbs (present tense)

The following verbs, *gustar* and *encantar*, are most commonly used to express what a person *likes* or *loves*, respectively. Literally translated: what *pleases* that person or what *delights* that person. Therefore, they are not commonly conjugated like the verbs that we have already seen nor will see in the future. In Spanish, liking something is not active, but rather it is passive. Think of a food that you like or don't like. Do you have control over whether you like it or not? Can you simply change your mind about it? Take a look at the following comparisons.

> In English, the subject does the liking and the thing being liked is the object.
> *Ej.* **I** like chocolate. (how it is commonly said in English)

> In Spanish, the subject does the pleasing and the object is the person that it pleases.
> *Ej.* Chocolate pleases **me**. (literal translation from Spanish)

Notice that in the following constructions, the subject (what is doing the pleasing) is always in the 3rd person. The only difference is whether the thing doing the pleasing is singular or plural. The person receiving the pleasure of this/these thing(s) is the object and is represented by the corresponding indirect-object pronoun.

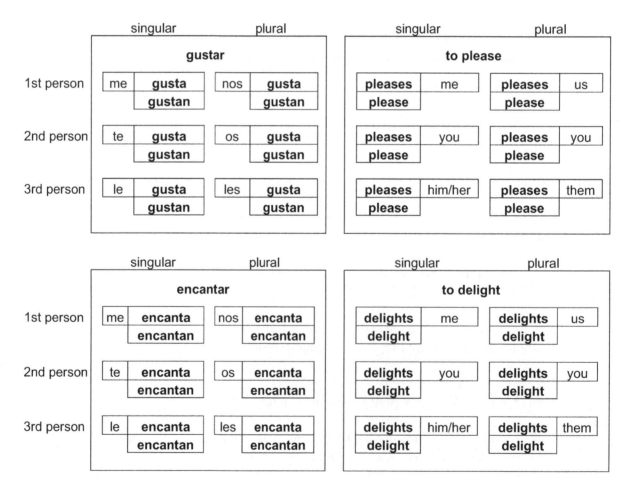

Los pronombres de complemento indirecto – Indirect-Object Pronouns

me – me	**nos** – us
te – you	**os** – you (Spain plural)
le – him / her / you (formal)	**les** – them / you (Latin America plural, formal)

Ej. (A mí) *me* gustan los coches. – I like cars. (Cars are pleasing to me.)

¿(A ti) *te* gusta cantar? – Do you like to sing? (Is singing pleasing to you?)

(A Pedro) <u>no</u> *le* encanta estudiar. – Pedro <u>doesn't</u> love to study.

(A mí y a María) *nos* encantan las flores. – We love flowers.

¿(A ti y a tus amigos) *os* gusta bailar? – Do you (all) like to dance?

(A Pedro y a María) *les* gusta leer. – Pedro and Maria like to read.

Regardless of the object of pleasure/delight, the subject in these examples is 3rd person, and is either singular or plural. Either "it pleases" or "they please." It would sound silly to say "it please" or "they pleases," so you could imagine how silly it would sound to say "*Me gusta los coches*" or "*Nos gustan bailar.*"

¡Ojo! If the subject of the verb *gustar* or *encantar* is an infinitive (verb – *bailar, leer*, etc.), even if there are multiple verbs as the subject, the convention is to use the singular form of *gustar* (*gusta*) or *encantar* (*encanta*).

Ej. Me encanta~~n~~ correr y nadar.
Nos gusta~~n~~ bailar y cantar.

Las preguntas – Questions

In English, there are several cues that tell us a sentence is a question: it starts with an interrogative word (who, what, why, etc.) and/or the subject/verb order is flipped, or the word "do" is added.

Ej. *How* <u>are you</u>? (<u>You are</u> …) – subject/verb order was flipped, with question word
<u>Are you</u> impatient? (<u>You are</u> impatient.) – subject/verb order was flipped
<u>Do</u> you have a minute? (You have a minute.) – "do" was added to the beginning

In Spanish, there are also several cues that tell us it's a question, but they aren't all the same as the ones in English. Starting with an interrogative word (*quién, qué, por qué*, etc.) and/or flipping the subject/verb order is the same, but there isn't a word like "do" that we can add to the beginning. Instead, an upside-down question mark is placed at the beginning of the question (not necessarily the beginning of the sentence). This is done for all questions, regardless of the other cues.

Ej. ¿*Cómo* <u>estás tú</u>? (<u>Tú estás</u> …) – subject/verb order was switched, with question word
¿<u>Eres tú</u> impaciente? (<u>Tú eres</u> impaciente.) – subject/verb order was switched
¿<u>Trabajas</u>? (Trabajas.) – The upside-down question mark is like "do."

Unidad 3

Los verbos regulares (el presente) – Regular Verbs (present tense)

You have already been introduced to many common verbs, within the context of what you like to do, by using the verbs *gustar* and *encantar*. All of the verbs were presented to you in their infinitive form. Remember: according to Webster, an infinitive is a verb form having the characteristics of both verb and noun. In English, it is usually used with the word *to*: *to walk*, *to swim*, etc. According to yours truly, it is the most basic and root form of a verb. To conjugate a verb is to change it so that the resulting form agrees with the subject.

> *Ej.* I walk. You walk. She walks. I swim. You swim. She swims.

In Spanish, unlike in the above examples, each subject (1st person, singular; 1st person, plural; 2nd person, singular; 2nd person, plural; 3rd person, singular; and 3rd person, plural), in most tenses, has a unique verb conjugation.

All verbs in Spanish fall into one of three categories, which is determined by their endings in the infinitive form: *-ar, -er, -ir*. Within each category, verbs are classified, within the given tense, as either regular or irregular. All regular verbs follow the same rules of conjugation for their respective category (regular *-ar*, regular *-er*, and regular *-ir*). Irregular verbs do not follow the same rules and their conjugations must be learned individually. Fortunately for learners of Spanish as a foreign language, most verbs are regular in their conjugations. Take a look at the following example of a regular present-tense *-ar* verb.

	singular		plural		singular		plural	
	hablar				**to speak**			
1st person	yo	**hablo**	nosotros	**hablamos**	I	speak	we	speak
2nd person	tú	**hablas**	vosotros	**habláis**	you	speak	you	speak
3rd person	él / ella / usted (Ud.)	**habla**	ellos / ellas / ustedes (Uds.)	**hablan**	he / she	speaks	they	speak

Notice that the stem of the verb (everything but the ending) does not change, only the ending. To conjugate regular verbs, you simply drop the infinitive ending: *-ar, -er, -ir*; and then add the corresponding conjugated ending.

¡Ojo! For simplicity, in these verb charts, *nosotros* and *vosotros* also represent their respective feminine forms: *nosotras* and *vosotras*.

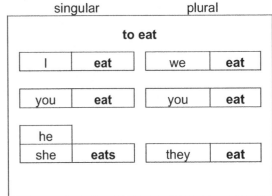

¡Ojo! Usted and *ustedes* are 2nd person, formal, but they are conjugated as 3rd person.

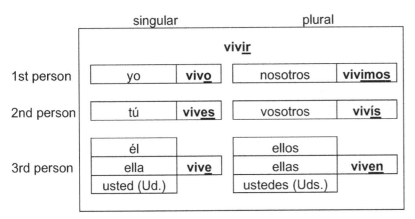
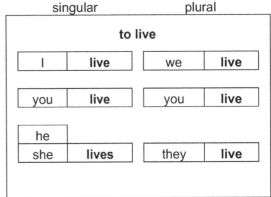

¡Ojo! The *vosotros* form is used primarily in Spain. In Latin America, *ustedes* serves as both the familiar and formal forms of *you, plural.*

La posesión y los adjetivos posesivos – Possession and Possessive Adjectives

mi(s) – my	**nuestro(s) / nuestra(s)** – our
tu(s) – your	**vuestro(s) / vuestra(s)** – your (Spain plural)
su(s) – his / her / your (formal)	**su(s)** – their / your (Latin America plural, formal)
de – of (used to clarify 3rd person)	

Ej. mi amigo – my friend
   mis amigos – my friends
   nuestro maestro – our (male) teacher
   nuestra maestra – our (female) teacher
   nuestros maestros – our (male, or male and female) teachers
   la calculadora de mi jefe – my boss's calculator (literally – the calculator of my boss)
   La maestra de mi amiga es amable. – My friend's teacher is kind.

Unidad 4

Los verbos irregulares (el presente) – Irregular Verbs (present tense)

You have already been introduced to regular present-tense verbs. There are two parts to every verb in Spanish: the stem and the ending. By definition, all regular verbs retain the stem of their infinitives and only their endings change.

hablar	**comer**	**vivir**
hablo	**como**	**vivo**
hablas	**comes**	**vives**
habla	**come**	**vive**
hablamos	**comemos**	**vivimos**
habláis	**coméis**	**vivís**
hablan	**comen**	**viven**

Irregular verbs do not follow these rules and their conjugations must be learned individually. There are several different types of irregular verbs; some are stem-changing verbs (which can be categorized by the type of change required); some change, remove, or add letters to retain their pronunciation; and some don't seem to follow any pattern at all. Take a look at the following examples of some irregular present-tense verbs. Notice the types of stem changes in parentheses.

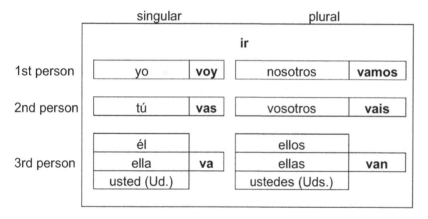

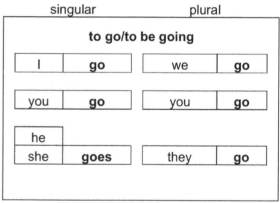

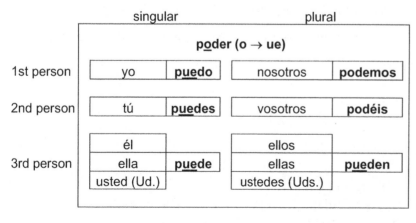

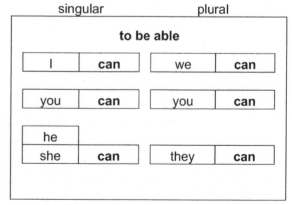

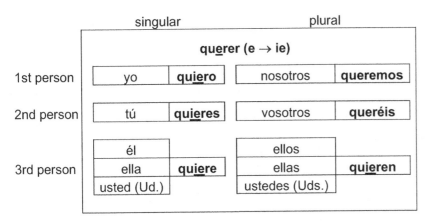

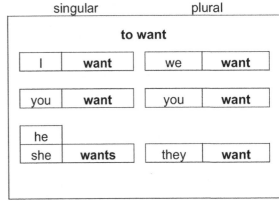

¡Ojo! *Usted* and *ustedes* are 2nd person, formal, but they are conjugated as 3rd person.

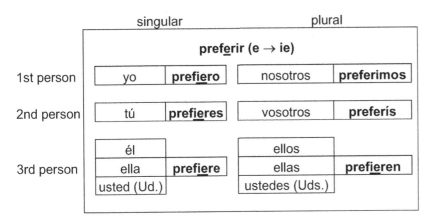

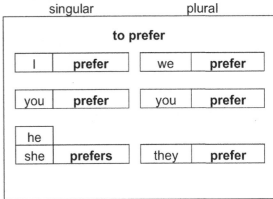

¡Ojo! The *vosotros* form is used primarily in Spain. In Latin America, *ustedes* serves as both the familiar and formal forms of *you, plural*.

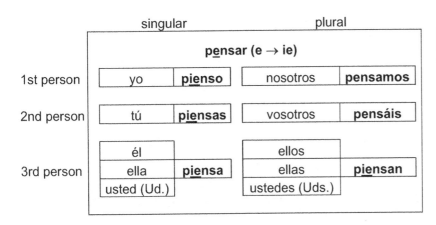

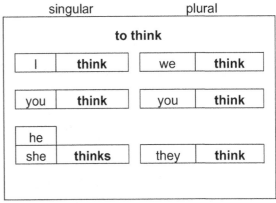

Sometimes the *yo* form has a unique change.

Ej. **ver** (to see / to watch) – yo ~~ve~~ **veo**   **dar** (to give) – yo ~~do~~ **doy**
     saber (to know) – yo ~~sabe~~ **sé**   **hacer** (to do / to make) – yo ~~hace~~ **hago**

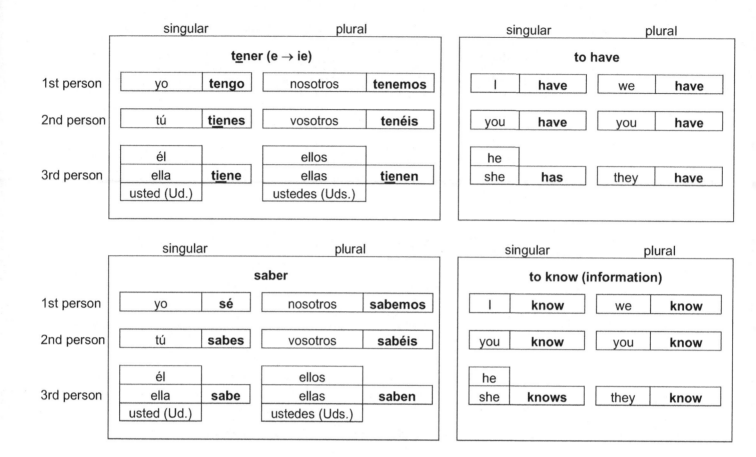

	singular		plural	
	tener (e → ie)			
1st person	yo	**tengo**	nosotros	**tenemos**
2nd person	tú	**tienes**	vosotros	**tenéis**
3rd person	él / ella / usted (Ud.)	**tiene**	ellos / ellas / ustedes (Uds.)	**tienen**

	singular		plural	
	to have			
1st person	I	**have**	we	**have**
2nd person	you	**have**	you	**have**
3rd person	he / she	**has**	they	**have**

	singular		plural	
	saber			
1st person	yo	**sé**	nosotros	**sabemos**
2nd person	tú	**sabes**	vosotros	**sabéis**
3rd person	él / ella / usted (Ud.)	**sabe**	ellos / ellas / ustedes (Uds.)	**saben**

	singular		plural	
	to know (information)			
1st person	I	**know**	we	**know**
2nd person	you	**know**	you	**know**
3rd person	he / she	**knows**	they	**know**

Los infinitivos y las estructuras compuestas – Infinitives and Compound Structures

Many verbs can be combined with infinitives to form compound structures. Take a look at the following examples below. Each conjugated verb can be conjugated according to any subject, but the second verb remains in the infinitive form no matter who the subject may be. I have included a few prepositions that signal the use of an infinitive as well.

Tengo que <u>estudiar</u>. – I have <u>to study</u>.

Quiero <u>comer</u>. – I want <u>to eat</u>.

¿Prefieres <u>correr</u>? – Do you prefer <u>to run</u>?

Necesitan <u>intentar</u>. – They need <u>to try</u>.

¿Puedo <u>ir</u> al baño? – Can I go to the bathroom?

Sabe <u>manejar</u>. – He knows how <u>to drive</u>.

Vamos a <u>viajar</u>. – We are going <u>to travel</u>.

Pienso <u>viajar</u>. – I plan <u>to travel</u>.

Intentan <u>nadar</u>. – They try <u>to swim</u>.

para <u>estudiar</u> – in order <u>to study</u>

después de <u>leer</u> – after <u>reading</u>

antes de <u>nadar</u> – before <u>swimming</u>

Notice that the verb structure *ir + a +* infinitive is one form of the future tense. Other verbs structures that can imply the future are *necesitar* + infinitive, *querer* + infinitive, and *pensar* + infinitive.

90

Unidad 5

"To Be" (*ser*/*estar*) or not "to Be" (*tener*)

You have already seen your first example in which Spanish uses the verb *tener* (to have) where English uses the verb "to be."

> *Ej.* ¿Cuántos años <u>tienes</u>? – How old <u>are you</u>?
> <u>Tengo</u> 34 años. – <u>I am</u> 34 years old.

By now, you're probably starting to get the idea that Spanish is not simply English with different words and that some phrases need to be learned as a whole to be truly understood. *Tener años* is a classic example, but it's not the only expression that uses *tener* instead of "to be." Here are a few expressions where *tener* is coupled with a noun, whereas "to be" is coupled with an adjective:

tener frío – to be cold	Tengo frío. – I am cold.
tener calor – to be hot	¿Tienes calor? – Are you hot?
tener sueño – to be sleepy	Mi hija tiene sueño. – My daughter is sleepy.
tener sed – to be thirsty	Tenemos sed. – We are thirsty.
tener hambre – to be hungry	¿Tienen hambre? – Are you (all) hungry?
tener miedo – to be afraid	Tengo miedo. – I am afraid.
tener prisa – to be in a hurry	Tenemos prisa. – We are in a hurry.

La adjetivación de sustantivos – Using Nouns as Adjectives

You've learned that all nouns have gender (*masculino* or *femenino*) and number (*singular* or *plural*) and that adjectives must agree in gender and number with the nouns they modify (p.81). While we most often use adjectives to modify nouns, it is important to note that we can also use other nouns to modify nouns. In English, we simply use the noun as though it were an adjective and *voilà*: *plastic* chair, *metal* table, *ham* sandwich, *chicken* soup, etc. In Spanish, the preposition *de* ("of" or "from") usually introduces the modifier.

> *Ej.* la sopa *de tomate*   la ensalada *de espinacas*
> el sándwich *de jamón y queso*   el jugo *de manzana*
> el pastel *de chocolate*   la leche *de almendra*

Since all nouns have gender and number, and we can use a noun to describe another noun, we have to consider each noun's gender and number independently. Any adjectives used must agree with the nouns they modify, even if the nouns they modify are modifying other nouns.

> *Ej.* <u>la</u> ensala<u>da</u> delicio<u>sa</u> *de verdur<u>as</u> fresc<u>as</u>*
> <u>los</u> sándwich<u>es</u> cuban<u>os</u> autéti<u>cos</u> *de jamón, puerco, ques<u>o</u> suiz<u>o</u>, pepinillo y mostaza*

¡Ojo! If the noun used as a modifier is generic, like *tomate* in *sopa de tomate*, then it's usually singular. If you made it plural: *sopa de tomate<u>s</u>*, you would be saying that multiple types of tomatoes were used in the making of it.

Unidad 6

Los adjetivos – Adjectives

You've been introduced to the concept of adjectives having gender and number as well as agreeing with the nouns they modify (p.81). They can be used with the verbs *ser* and *estar*.

> *Ej.* El carro es <u>negro</u>.   Las casas son <u>pequeñas</u>.
> La comida está <u>fría</u>.   Mis amigos están <u>enfermos</u>.

They can also be used without *ser* or *estar*. Remember that adjectives almost always follow the nouns they modify. You can also use more than one adjective to describe the same noun.

> *Ej.* Yo prefiero el carro <u>negro</u> y <u>amarillo</u>.   No me gustan las casas <u>pequeñas</u>.

Don't be thrown off by words like *persona* or *masculino/a* and *femenino/a*; just follow the rules.

> *Ej.* Juan es un<u>a</u> person<u>a</u> atractiv<u>a</u>.   "Problema" es un<u>a</u> palabr<u>a</u> masculin<u>a</u>.

Los adverbios – Adverbs

Adjectives modify nouns, whereas adverbs modify verbs (and adjectives). Nouns have gender and number, therefore adjectives have corresponding gender and number. Verbs, on the other hand, do not have gender or number, therefore adverbs, likewise, do not have gender or number.

> *Ej.* Mi hermana juega <u>bien</u>.   Nuestros tíos cantan <u>mal</u>.
> Mi hermano juega <u>bien</u>.   Nuestra tía canta <u>mal</u>.

In English, we can add "ly" to many adjectives to turn them into adverbs. Likewise, in Spanish, we can add *-mente* to the **feminine** form of many adjectives to make adverbs.

> *Ej.* quick   → quick<u>ly</u>   rápido/**a** → rápid**a**<u>mente</u>
> sincere → sincere<u>ly</u>   sincero/**a** → sincera<u>mente</u>
> simple → simp<u>ly</u>   simple   → simple<u>mente</u>
> formal → formal<u>ly</u>   formal   → formal<u>mente</u>

Los comparativos – Comparatives

Comparatives, as the name implies, make comparisons between two things either with adjectives or adverbs. In the case of adjectives, the adjectives in question do not modify both nouns; they only modify the first one. In the case of adverbs, there is no issue.

> *Ej.* Mi tí<u>o</u> es *más* alt<u>o</u> *que* mi papá.   Tu herman<u>a</u> es *más* cariños<u>a</u> *que* tu prima.
> Mi tí<u>o</u> es *más* alt<u>o</u> *que* mi mamá.   Tu herman<u>a</u> es *más* cariños<u>a</u> *que* tus primos.
>
> Mi hermano corre *más* rápidamente *que* <u>yo</u>. (more quickly than <u>I do</u>/me)
> Nuestros primos corren *más* rápidamente *que* <u>nosotros</u>. (more quickly than <u>we do</u>/us)

¡Ojo! In English, we often use "me/I," "us/we," and "them/they" interchangeably. This is not the case in Spanish. For these comparatives, always use subject pronouns (*yo, tú, él/ella*, etc.).

Unidad 7

Los pronombres de complemento directo – Direct-Object Pronouns

lo – it (masculine)	**la** – it (feminine)
los – them (masculine / masculine and feminine)	**las** – them (feminine)

As in English, pronouns (*pronombres*) in Spanish are used to replace nouns (*sustantivos*). What is different from English is their placement with respect to the verb: before a conjugated verb or attached to an infinitive.

> *Ej.* ¿Quieres <u>la blusa</u>?   ¿Tienes <u>los pantalones</u>?
> No, no <u>la</u> quiero. – No, I don't want <u>it</u>.   Sí, <u>los</u> tengo. – Yes, I have <u>them</u>.
>
> ¿Quieres llevar <u>esta corbata</u>?
> No, no <u>la</u> quiero llevar.   or   No, no quiero llevar<u>la</u>.

Las preguntas – Questions

There are several phrases you can use to ask people how they like something (food, clothing, etc.). Your inclination is probably to translate the word "how" as *cómo* and finish it off with the verb *gustar*. This would make sense in Spanish, but it probably would not mean what you think.

> *Ej.* ¿Cómo te gusta tu café? – How do you like (prefer) your coffee?
> Me gusta mi café con leche. – I like (prefer) my coffee with milk.

To inquire about someone's experience with a specific thing, use the verb *estar* with *cómo*.

> *Ej.* ¿Cómo está tu café? – How is your coffee?
> Mi café está caliente pero muy bueno. – My coffee is hot, but very good (tasty).

To ask someone's opinion of a specific thing, use the verb *parecer* with *qué.*

> *Ej.* ¿Qué te parece esta camisa? – How does this shirt seem (look) to you?
> Esa camisa me parece muy bonita. – That shirt seems (looks) very pretty to me.

The phrase *¿qué tal?* is quite versatile. By itself it translates best as "How are things?" Even though it's not a verb, you can use it with an object to ask how it is.

> *Ej.* ¿Qué tal la sopa? – How's the soup? / How about the soup?
> La sopa está deliciosa. – The soup is delicious.

You can also use it in conjunction with verbs like *gustar, estar, parecer,* etc., which then translates to "how" in the way that *cómo* couldn't in the first example of this section.

> *Ej.* ¿Qué tal te gusta tu café?
> ¿Qué tal te parecen estos pantalones?
> ¿Qué tal está tu burrito?

Unidad 8

El presente progresivo – Progressive Present

The present tense is most often used to describe habitual action, and words like *siempre*, *nunca*, *todos los días*, *de vez en cuando*, etc. describe the frequency of that action. The present tense can also be used to describe ongoing action that is taking place in the moment (right now).

This construction has two components: the verb *estar*, conjugated in the present tense, and the gerund form (-ing) of the action verb. This is called the progressive present.

> *Ej.* ¿Qué **estás** hac<u>iendo</u>? – What **are you** do<u>ing</u>?
> **Estoy** desayun<u>ando</u>. – **I am** eat<u>ing</u> breakfast.

Review the verb *estar* in the present tense and notice the construction of the gerund (-ing).

estar – to be		-ing
estoy	estamos	-ar → -ando
estás	estáis	-er → -iendo
está	están	-ir → -iendo

¡Ojo! The verb *estar* is conjugated in the present tense according to the subject of the action. The action verb in the gerund (-ing) is not conjugated; it is an adverb, which has no subject or gender.

> *Ej.* **Estoy** jug<u>ando</u>. – **I am** play<u>ing</u>.   **Estamos** jug<u>ando</u>. – **We are** play<u>ing</u>.
> **Estás** jug<u>ando</u>. – **You are** play<u>ing</u>.   **Estáis** jug<u>ando</u>. – **You (all) are** play<u>ing</u>.
> **Está** jug<u>ando</u>. – **S/he is** play<u>ing</u>.   **Están** jug<u>ando</u>. – **They are** play<u>ing</u>.
>
> **Estoy** com<u>iendo</u>. – **I am** eat<u>ing</u>.   **Estamos** com<u>iendo</u>. – **We are** eat<u>ing</u>.
> **Estás** com<u>iendo</u>. – **You are** eat<u>ing</u>.   **Estáis** com<u>iendo</u>. – **You (all) are** eat<u>ing</u>.
> **Está** com<u>iendo</u>. – **S/he is** eat<u>ing</u>.   **Están** com<u>iendo</u>. – **They are** eat<u>ing</u>.
>
> **Estoy** escrib<u>iendo</u>. – **I am** writing.   **Estamos** escrib<u>iendo</u>. – **We are** writing.
> **Estás** escrib<u>iendo</u>. – **You are** writing.   **Estáis** escrib<u>iendo</u>. – **You (all) are** writing.
> **Está** escrib<u>iendo</u>. – **S/he is** writing.   **Están** escrib<u>iendo</u>. – **They are** writing.

- **The gerund: noun or adverb?**

In English, the gerund (-ing) form can be either a noun or an adverb.
> *Ej.* Running (noun) is good for you.   She spends her days dreaming (adverb).

In Spanish, the gerund form can only be used as an adverb. If you want the noun form for -ing, use the infinitive. This means the infinitive is used as the subject of another verb as well as after a preposition (*por*, *para*, *sin*, *con*, *de*, etc.) whether the translation to English is "to __" or "__ing."

> *Ej.* ~~Corriendo~~ Corr<u>er</u> es bueno para ti.   Ella pasa sus días soñ<u>ando</u> (adverbio).
> Me gusta ~~corriendo~~ correr. – I like <u>to run</u>. / I like <u>running</u>.
> sin correr – without running, después de comer – after eating

Unidad 9

Los verbos irregulares (el presente) – Irregular Verbs (present tense)

You should already be familiar with the concept of stem-changing verbs. Here is a review of two irregular verbs that we have already studied.

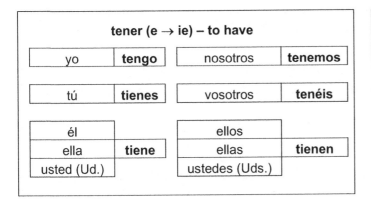

tener (e → ie) – to have			
yo	**tengo**	nosotros	**tenemos**
tú	**tienes**	vosotros	**tenéis**
él / ella / usted (Ud.)	**tiene**	ellos / ellas / ustedes (Uds.)	**tienen**

preferir (e → ie) – to prefer			
yo	**prefiero**	nosotros	**preferimos**
tú	**prefieres**	vosotros	**preferís**
él / ella / usted (Ud.)	**prefiere**	ellos / ellas / ustedes (Uds.)	**prefieren**

Notice that *tener* has a unique change in the 1st person, singular form (*yo*). Here are two more verbs that have a similar change in the 1st person, singular form in the present, but the rest of the conjugations are regular.

hacer – to do / to make			
yo	**hago**	nosotros	**hacemos**
tú	**haces**	vosotros	**hacéis**
él / ella / usted (Ud.)	**hace**	ellos / ellas / ustedes (Uds.)	**hacen**

poner – to put / to place / to set			
yo	**pongo**	nosotros	**ponemos**
tú	**pones**	vosotros	**ponéis**
él / ella / usted (Ud.)	**pone**	ellos / ellas / ustedes (Uds.)	**ponen**

The verb *hay* is a very useful word. It means *there is* or *there are* and can be used in similar situations as the verb *tener*. Whereas *tener,* when conjugated, has a subject, and therefore tells us who possesses a certain item, *hay* is generic and is used when it is not necessary to express who an item or items belong to.

> *Ej.* **Yo tengo** una cama en mi habitación.
> **I have** a bed in my bedroom.
>
> **Hay** una cama en mi habitación.
> **There is** a bed in my bedroom.

Los pronombres de complemento directo – Direct-Object Pronouns

lo – it (masculine)	**la** – it (feminine)
los – them (masculine / masculine and feminine)	**las** – them (feminine)

As in English, pronouns (*pronombres*) in Spanish are used to replace nouns (*sustantivos*). What is different from English is their placement with respect to the verb.

> *Ej.* How often do you <u>clean</u> **the bathroom**?
> I <u>clean</u> **it** every Saturday.
>
> ¿Con qué frecuencia <u>limpias</u> **el baño**?
> Yo **lo** <u>limpio</u> todos los sábados.

Notice that *el baño* is a masculine noun and therefore it is replaced with the appropriate masculine, singular pronoun: *lo*.

Also notice that in Spanish, the pronoun comes immediately before the conjugated verb whereas in English, the pronoun comes after the verb. When you have two verbs in Spanish, one conjugated (*prefiero*) and one in its infinitive form (*limpiar*), the pronoun has two correct placements.

> *Ej.* Do you <u>prefer</u> <u>to clean</u> **the kitchen** tonight or tomorrow night?
> I <u>prefer</u> <u>to clean</u> **it** tonight.
>
> ¿<u>Prefieres</u> <u>limpiar</u> **la cocina** esta noche o mañana por la noche?
> Yo **la** <u>prefiero</u> <u>limpiar</u> esta noche.

Notice that in the above example, the feminine pronoun (*la*) replaces the feminine noun (*la cocina*) and is correctly placed directly before the conjugated verb *prefiero*. Below, we will see its alternate placement: attached to the end of the infinitive.

> *Ej.* ¿<u>Prefieres</u> <u>limpiar</u> **la cocina** esta noche o mañana por la noche?
> Yo <u>prefiero</u> <u>limpiar</u>**la** esta noche.

Both of these placements are equally correct and there is no specific preference in either case; usually the placement will be determined by the speaker/writer based on whichever one rolls off the tongue most easily. Again, we only have this option when we have both a conjugated verb and an infinitive together. If we *only* have a conjugated verb (*limpio*), the pronoun *must* be placed directly before the verb. If we *only* have an infinitive (*limpiar*), the pronoun *must* be attached to the end of the verb.

> *Ej.* Voy a la cocina para <u>limpiar</u>**la**.
> **La** <u>limpio</u> después de <u>usar</u>**la**.

Unidad 10

Los verbos irregulares (el presente) – Irregular Verbs (present tense)

Here is a review of some irregular verbs.

tener (e → ie) – to have			
yo	**tengo**	nosotros	**tenemos**
tú	**tienes**	vosotros	**tenéis**
él / ella / usted (Ud.)	**tiene**	ellos / ellas / ustedes (Uds.)	**tienen**

pensar (e → ie) – to think			
yo	**pienso**	nosotros	**pensamos**
tú	**piensas**	vosotros	**pensáis**
él / ella / usted (Ud.)	**piensa**	ellos / ellas / ustedes (Uds.)	**piensan**

The following two verbs both mean *to be* in English but they have separate uses in Spanish.

- **Estar**: emotions, physical or mental states of being, and location
  (These circumstances can change frequently, from day to day or moment to moment.)

    Ej. Yo <u>estoy</u> contento. – I am happy. (emotion)
    Tú <u>estás</u> enfermo. – You are sick. (physical state of being)
    Ella <u>está</u> loca. – She is crazy. (mental state of being)
    Nosotros <u>estamos</u> en clase. – We are in class. (location)

- **Ser**: origins, time, days, dates, professions, physical characteristics, and personality traits
  (These characteristics are usually permanent, but may change over long periods of time.)

    Ej. Yo <u>soy</u> de Colorado. – I am from Colorado. (origin)
    Hoy <u>es</u> sábado. – Today is Saturday. (days)
    Ella <u>es</u> médica. – She is a doctor. (profession)
    Nosotros <u>somos</u> altos. – We are tall. (physical characteristic)
    Ellos <u>son</u> simpáticos. – They are nice. (personality trait)

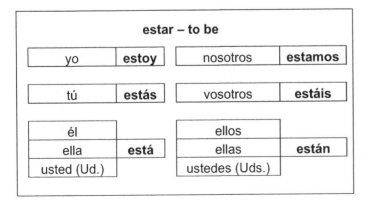

estar – to be			
yo	**estoy**	nosotros	**estamos**
tú	**estás**	vosotros	**estáis**
él / ella / usted (Ud.)	**está**	ellos / ellas / ustedes (Uds.)	**están**

ser – to be			
yo	**soy**	nosotros	**somos**
tú	**eres**	vosotros	**sois**
él / ella / usted (Ud.)	**es**	ellos / ellas / ustedes (Uds.)	**son**

Los pronombres de complemento indirecto – Indirect-Object Pronouns

me – me		**nos** – us	
te – you		**os** – you (Spain plural)	
le – him / her / you (formal)		**les** – them / you (Latin America plural, formal)	

You have studied the verbs *gustar* and *encantar*, which, when translated into English, cause problems between subject and object.

English: "I like the class." – "I" is the subject and "the class" is the object.
Spanish: "The class pleases me." – "The class" is the subject and "me" is the object.

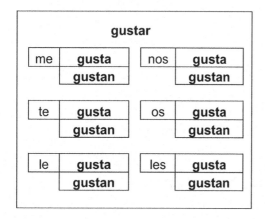
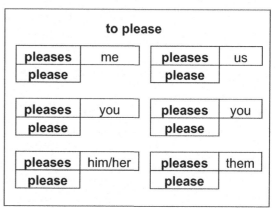

Another verb that follows a similar pattern is the verb *doler* (to ache/to hurt). It is used with body parts and is almost always conjugated in the 3rd person: singular (one body part that hurts) or plural (multiple body parts that hurt). **The indirect object (pronoun) indicates the person whose body part(s) hurt(s) and is completely independent of the conjugation of the verb *doler*.**

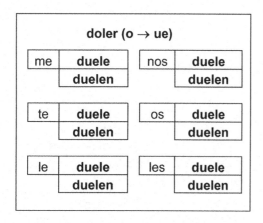
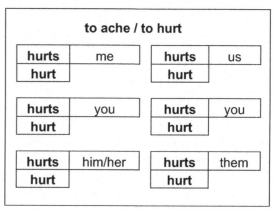

Ej. Me duele la rodilla. – My knee hurts.   ¿Te duele la rodilla? – Does your knee hurt?
     Me duelen las rodillas. – My knees hurt. ¿Te duelen las rodillas? Do your knees hurt?

¡Ojo! When separate singular nouns come after the verb, the verb can be either singular or plural.

    Ej. Me duel<u>e</u> el estómago y la cabeza.   or   Me duel<u>en</u> el estómago y la cabeza.

Double Negatives

Negative words like *nunca*, *nada*, *nadie*, and *ninguno* have affirmative meanings, as well, so what looks like a double negative is really an affirmation of the negative.

> *Ej.* No lo hago *nunca*. – I don't *ever* do it.
> No nos gusta *ninguno*. – We don't like *any* (of them).
> No hay *nadie* aquí. – There isn't *anyone* here.
> No tiene *nada*. – She doesn't have *anything*.

Los verbos reflexivos – Reflexive Verbs

The <u>subject</u> of a sentence/phrase is the person or thing that does the action of the verb or is otherwise described by that verb if it is not an action.

> *Ej.* <u>Yo</u> llamo al médico cuando estoy enfermo. – <u>I</u> call the doctor when I am sick.

The <u>object</u> of a sentence/phrase is the person or thing that receives the benefit, consequence, effect, etc. of the verb either directly or indirectly.

> *Ej.* Yo llamo <u>al médico</u> cuando estoy enfermo. – I call <u>the doctor</u> when I am sick.
> Yo <u>lo</u> llamo cuando estoy enfermo. – I call <u>him</u> when I am sick.

When the <u>subject</u> and <u>object</u> of a sentence/phrase are the same person, the verb is considered reflexive. This means that the subject does an action to itself, for itself, etc. The most common use of reflexive verbs is for those describing one's daily routine (Unit 13). There are many other uses of reflexive verbs in Spanish and many do not translate well into English, so until you understand all of the subtle uses and meanings of reflexive verbs, you may just have to accept their conjugation rules as they are.

> *Ej.* <u>Yo</u> <u>me</u> llamo David. – <u>I</u> call <u>myself</u> David (my name is David).

Los pronombres reflexivos – Reflexive Pronouns

me – myself	**nos** – ourselves
te – yourself	**os** – yourselves (Spain plural)
se – himself / herself / yourself (formal)	**se** – themselves / yourselves (Latin America plural, formal)

A reflexive verb looks like any other verb, whether regular or irregular in any given verb tense, with the exception of the reflexive pronoun that accompanies it. It is this pronoun that makes the verb reflexive.

¡Ojo! The reflexive pronoun must match the subject in person (1st, 2nd, 3rd) and number (s., pl.).

Take a look at the following reflexive verbs in the **present tense** and notice that the reflexive pronouns match each subject and also notice their placement.

	singular		plural	
llamarse – to call oneself				
1st person	yo	**me llamo**	nosotros	**nos llamamos**
2nd person	tú	**te llamas**	vosotros	**os llamáis**
3rd person	él / ella / usted (Ud.)	**se llama**	ellos / ellas / ustedes (Uds.)	**se llaman**

	singular		plural	
sentirse (e → ie) – to feel				
1st person	yo	**me siento**	nosotros	**nos sentimos**
2nd person	tú	**te sientes**	vosotros	**os sentís**
3rd person	él / ella / usted (Ud.)	**se siente**	ellos / ellas / ustedes (Uds.)	**se sienten**

	singular		plural	
quedarse – to stay / to remain				
1st person	yo	**me quedo**	nosotros	**nos quedamos**
2nd person	tú	**te quedas**	vosotros	**os quedáis**
3rd person	él / ella / usted (Ud.)	**se queda**	ellos / ellas / ustedes (Uds.)	**se quedan**

	singular		plural	
		mejorarse – to get better		
1st person	yo	**me mejoro**	nosotros	**nos mejoramos**
2nd person	tú	**te mejoras**	vosotros	**os mejoráis**
3rd person	él / ella / usted (Ud.)	**se mejora**	ellos / ellas / ustedes (Uds.)	**se mejoran**

	singular		plural	
		soplarse (la nariz) – to blow one's (nose)		
1st person	yo	**me soplo**	nosotros	**nos soplamos**
2nd person	tú	**te soplas**	vosotros	**os sopláis**
3rd person	él / ella / usted (Ud.)	**se sopla**	ellos / ellas / ustedes (Uds.)	**se soplan**

Reflexive pronouns follow the same placement rules as indirect-object pronouns (pp.85, 98) and direct-object pronouns (pp.93, 96) – immediately before a conjugated verb or attached to the end of an infinitive.

> *Ej.* Yo **me** siento fatal.
> Ella y yo **nos** sentimos fatal.
>
> Yo debo tomar mucha agua y descansar mucho para mejorar**me**.
> Ella y yo debemos tomar mucha agua y descansar mucho para mejorar**nos**.

When there are two verbs together, one conjugated (*debo*) and one in its infinitive form (*quedarse*), the speaker/writer has an option with respect to the placement of the pronoun.

> *Ej.* Me debo quedar en la cama. (immediately before the conjugated verb)
> Debo quedarme en la cama. (attached to the end of the infinitive)

Unidad 11

Los verbos (el pretérito) – Verbs (preterite/past tense)

In Spanish, as in most languages, there are many different verb tenses. So far, we have only studied the present tense although you may have seen or heard other tenses before. It is time to expand on your understanding of verb tenses by introducing one of the past tenses: the preterite. This tense is used to talk about events that happened at a specific time or a specific number of times in the past. Some words that would signal the preterite are the following:

ayer – yesterday	la semana pasada – last week
anteayer – the day before yesterday	el año pasado – last year
anoche – last night	hace dos días – two days ago
el sábado pasado – last Saturday	hace tres semanas – three weeks ago

As you already know, all verbs in Spanish fall into one of three categories, which is determined by their endings in the infinitive form: *-ar, -er, -ir*. Within each category, verbs are classified, within the given tense, as either regular or irregular. All regular verbs follow the same rules of conjugation for their respective category (regular *-ar*, regular *-er*, and regular *-ir*). Irregular verbs do not follow the same rules and their conjugations must be learned individually. It is important to understand that each tense has unique endings. Take a look at the following example of a regular preterite-tense *-ar* verb. Notice the differences from the present, especially accent marks.

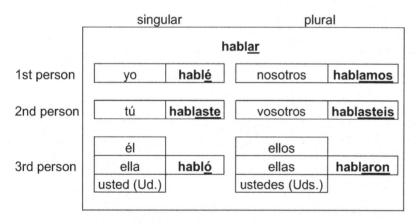
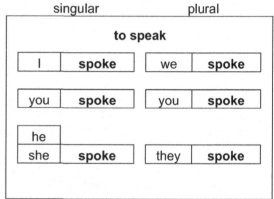

Notice that the stem of the verb (everything but the ending) does not change, only the ending. To conjugate regular verbs, you simply drop the infinitive ending: *-ar, -er, -ir*; and add the corresponding conjugated ending.

¡Ojo! The *nosotros* forms for *-ar* and *-ir* verbs are the same in the present and the preterite tenses. The only way to determine whether the conjugation is present or preterite is by understanding the context of the sentence; key words/phrases such as *todos los días* and *ayer* are the biggest indicators.

	singular		plural	
	comer			
1st person	yo	**comí**	nosotros	**comimos**
2nd person	tú	**comiste**	vosotros	**comisteis**
3rd person	él / ella / usted (Ud.)	**comió**	ellos / ellas / ustedes (Uds.)	**comieron**

	singular		plural	
	to eat			
1st person	I	ate	we	ate
2nd person	you	ate	you	ate
3rd person	he / she	ate	they	ate

¡Ojo! Usted and *ustedes* are 2nd person, formal, but they are conjugated as 3rd person.

	singular		plural	
	vivir			
1st person	yo	**viví**	nosotros	**vivimos**
2nd person	tú	**viviste**	vosotros	**vivisteis**
3rd person	él / ella / usted (Ud.)	**vivió**	ellos / ellas / ustedes (Uds.)	**vivieron**

	singular		plural	
	to live			
1st person	I	lived	we	lived
2nd person	you	lived	you	lived
3rd person	he / she	lived	they	lived

¡Ojo! The *vosotros* form is used primarily in Spain. In Latin America, *ustedes* serves as both the familiar and formal forms of *you, plural*.

Take a look at the following sentences that contrast the present tense with the preterite tense. Notice the key words/phrases that signal frequency.

Ej. Mónica **generalmente** come en casa, pero **ayer**, comió en un restaurante.

Les <u>gusta</u> jugar al béisbol durante el verano, pero **el verano pasado**, no <u>jugaron</u>.

Normalmente, <u>estudiamos</u> en la biblioteca, pero **ayer**, <u>estudiamos</u> en la cafetería.

Los verbos irregulares (el pretérito) – Irregular Verbs (preterite/past tense)

Just like the present tense, the preterite tense has irregular verbs. Some irregular verbs in the present are also irregular in the preterite, but not always. No verb is inherently irregular; their irregularities are tense specific. We will study a few different types of preterite irregulars in the next unit, but for now, here are a few common ones to get you started.

¡Ojo! These irregular verbs in the preterite tense do not have accent marks.

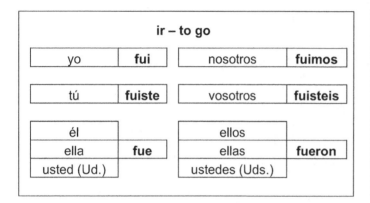

ir – to go			
yo	**fui**	nosotros	**fuimos**
tú	**fuiste**	vosotros	**fuisteis**
él / ella / usted (Ud.)	**fue**	ellos / ellas / ustedes (Uds.)	**fueron**

ser – to be			
yo	**fui**	nosotros	**fuimos**
tú	**fuiste**	vosotros	**fuisteis**
él / ella / usted (Ud.)	**fue**	ellos / ellas / ustedes (Uds.)	**fueron**

Notice that *ir* and *ser* have the same conjugations in the preterite but their meanings remain different. The way to determine whether a conjugation is from the verb *ir* or *ser*, you must understand the context of the sentence.

Ej. Fue al cine el sábado pasado.
He <u>went</u> to the movies last Saturday. vs. He ~~was~~ to the movies last Saturday.

Ej. Mi abuelo <u>fue</u> ingeniero.
My grandpa <u>was</u> an engineer. vs. My grandpa ~~went~~ an engineer.

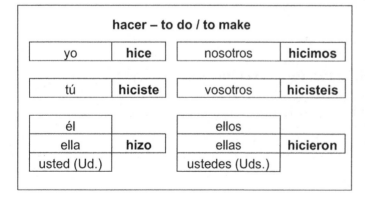

hacer – to do / to make			
yo	**hice**	nosotros	**hicimos**
tú	**hiciste**	vosotros	**hicisteis**
él / ella / usted (Ud.)	**hizo**	ellos / ellas / ustedes (Uds.)	**hicieron**

ver – to see / to watch (TV, movies, etc.)			
yo	**vi**	nosotros	**vimos**
tú	**viste**	vosotros	**visteis**
él / ella / usted (Ud.)	**vio**	ellos / ellas / ustedes (Uds.)	**vieron**

Notice the spelling change from *c* to *z* in the 3rd person, singular category (*él, ella, Ud.*).

Unidad 12

Los verbos irregulares (el presente) – Irregular Verbs (present tense)

You should now be aware that there are different types of irregular verbs. Some require a stem change (*poder, querer*), while others require a complete change (*ser, ir*). There are also some that have a unique change in the 1st person, singular form *yo* (*hacer, tener*). Take a look at some other irregular verbs that follow this pattern and notice the unique changes with *yo*.

poner – to put / to place / to set

yo	**pongo**	nosotros	**ponemos**
tú	**pones**	vosotros	**ponéis**
él / ella / usted (Ud.)	**pone**	ellos / ellas / ustedes (Uds.)	**ponen**

hacer – to do / to make

yo	**hago**	nosotros	**hacemos**
tú	**haces**	vosotros	**hacéis**
él / ella / usted (Ud.)	**hace**	ellos / ellas / ustedes (Uds.)	**hacen**

tener (e → ie) – to have

yo	**tengo**	nosotros	**tenemos**
tú	**tienes**	vosotros	**tenéis**
él / ella / usted (Ud.)	**tiene**	ellos / ellas / ustedes (Uds.)	**tienen**

salir – to go out / to leave

yo	**salgo**	nosotros	**salimos**
tú	**sales**	vosotros	**salís**
él / ella / usted (Ud.)	**sale**	ellos / ellas / ustedes (Uds.)	**salen**

traer – to bring

yo	**traigo**	nosotros	**traemos**
tú	**traes**	vosotros	**traéis**
él / ella / usted (Ud.)	**trae**	ellos / ellas / ustedes (Uds.)	**traen**

venir (e → ie) – to come

yo	**vengo**	nosotros	**venimos**
tú	**vienes**	vosotros	**venís**
él / ella / usted (Ud.)	**viene**	ellos / ellas / ustedes (Uds.)	**vienen**

Conocer vs. saber

You may have studied the verb *saber* before, but you may not have realized that there is another verb with the same translation to English: *conocer*. Both mean "to know" in English, but each has a unique use in Spanish.

- **Conocer**

Conocer is used when talking about personal experiences that cannot be summarized by mere facts. To know someone personally is a much more abstract concept than to simply know details about that same person. *Conocer*, however, is not limited to people; it can also refer to anything you can be familiar with: a place, a song, a feeling, etc.

> *Ej. Mi mamá **conoce** a tu amiga.* (personally)

> *¿**Conoces** muy bien la ciudad de Denver?* (personally)

¡Ojo! – The *a* in the first example, right before *tu amiga*, is called the "personal *a*" and is used to distinguish the subject of the sentence from the direct object of the sentence when the direct object is a person.

- **Saber**

Saber, in contrast, is used when talking about details, facts or other information that can answer the questions *¿quién? ¿cuándo? ¿dónde? ¿por qué? ¿cómo? ¿cuánto? ¿qué?* and *¿cuál?*

> *Ej. Mi mamá **sabe** quién es tu amiga.* (information)

> *¿**Sabes** dónde está Alejandra?* (information)

As with the verbs on the previous page, *saber* and *conocer* in the present tense have unique changes in the 1st person, singular form *yo*.

conoce**r** – to know (personally)			
yo	**conozco**	nosotros	**conocemos**
tú	**conoces**	vosotros	**conoc<u>é</u>is**
él / ella / usted (Ud.)	**conoce**	ellos / ellas / ustedes (Uds.)	**conocen**

saber – to know (information)			
yo	**sé**	nosotros	**sabemos**
tú	**sabes**	vosotros	**sab<u>é</u>is**
él / ella / usted (Ud.)	**sabe**	ellos / ellas / ustedes (Uds.)	**saben**

Los verbos irregulares (el pretérito) – Irregular Verbs (preterite/past tense)

You have already been introduced to regular preterite-tense verbs. There are two parts to every verb in Spanish: the stem and the ending. By definition, all regular verbs retain the stem of their infinitives and only their endings change.

hablar	comer	vivir
hablé	comí	viví
hablaste	comiste	viviste
habló	comió	vivió
hablamos	comimos	vivimos
hablasteis	comisteis	vivisteis
hablaron	comieron	vivieron

As you know, irregular verbs do not follow these rules and their conjugations must be learned individually. What you may not know yet is that *irregular* is verb-tense specific. That means that irregular verbs in the present are not necessarily irregular in the preterite or any other verb tense for that matter. As in the present tense, there are several different types of irregular verbs; some are stem-changing verbs (which can be categorized by the type of change required), some change, remove, or add letters to retain their pronunciation, and some don't seem to follow any pattern at all. Take a look at the following examples of some irregular present-tense verbs and compare them with their preterite-tense conjugations.

jugar (u → ue) – presente			
yo	juego	nosotros	jugamos
tú	juegas	vosotros	jugáis
él / ella / usted (Ud.)	juega	ellos / ellas / ustedes (Uds.)	juegan

jugar – pretérito			
yo	jugué	nosotros	jugamos
tú	jugaste	vosotros	jugasteis
él / ella / usted (Ud.)	jugó	ellos / ellas / ustedes (Uds.)	jugaron

Notice that the preterite of *jugar* in the 1st person, singular form requires a *u* before the ending to maintain the proper pronunciation of the hard *g* sound. This change is coincidental and has nothing to do with the fact that *jugar* is irregular in the present tense. This change is required for all verbs ending in *gar*. Verbs ending in *car* and *zar* also require a spelling change in the 1st person, singular form in order to maintain correct pronunciation.

Ej.   **sacar** – to take out   **comenzar** – to start
          yo **saqué**   yo **comencé**
          tú **sacaste**   tú **comenzaste**
          él **sacó**   él **comenzó**

Verbs that end in *gar*, *car*, and *zar* have unique changes in the *yo* form in the preterite. This is due to the dual sounds of *g* and *c*. When followed by an *e* or *i*, *c* and *g* have a soft sound. When followed by an *a*, *o*, or *u*, they have a hard sound. In the case of the preterite, the *yo* form ending of *-ar* verbs is an *é*, which deviates from the other endings that start with either *a* or *o*. Take a look at the following pronunciation categories to better understand what's happening when we conjugate these *-gar*, *-car*, and *-zar* verbs in the preterite. Notice that *-guar* verbs (*averiguar*) also have a change (*averigüé*), but *-jar* verbs do not (*trabajé*). Also, watch out for *-ger* (*yo recojo*).

ga	gue
go	gui
gu	

ja	ge / je
jo	gi / ji
ju	

gua	güe
guo	güi
~~guu~~	

ca	que
co	qui
cu	

za	ce / ~~ze~~
zo	ci / ~~zi~~
zu	

jugo (Span.)   **ju**go (Span.)   a**gua** (Span.)   **co**lor (Span.)   **za**pato (Span.)
guess (Eng.)   **ha**ppy (Eng.)   i**gua**na (Eng.)   **cu**t (Eng.)   **ce**lebrate (Eng.)

➢ The Spanish *g* can either sound similar to the English *g* (*golf*) or the English *h* depending on the letter that follows it.

➢ The Spanish *j* sounds similar to the English *h* regardless of the letter that follows it.

➢ The *u* in *gue* and *gui* tells you which *g* sound to use, but it is silent, unless you have ¨ ("la crema") on top (*ü*). Seriously, it's called *crema*, but you can call it "*diéresis*," if you want.

➢ The Spanish *c* sounds similar to the English *k* or the English *s* depending on the letter that follows it.

➢ The Spanish *z* sounds similar to the English *s* regardless of the letter that follows it. Note that the Spanish *z* is never pronounced like the English *z*; "zzzzzzz" no eggzzzzzziste.

The *yo* forms in the preterite are affected by these changes as are the preterite forms of *hacer*: **hice** (~~hize~~), hi**zo** (~~hico~~), but these pronunciation categories do not apply exclusively to verbs.

> *Ej.* lápi**z** vs. lápi**ce**s (*pencil*)   pe**z** vs. pe**ce**s (*fish*)

Other pronunciation problems arise with *-eer* and some *-aer* verbs in the preterite. In Spanish verbs, the vowel combinations *eio* and *aio* do not exist due to the weak pronunciation that would result, so *y* ("*i griega*" – "Greek i") substitutes for *i* ("*i*" or "*i latina*" – "i" or "Latin i") in the 3rd person conjugations to give them a stronger pronunciation. Notice the irregular accent marks.

leer – to read			
yo	leí	nosotros	leímos
tú	leíste	vosotros	leísteis
él / ella / usted (Ud.)	leyó	ellos / ellas / ustedes (Uds.)	leyeron

creer – to believe			
yo	creí	nosotros	creímos
tú	creíste	vosotros	creísteis
él / ella / usted (Ud.)	creyó	ellos / ellas / ustedes (Uds.)	creyeron

Los verbos irregulares (el pretérito) – Irregular Verbs (preterite/past tense)

As stated last unit (p.104), irregular verbs are tense specific. That said, there are some things we can observe that might help us identify irregulars from one tense to another. Take a look at some examples of stem-changing verbs in the present and what their preterite conjugations look like.

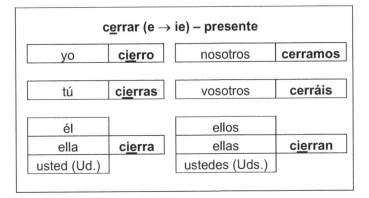

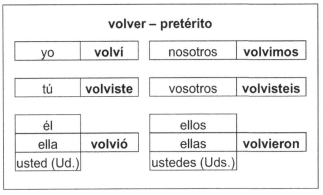

You can see that in the case of *cerrar* and *volver* above, the verbs are stem-changing in the present, but they are both regular in the preterite. This is typical both of *-ar* and *-er* verbs.

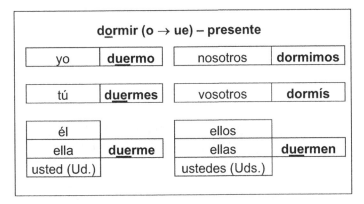

In the case of *-ir* verbs, stem-changing verbs in the present are irregular in the preterite and, in most cases, the preterite tense also requires a stem change in the 3rd person (*él / ellos*). Sometimes the stem changes are the same between tenses and sometimes they are different.

Unidad 13

Los verbos reflexivos – Reflexive Verbs

The <u>subject</u> of a sentence/phrase is the person or thing that does the action of the verb or is otherwise described by that verb if it is not an action.

> *Ej.* <u>Joaquín</u> lava el carro. – <u>Joaquin</u> washes the car.

The <u>object</u> of a sentence/phrase is the person or thing that receives the benefit, consequence, effect, etc. of the verb either directly or indirectly.

> *Ej.* Joaquín lava el <u>carro</u>. – Joaquin washes the <u>car</u>.

Of course, the <u>object</u> can be substituted with an <u>object pronoun</u> if the object in question has already been established (pp.93, 96).

> *Ej.* Joaquín <u>lo</u> lava. – Joaquin washes <u>it</u>.

When the <u>subject</u> and <u>object</u> of a sentence/phrase are the same person, the verb is considered reflexive. This means that the subject does an action to itself, for itself, etc. The most common use of reflexive verbs is for those describing one's daily routine. But there are many other uses of reflexive verbs in Spanish and many do not translate well into English. Until you understand all of the subtle uses and meanings of reflexive verbs, you may just have to accept their conjugation rules as they are.

> *Ej.* <u>Joaquín</u> <u>se</u> lava (el pelo). – <u>Joaquin</u> washes <u>himself</u> (his own hair).

Los pronombres reflexivos – Reflexive Pronouns

me – myself	**nos** – ourselves
te – yourself	**os** – yourselves (Spain plural)
se – himself / herself / yourself (formal)	**se** – themselves / yourselves (Latin America plural, formal)

A reflexive verb looks like any other verb, whether regular or irregular in any given verb tense, with the exception of the reflexive pronoun that accompanies it. It is this pronoun that makes the verb reflexive.

¡Ojo! The reflexive pronoun must match the subject in person (1st, 2nd, 3rd) and number (s., pl.).

Take a look at the following verbs in the **present tense** and notice the differences between the reflexive versions and the non-reflexive versions. Both are correct but have different meanings.

vestirse (e → i) – to get dressed			
yo	me visto	nosotros	nos vestimos
tú	te vistes	vosotros	os vestís
él / ella / usted (Ud.)	se viste	ellos / ellas / ustedes (Uds.)	se visten

vestir (e → i) – to dress (someone else)			
yo	visto	nosotros	vestimos
tú	vistes	vosotros	vestís
él / ella / usted (Ud.)	viste	ellos / ellas / ustedes (Uds.)	visten

Ej. <u>Yo</u> <u>me</u> visto. – I get dressed (I dress myself). – subject and object are the same

<u>Yo</u> visto <u>a mi hijo</u>. – I dress my son. – subject and object are different

bañarse – to take a bath			
yo	me baño	nosotros	nos bañamos
tú	te bañas	vosotros	os bañáis
él / ella / usted (Ud.)	se baña	ellos / ellas / ustedes (Uds.)	se bañan

bañar – to give (someone else) a bath			
yo	baño	nosotros	bañamos
tú	bañas	vosotros	bañáis
él / ella / usted (Ud.)	baña	ellos / ellas / ustedes (Uds.)	bañan

Ej. <u>Yo</u> <u>me</u> baño. – I take a bath (I bathe myself). – subject and object are the same

<u>Yo</u> baño <u>a mi hijo</u>. – I give my son a bath. – subject and object are different

Reflexive pronouns follow the same placement rules as indirect-object pronouns (pp.85, 98) and direct-object pronouns (pp.93, 96) – immediately before a conjugated verb or attached to the end of an infinitive. When there are two verbs together, one conjugated (*voy*) and one in its infinitive form (*vestirse*), the speaker/writer has an option with respect to the placement of the pronoun.

Ej. <u>Me voy</u> a vestir en mi dormitorio. – I'm going to get dressed in my bedroom.

Voy a <u>vestirme</u> en mi dormitorio.

Todos los días, <u>me visto</u> en mi dormitorio después de <u>bañarme</u>.

Now take a look at the same verbs in the **preterite tense**. A verb can be reflexive regardless of its tense

vestirse (e → i) – to get dressed			
yo	me vestí	nosotros	nos vestimos
tú	te vestiste	vosotros	os vestisteis
él / ella / usted (Ud.)	se vistió	ellos / ellas / ustedes (Uds.)	se vistieron

vestir (e → i) – to dress (someone else)			
yo	vestí	nosotros	vestimos
tú	vestiste	vosotros	vestisteis
él / ella / usted (Ud.)	vistió	ellos / ellas / ustedes (Uds.)	vistieron

Ej. <u>Yo</u> <u>me</u> vestí. – I got dressed (I dressed myself). – subject and object are the same

<u>Yo</u> vestí <u>a mi hijo</u>. – I dressed my son. – subject and object are different

bañarse – to take a bath			
yo	me bañé	nosotros	nos bañamos
tú	te bañaste	vosotros	os bañasteis
él / ella / usted (Ud.)	se bañó	ellos / ellas / ustedes (Uds.)	se bañaron

bañar – to give (someone else) a bath			
yo	bañé	nosotros	bañamos
tú	bañaste	vosotros	bañasteis
él / ella / usted (Ud.)	bañó	ellos / ellas / ustedes (Uds.)	bañaron

Ej. <u>Yo</u> <u>me</u> bañé. – I took a bath (I bathed myself). – subject and object are the same

<u>Yo</u> bañé <u>a mi hijo</u>. – I gave my son a bath. – subject and object are different

Reflexive pronouns follow the same placement rules as indirect-object pronouns (pp.85, 98) and direct-object pronouns (pp.93, 96) – immediately before a conjugated verb or attached to the end of an infinitive. When there are two verbs together, one conjugated (*fui*) and one in its infinitive form (*vestirse*), the speaker/writer has an option with respect to the placement of the pronoun.

Ej. <u>Me</u> <u>fui</u> a vestir en mi dormitorio.

Fui a <u>vestirme</u> en mi dormitorio.

Ayer, <u>me vestí</u> en mi dormitorio después de <u>bañarme</u>.

Unidad 14

We have covered the concept of direct-object pronouns (pp.93, 96) and we have also covered reflexive pronouns (pp.99-101, 110-112), so let's review.

Los pronombres de complemento directo – Direct-Object Pronouns

lo – it (masculine)	**la** – it (feminine)
los – them (masculine / masculine and feminine)	**las** – them (feminine)

The best way to understand the use of direct objects is to think of them as answering the question "*what?*"

> *Ej.* Did you buy **the shirt**?
> Yes, I bought **it** last weekend.
>
> ¿Compraste la camisa?
> Sí, **la** compré el fin de semana pasado.

Notice that *la camisa* is a feminine noun and therefore it is replaced with the appropriate feminine, singular pronoun: *la*.

Also notice that in Spanish, the pronoun comes immediately before the conjugated verb whereas in English, the pronoun comes after the verb. When you have two verbs in Spanish, one conjugated (*voy*) and one in its infinitive form (*llevar*), the pronoun has two correct placements.

> *Ej.* Are you going to wear your new **suit** to the party?
> No, I'm going to wear **it** to church.
>
> ¿<u>Vas a llevar</u> tu **traje** nuevo a la fiesta?
> No, **lo** <u>voy a</u> <u>llevar</u> a la iglesia.

Notice that in the above example, the masculine pronoun (*lo*) replaced the masculine noun (*el traje*) and is correctly placed directly before the conjugated verb *voy*. Below, we will see its alternate placement: attached to the end of the infinitive.

> *Ej.* ¿<u>Vas a llevar</u> tu **traje** nuevo a la fiesta?
> No, <u>voy a</u> <u>llevar**lo**</u> a la iglesia.

Both of these placements are equally correct and there is no specific preference in either case; usually the placement will be determined by the speaker/writer based on whichever one rolls off the tongue the easiest. Again, we only have this option when we have both a conjugated verb and an infinitive together. If we *only* have a conjugated verb (*llevo*), the pronoun *must* be placed directly before the verb. If we *only* have an infinitive (*llevar*), the pronoun *must* be attached to the end of the verb.

Remember: when the subject and object of a sentence/phrase are the same person, the verb is considered *reflexive*. This means that the subject does an action to itself, for itself, etc.

Los pronombres reflexivos – Reflexive Pronouns

me – myself	**nos** – ourselves
te – yourself	**os** – yourselves (Spain plural)
se – himself / herself /	**se** – themselves /
yourself (formal)	yourselves (Latin America plural, formal)

A reflexive verb looks like any other verb, whether regular or irregular in any given verb tense, with the exception of the reflexive pronoun that accompanies it. It is this pronoun that makes the verb reflexive.

¡Ojo! The reflexive pronoun must match the subject in person (1st, 2nd, 3rd) and number (s., pl.).

Combinar dos complementos – Combining Two Objects

Mastering the sentence structure of Spanish is a difficult task, especially where object pronouns are concerned, so when you combine two objects in the same sentence, it becomes even more difficult. Take a look at the following examples of combined objects.

> *Ej.* ¿<u>Te</u> probaste <u>el suéter</u> en la tienda?　　Did you try on <u>the sweater</u> at the store?
> Sí, <u>me lo</u> probé antes de comprarlo.　　Yes, I tried <u>it</u> on before buying it.

In the above example, we have the reflexive verb *probarse* combined with the direct object *el suéter,* which is both masculine and singular. The direct object is then replaced with the corresponding pronoun: *lo* (masculine, singular).

> *Ej.* ¿<u>Se</u> ponen <u>la ropa</u> en el baño?　　Do you put your <u>clothing</u> on in the bathroom?
> No, <u>nos la</u> ponemos en el dormitorio.　　No, we put <u>it</u> on in the bedroom.

Whether you have only one object pronoun or are combining two, the placement rules still apply: immediately before a conjugated verb (*me lo* pongo) or attached to the end of an infinitive (ponér*melo*), but you must also place them in the proper order with respect to each other. If you are not sure which order to put them in, don't stress out; "ME LO" out. That is to say that the reflexive pronoun goes first and the direct-object pronoun goes second (*nos la, te los,* etc.).

Los verbos irregulares (el pretérito) – Irregular Verbs (preterite/past tense)

poner – to put		dar – to give		traer – to bring	
puse	pusimos	di	dimos	traje	trajimos
pusiste	pusisteis	diste	disteis	trajiste	trajisteis
puso	pusieron	dio	dieron	trajo	trajeron

Los comparativos – Comparatives

Comparatives, you may remember (p.92), make comparisons between two nouns. They can be used with adjectives, but the adjectives cannot always agree in gender and number with both nouns. This means that we have to treat the first part of the phrase as though it were the entire phrase, and then tack on the second noun afterward.

> *Ej.* La corbata es *más* barata.   El chaleco es *menos* bonito.
> La corbata es *más* barata *que* el chaleco. El chaleco es *menos* bonito *que* la corbata.
>
> Los anillos son *tan* caros *como* la blusa. (The rings are *as* expensive *as* the blouse.)
> La blusa es *tan* cara *como* los anillos. (The blouse is *as* expensive *as* the rings.)

- **Common comparative pitfall**

The phrase "more than" is not always a comparative. If you are talking about money and you say you have *more than* your friend, it's a comparative (comparison between you and your friend), but if you are saying you have *more than* $100 in your wallet, you are not comparing what you have to what $100 have, therefore it is not a comparative. This "than" is translated as *de*, not *que*. Think of it as "more *of* the same units." More than $100 is $101 (same units); it's not "I have."

> *Ej.* Tengo *más **de*** $100 en mi cartera.
> La blusa cuesta *menos **de*** $20.
> Hay *más **de*** 40 estudiantes en la clase.

La sustantivación de adjetivos – The Nominalization (Noun-ing) of Adjectives

Using direct-object pronouns is not the only way to avoid repetition of a noun. We can also turn adjectives into nouns. Consider the following phrases.

"Which skirt do you prefer: the tight skirt or the loose skirt?"

Skirt, skirt, skirt. How many times do we need to say "skirt"? Exactly once, using "one" instead.

"Which skirt do you prefer: the tight one or the loose one?"

In Spanish, this is accomplished by eliminating the noun, but leaving the article (*el, la,* etc.).

> *Ej.* ¿Qué falda prefieres: la ~~falda~~ apretada o la ~~falda~~ floja?
> Prefiero la ~~falda~~ apretada. (I prefer the tight one.)
> La ~~falda~~ que prefiero es la ~~falda~~ apretada. (The one I prefer is the tight one.)
>
> ¿Te gusta más el chaleco de rayas o el ~~chaleco~~ de cuadros?
> Me gusta más el de cuadros. (I prefer the plaid one.)
>
> ¿Cuál vestido es más elegante: el flojo y floreado o el corto y negro?
> Creo que el corto y negro es más elegante.

Unidad 15

We have covered the concept of subject-verb agreement unit after unit, and we have also covered the concept of indirect-object (pp.85, 98) and direct-object pronouns (pp.93, 96, 113-114). Independently, they are fairly basic concepts and are easily understood, but the sentence structure of Spanish creates problems for students when object pronouns are used.

¡Ojo! **The most important thing to remember is that verbs can only be conjugated to subjects, never to objects. The subject does the action, the object receives the benefit or consequence of the action or is otherwise impacted by it.**

Los pronombres de complemento indirecto – Indirect-Object Pronouns

me – me	**nos** – us
te – you	**os** – you (Spain plural)
le – him / her / you (formal)	**les** – them / you (Latin America plural, formal)

The best way to understand the use of indirect objects is to think of them as answering the questions: "*to whom?*" or "*for whom?*"

> *Ej.* Yo le pedí al mesero una ensalada. – I asked the waiter for a salad.
> Yo le pedí una ensalada. – I asked him for a salad.

In English, pronouns always replace nouns. In Spanish, in contrast, although they may replace nouns, they also may accompany them. In the case of indirect-object pronouns, it is most common to use the pronoun whether or not you use the noun, as you can see in the examples above.

There are two reasons to use the noun even when you use an indirect-object pronoun:

> ➤ to clarify the pronoun (*le, nos, os, les*)
> *Ej.* Mi mamá nos sirve la cena a mí y a mi hermano.

> ➤ to add emphasis
> *Ej.* A ti te gusta, pero a mí no (me gusta). – *You* like it, but *I* don't (like it).

In the case of *me* and *te*, there is never a need to clarify, but there may be a need to add emphasis. In English, we simply change our intonation to show that emphasis.

- **Common subject/object pitfall**

Be sure to keep your subject/object pronouns straight when concurring with someone.

> *Ej.* Juan – "Me gustan los tacos." ("Tacos please me.")
> María – "Yo, también." ("I also please you.") Are you sure that's what you mean?
> – "A mí, también." ("They also please me.") Now you're talking.

116

Los pronombres de complemento directo – Direct-Object Pronouns

lo – it (masculine)	**la** – it (feminine)
los – them (masculine / masculine and feminine)	**las** – them (feminine)

We have already studied direct-object pronouns (pp.93, 96, 113-114), so let's review.

> *Ej.* Did you already <u>order</u> **the enchiladas**?
> Yes, I <u>ordered</u> **them** already.
>
> ¿Ya <u>pediste</u> **las enchiladas**?
> Sí, ya **las** <u>pedí</u>.

Notice that *las enchiladas* is a feminine, plural noun and therefore it is replaced with the feminine, plural pronoun: *las*.

Combinar dos complementos – Combining Two Objects

Let's review the concept of combining two objects in the same sentence. Last unit, we combined direct-object pronouns with reflexive pronouns. This unit we will combine direct-object pronouns with indirect-object pronouns. Oh, yeah, and don't forget to "ME LO" out!

> *Ej.* ¿<u>Te</u> sirvió el mesero tu <u>sopa</u>?   Did the waiter serve <u>you</u> your <u>soup</u>?
> Sí, <u>me la</u> sirvió.   Yes, he served <u>it</u> <u>to me</u>.
>
> ¿<u>Me</u> va a traer mi <u>ensalada</u>?   Is she going to bring <u>me</u> my <u>salad</u>?
> Sí, <u>te la</u> va a traer ahora mismo.   Yes, she's going to bring <u>it</u> <u>to you</u> right now.
>   or
> ¿Va a traer<u>me</u> mi <u>ensalada</u>?
> Sí, va a traér<u>tela</u> ahora mismo

When the indirect-object pronouns *le* or *les* are combined with the direct-object pronouns *lo / la* or *los / las*, the *le* or *les* must be changed to *se*. This is to avoid the alliteration (repetition of a consonant sound), not because it is reflexive.

> *Ej.* ¿<u>Le</u> pediste <u>los tenedores</u>?   Did you ask <u>her</u> for <u>forks</u>?
> Sí, ~~le los~~ <u>se los</u> pedí hace 5 minutos.   Yes, I asked <u>her</u> for <u>them</u> 5 minutes ago.

Whether you have only one object pronoun or are combining two, the placement rules still apply: immediately before a conjugated verb (*me lo* sirvió) or attached to the end of an infinitive (servír*melo*). If you are still confused about which pronoun to put first, you may prefer the acronym R.I.D. (reflexive, indirect, direct). Apply it and *rid* yourself of the confusion.

Unidad 16

Los verbos irregulares (el presente y el pretérito) – Irregular Verbs (present and preterite)

In this unit, we will compare and contrast the present-tense conjugations with the preterite-tense conjugations of several irregular verbs. Remember that "irregular" is tense specific, which means that irregular in one tense does not mean irregular in another tense. Compare and contrast the following irregular verbs in the present and preterite.

presente   **pretérito**

p<u>e</u>rder (e → ie) – to lose

p<u>ie</u>rdo	perdemos	
p<u>ie</u>rdes	perdéis	
p<u>ie</u>rde	p<u>ie</u>rden	

perder

perdí	perdimos
perdiste	perdisteis
perdió	perdieron

div<u>e</u>rtirse (e → ie) – to have fun

me div<u>ie</u>rto	nos divertimos
te div<u>ie</u>rtes	os divertís
se div<u>ie</u>rte	se div<u>ie</u>rten

div<u>e</u>rtirse (e → i)

me divertí	nos divertimos
te divertiste	os divertisteis
se div<u>i</u>rtió	se div<u>i</u>rtieron

Remember that stem-changing verbs in the present tense follow the basic guidelines below in the preterite. As you know, there are exceptions to almost every rule.

> ➤ **-ar** → regular

> ➤ **-er** → regular

> ➤ **-ir** → irregular, usually stem-changing in the 3rd person

The following irregular verbs require a change to maintain the pronunciation of certain consonants. This change is required in the 1st person, singular form (*yo*) in the preterite due to the *e* ending. These changes apply to all *-gar*, *-car*, and *-zar* verbs. For further review of this pronunciation issue, see pages 107-108.

ju**gar** – to play (games)	to**car** – to play (instruments)	empe**zar** – to begin
yo ju**gu<u>é</u>**	yo to**qu<u>é</u>**	yo empe**c<u>é</u>**
tú jugaste	tú tocaste	tú empezaste

pa**gar** – to pay (for)	sa**car** – to take out	almor**zar** – to eat
yo pa**gu<u>é</u>**	yo sa**qu<u>é</u>**	yo almor**c<u>é</u>**
tú pagaste	tú sacaste	tú almorzaste

col**gar** – to hang (up)	masti**car** – to chew	lan**zar** – to throw
yo col**gu<u>é</u>**	yo masti**qu<u>é</u>**	yo lan**c<u>é</u>**
tú colgaste	tú masticaste	tú lanzaste

Here is a review of the verbs *ser*, *ir* and *ver*. Remember that *ser* and *ir* have the same conjugations in the preterite tense but their meanings remain different. They can be distinguished only by context.

presente   **pretérito**

	ir – to go		**ir**	
voy	vamos	fui	fuimos
vas	vais	fuiste	fuisteis
va	van	fue	fueron

	ser – to be		**ser**	
soy	somos	fui	fuimos
eres	sois	fuiste	fuisteis
es	son	fue	fueron

	ver – to see		**ver**	
veo	vemos	vi	vimos
ves	veis	viste	visteis
ve	ven	vio	vieron

¡Ojo! The *vosotros* forms in the present, and the *yo,* and *él/ella/Ud.* forms in the preterite are monosyllabic (one syllable) and therefore are too short to require an accent mark.

There are many preterite verbs that have an irregular stem change as well as irregular endings. The good thing is that almost all of them have the same irregular endings. You've already seen some of them, but here are the most common verbs that share these irregular endings.

presente   **pretérito**

	hacer – to do / to make		**hacer (hic/z)**	
hago	hacemos	**hice**	**hicimos**
haces	hacéis	**hiciste**	**hicisteis**
hace	hacen	**hizo**	**hicieron**

	estar – to be		**estar (estuv)**	
estoy	estamos	**estuve**	**estuvimos**
estás	estáis	**estuviste**	**estuvisteis**
está	están	**estuvo**	**estuvieron**

	poder (o → ue) – to be able		**poder (pud)**	
puedo	podemos	**pude**	**pudimos**
puedes	podéis	**pudiste**	**pudisteis**
puede	pueden	**pudo**	**pudieron**

¡Ojo! These irregular verbs in the preterite tense do not have accent marks.

presente		pretérito	

poner – to put / to place / to set **poner (pus)**

pongo	ponemos	**pus**e	**pus**imos
pones	ponéis	**pus**iste	**pus**isteis
pone	ponen	**pus**o	**pus**ieron

querer (e → ie) – to want **querer (quis)**

quiero	queremos	**quis**e	**quis**imos
quieres	queréis	**quis**iste	**quis**isteis
quiere	quieren	**quis**o	**quis**ieron

saber – to know (information) **saber (sup)**

sé	sabemos	**sup**e	**sup**imos
sabes	sabéis	**sup**iste	**sup**isteis
sabe	saben	**sup**o	**sup**ieron

tener (e → ie) – to have **tener (tuv)**

tengo	tenemos	**tuv**e	**tuv**imos
tienes	tenéis	**tuv**iste	**tuv**isteis
tiene	tienen	**tuv**o	**tuv**ieron

venir (e → ie) – to come **venir (vin)**

vengo	venimos	**vin**e	**vin**imos
vienes	venís	**vin**iste	**vin**isteis
viene	vienen	**vin**o	**vin**ieron

Verbs whose irregular stems end in *j* have a modification in the 3rd person, plural form.

decir (e → i) – to say / to tell **decir (dij)**

digo	decimos	**dij**e	**dij**imos
dices	decís	**dij**iste	**dij**isteis
dice	dicen	**dij**o	**dij**eron (no *i*)

traer – to bring **traer (traj)**

traigo	traemos	**traj**e	**traj**imos
traes	traéis	**traj**iste	**traj**isteis
trae	traen	**traj**o	**traj**eron (no *i*)

These irregular preterite verbs above are also irregular in the present in some way or another. Below is a very useful and unique verb: *dar*. Notice the similarities between *dar* and *ir* in the present and *dar* and *ver* in the preterite.

dar – to give (like *ir*) **dar** (like *ver*)

doy	damos	di	dimos
das	dais	diste	disteis
da	dan	dio	dieron

El presente progresivo – Progressive Present

You have learned that the main use of the present tense is to describe habitual action, and words like *siempre, nunca, todos los días, de vez en cuando,* etc. describe the frequency of that action. This, however, is not the only use of the present tense. The present tense can also be used to describe ongoing action that is taking place in the moment (right now).

> *Ej.* ¿Adónde vas (ahora)? – Where are you going (now)?
> Voy a la escuela (ahora). – I am going to school (now).

This use of the present could, in certain circumstances, be confused with habitual action. Although non-verbal cues (a person opening a door about to leave the house) or the word *ahora* would clarify the above conversation, without those non-verbal cues or clarifying words, it could be interpreted as habitual action.

> *Ej.* ¿Adónde vas (cada mañana)? – Where do you go (every morning)?
> Voy a la escuela (cada mañana). – I go to school (every morning).

To clarify this possible confusion, a modification of the present tense could be used: the progressive present. You've seen it before (p.94). This construction has two components: the verb *estar*, conjugated in the present tense, and the gerund form (-ing) of the action verb.

> *Ej.* ¿Qué **están** hac<u>iendo</u>? – What **are you (all)** do<u>ing</u>?
> **Estamos** desayun<u>ando</u>. – **We are** eat<u>ing</u> breakfast.

Review the verb *estar* in the present tense and notice the construction of the gerund (-ing).

estar – to be		-ing
estoy	estamos	-ar → -ando
estás	estáis	-er → -iendo
está	están	-ir → -iendo

¡Ojo! The verb *estar* is conjugated in the present tense according to the subject of the action. The action verb in the gerund (-ing) is not conjugated; it is an adverb, which has no subject or gender.

> *Ej.* **Estoy** com<u>iendo</u>. – **I am** eat<u>ing</u>.
> **Estás** com<u>iendo</u>. – **You are** eat<u>ing</u>.

There are irregular forms, and the changes are the same as the changes in stem-changing verbs in the preterite (3rd person). This means that -*ir* verbs are mainly affected.

> *Ej.* d<u>o</u>rmir (o → ue) – present   **d<u>o</u>rmir (o → u) – preterite**
> Mi hermano d<u>u</u>rmió mucho anoche. – My brother slept a lot last night.
> Mi hermano está d<u>u</u>rmiendo ahora. – My brother is sleeping right now.

Some verbs have an irregular gerund to break up the vowel sounds, whereas others, just because.

> *Ej.* le<u>y</u>endo ~~leiendo~~ (leer), tra<u>y</u>endo ~~traiendo~~ (traer), <u>y</u>endo ~~iendo~~ (ir), p<u>u</u>diendo (poder) d<u>i</u>ciendo (decir), v<u>i</u>niendo (venir)

Unidad 17

Los verbos regulares (el imperfecto) – Regular Verbs (imperfect tense)

In this unit, we will focus on habitual action, which, as you know, cannot be represented by the preterite tense. So far, that has left the present tense as its sole representative. Now you will be introduced to the other past tense in Spanish – the imperfect tense. The imperfect tense is used to describe habitual action in the past (things that you used to do). There are other uses of the imperfect tense (p.154), but habitual action will be our focus here. As with the preterite, there are only two categories of verb endings: -ar and -er/-ir. Take a look at the following regular verbs in the imperfect tense.

<table>
<tr><td colspan="2" align="center">jug<u>ar</u> – to play</td><td colspan="2" align="center">corr<u>er</u> – to run</td></tr>
<tr><td>jug<u>aba</u></td><td>jug<u>ába</u>mos</td><td>corr<u>ía</u></td><td>corr<u>ía</u>mos</td></tr>
<tr><td>jug<u>aba</u>s</td><td>jug<u>aba</u>is</td><td>corr<u>ía</u>s</td><td>corr<u>ía</u>is</td></tr>
<tr><td>jug<u>aba</u></td><td>jug<u>aba</u>n</td><td>corr<u>ía</u></td><td>corr<u>ía</u>n</td></tr>
</table>

<table>
<tr><td colspan="2" align="center">escrib<u>ir</u> – to write</td></tr>
<tr><td>escrib<u>ía</u></td><td>escrib<u>ía</u>mos</td></tr>
<tr><td>escrib<u>ía</u>s</td><td>escrib<u>ía</u>is</td></tr>
<tr><td>escrib<u>ía</u></td><td>escrib<u>ía</u>n</td></tr>
</table>

¡Ojo! The *yo* and *él/ella/Ud.* forms are always the same as each other in the imperfect tense, so it's much more important that you use subject pronouns to maintain clarity.

> *Ej.* <u>Él</u> escribía muchas cartas de niño.
> <u>Yo</u> escribía muchas cartas de niño.

¡Ojo! Regular -ar verbs in the imperfect have an accent mark on the first *a* in the *nosotros* form. Regular -er and -ir verbs in the imperfect all have accent marks on the first *i*.

The following is a review of some key words/phrases that signal habitual or routine action (whether present or past) and describe its frequency:

(casi) siempre – (almost) always	de vez en cuando – from time to time
(casi) nunca – (almost) never	por lo general – in general
(casi) todos los días – (almost) every day	generalmente – generally
cada semana – each week	normalmente – normally
a menudo – often	típicamente – typically
muchas veces – many times	frecuentemente – frequently
a veces – sometimes	constantemente – constantly
raras veces – rarely	

Los verbos irregulares (el imperfecto) – Irregular Verbs (imperfect tense)

You have already been introduced to regular imperfect-tense verbs. As you know, there are two parts to every verb in Spanish: the stem and the ending. By definition, all regular verbs retain the stem of their infinitives and only their endings change.

hablar	comer	vivir
hablaba	comía	vivía
hablabas	comías	vivías
hablaba	comía	vivía
hablábamos	comíamos	vivíamos
hablabais	comíais	vivíais
hablaban	comían	vivían

As with all verb tenses in Spanish, there are regular verbs and there are irregular verbs. The present and preterite tenses have countless irregular verbs, but in the imperfect tense, you can literally count the number of irregular verbs on one hand – three (*ser, ir, ver*). Take a look at these irregular verbs in both the present and imperfect tenses.

presente   **imperfecto**

ser – to be   **ser**

soy	somos		era	éramos
eres	sois		eras	erais
es	son		era	eran

ir – to go   **ir**

voy	vamos		iba	íbamos
vas	vais		ibas	ibais
va	van		iba	iban

ver – to see / to watch   **ver**

veo	vemos		veía	veíamos
ves	veis		veías	veíais
ve	ven		veía	veían

¡Ojo! The **NOSOTROS** form in the **IMPERFECT ALWAYS** has an **ACCENT MARK** whether the verb is regular, irregular, *-ar*, *-er*, or *-ir*.

Unidad 18

Los acentos escritos – Written Accent Marks

We have discussed accent marks throughout this course and they may still seem confusing and arbitrary, but when it comes to conjugating verbs, there are a few simple rules to remember and all of your accent-mark woes will be a thing of the past.

- The **present** tense: the *vosotros* form **almost always** has an accent mark.

  ➢ If the verb is an *-ar* verb, the accent mark goes over the *a*.   habl<u>ar</u> → habláis
  If the verb is an *-er* verb, the accent mark goes over the *e*.   com<u>er</u> → coméis
  If the verb is an *-ir* verb, the accent mark goes over the *i*.   viv<u>ir</u> → viv<u>ís</u>

  The exceptions are conjugations that are monosyllabic (one syllable): *sois, vais, veis, dais,* etc.

- The **preterite** tense: the *yo* and the *él/ella/Ud.* forms **normally** have an accent mark on the last letter of the ending.

  ➢ habl<u>é</u>   com<u>í</u>   viv<u>í</u>
  habl<u>aste</u>   com<u>iste</u>   viv<u>iste</u>
  habl<u>ó</u>   com<u>ió</u>   viv<u>ió</u>

  The exceptions are conjugations that are monosyllabic: *fui, fue, vi, vio, di, dio,* etc. and conjugations with irregular endings: *tuve, puse, traje, estuvo, quiso, dijo, supo,* etc.

  ➢ Irregular verbs that have regular endings still have accent marks:
    jugué, toqué, comencé, etc.

- The **imperfect** tense: **all six conjugations forms** of *-er*, and *-ir* verbs **almost always** have an accent mark on the first *i* of the ending.

  ➢ com<u>í</u>a   com<u>í</u>amos   viv<u>í</u>a   viv<u>í</u>amos
  com<u>í</u>as   com<u>í</u>ais   viv<u>í</u>as viv<u>í</u>ais
  com<u>í</u>a   com<u>í</u>an   viv<u>í</u>a   viv<u>í</u>an

  The exceptions are the irregular verbs with irregular endings: *ser, ir.*

  The *nosotros* form **always** has an accent mark on the first letter of the ending.

  ➢ habl<u>á</u>bamos, com<u>í</u>amos, viv<u>í</u>amos, ve<u>í</u>amos, <u>é</u>ramos, <u>í</u>bamos

We have covered the concept of subject-verb agreement unit after unit since the beginning, and we have also covered the concept of indirect-object (pp.85, 98, 116-117), direct-object (pp.93, 96, 113-114, 117), and reflexive pronouns (pp.99-101, 110-112). Independently, they are fairly basic concepts and are easily understood, but the sentence structure of Spanish creates problems for students when object pronouns are used.

¡Ojo! **The most important thing to remember is that verbs can only be conjugated to subjects, never to objects. The subject does the action, the object receives the benefit or consequence of the action or is otherwise impacted by it.**

Los pronombres de complemento indirecto – Indirect-Object Pronouns

me – me	**nos** – us
te – you	**os** – you (Spain plural)
le – him / her / you (formal)	**les** – them / you (Latin America plural, formal)

The best way to understand the use of indirect objects is to think of them as answering the following questions: *"to whom?"* or *"for whom?"*

> *Ej.* Yo le di un regalo a mi hermano. – I gave a gift to my brother.
> Yo le di un regalo. – I gave a gift to him.

In English, pronouns always replace nouns. In Spanish, in contrast, although they may replace nouns, they also often accompany them. In the case of indirect-object pronouns, it is most common to use the pronoun whether you use the noun or not. A general guideline is that you can sometimes leave out the pronoun if the noun is 3rd person, but not for 1st or 2nd person nouns. If you always use the indirect-object pronouns, regardless of person, you can never go wrong.

There are two reasons to use the noun even when you use an indirect-object pronoun:

> ➤ to clarify the pronoun (*le, nos, os, les*)
> *Ej.* Mi mamá nos sirve la cena a mí y a mi hermano.
> Yo les di $100 a mis hijos para la Navidad.

> ➤ to add emphasis
> *Ej.* A ti te gusta, pero a mí no (me gusta). – *You* like it, but *I* don't (like it).

In the case of *me* and *te*, there is never a need to clarify, but there may be a need to add emphasis. In English, we simply change our intonation to show that emphasis.

¡Ojo! Indirect-object pronouns typically represent people or animals because they are capable of receiving the action or direct object, but sometimes they are used to represent inanimate objects.

> *Ej.* Le eché un poco de sal a la sopa.

Los pronombres de complemento directo – Direct-Object Pronouns

me – me	**nos** – us
te – you	**os** – you (Spain plural)
lo – him / it (masculine)	**los** – them (masculine / masculine and feminine)
la – her / it (feminine)	**las** – them (feminine)

In contrast to indirect objects almost always being animate (living), we have studied direct objects as inanimate (not living), but direct objects are as commonly animate as they are inanimate.

The best way to understand the use of direct objects is to think of them as answering the following questions: "*whom?*" or "*what?*"

> *Ej.* ¿Tienes tu <u>mochila</u> aquí?   Do you have your <u>backpack</u> here?
> Sí, yo <u>la</u> tengo conmigo.   Yes, I have <u>it</u> with me.
>
> ¿Abrazas a tu <u>abuela</u>?   Do you hug your <u>grandma</u>?
> Sí, yo <u>la</u> abrazo cada vez que <u>la</u> veo.   Yes, I hug <u>her</u> each time I see <u>her</u>.

In the examples above, it is easy to identify the backpack as a direct object because it answers the question "*what?*" but it is more difficult to identify the grandma as a direct object as opposed to an indirect object because it is a person. When trying to determine whether you need an indirect-object pronoun (*le, les*) or a direct-object pronoun (*lo / la, los / las*), ask yourself this:

> Do I hug *to* my grandma (*to* whom; indirect) or do I hug my grandma (whom; direct)?

This is not a perfect, fail-safe system, as not everything will translate perfectly to and from English, but it gives you a basic understanding of the difference between direct and indirect.

- **La "*a* personal" – The "personal *a*"**

This is a difficult concept to understand for students because it doesn't exist in most languages. Since the sentence structure of the Spanish language is so flexible, it would be much harder to distinguish the subject from the object in context without the "personal *a*." In English, the subject and object can be easily identified by their placement in the sentence.

> *Ej.* I love my dad. "I" (subject doing the loving) comes before the verb and "my dad" (object receiving the love) comes after the verb.

In Spanish, the subject or object can come first, leaving the reader/listener in need of other cues.

> *Ej.* Yo amo <u>a</u> mi papá. *Yo* (subject doing the loving) is not preceded by *a* whereas *mi papá* (object receiving the love) is preceded by *a*.

Although this *a* has no translation in English, it is required for direct objects that are people (optional with animals) but not before a direct-object pronoun (*me, te, lo / la, nos, os, los / las*).

126

When the subject and object (indirect or direct) of a sentence/phrase are the same person, the verb is considered *reflexive*. This means that the subject does an action to itself, for itself, etc.

Los pronombres reflexivos – Reflexive Pronouns

me – myself	**nos** – ourselves
te – yourself	**os** – yourselves (Spain plural)

se – himself / herself /
     yourself (formal)
	se – themselves /
	     yourselves (Latin America plural, formal)

A reflexive verb looks like any other verb, whether regular or irregular in any given verb tense, with the exception of the reflexive pronoun that accompanies it. It is this pronoun that makes the verb reflexive.

¡Ojo! The reflexive pronoun must match the subject in person (1st, 2nd, 3rd) and number (s., pl.).

Combinar dos complementos – Combining Two Objects

Mastering the sentence structure of Spanish is a difficult task, especially where object pronouns are concerned, so when you combine two objects in the same sentence, it becomes even more difficult. Take a look at the following examples of combined objects.

Ej. ¿Quién <u>te</u> regaló esa <u>computadora</u>?   Who gave <u>you</u> that <u>computer</u>?
       Mi mamá <u>me la</u> regaló.   My mom gave <u>it</u> <u>to me</u>.

     ¿<u>Te</u> lavas el <u>pelo</u> cuando te bañas?   Do you wash your <u>hair</u> when you bathe?
     Sí, <u>me lo</u> lavo cada vez que me baño.   Yes, I wash <u>it</u> each time I bathe.

Notice that in the first example, there is an <u>indirect</u>-object pronoun combined with a <u>direct</u>-object pronoun, whereas in the second example, there is a <u>reflexive</u> pronoun combined with a <u>direct</u>-object pronoun. When the indirect-object pronouns *le* or *les* are combined with the direct-object pronouns *lo / la* or *los / las*, the *le* or *les* must be changed to *se*. This is to avoid the alliteration (repetition of a consonant sound), not because it is reflexive.

Ej. ¿Quién <u>le</u> regaló esa <u>computadora</u>?   Who gave <u>her</u> that <u>computer</u>?
       Mi mamá ~~le la~~ <u>se la</u> regaló.   Mi mom gave <u>it</u> <u>to her</u>.

As you hopefully remember, object pronouns, whether direct, indirect, or reflexive, are placed separately before a conjugated verb (*me lo sirvió*) or attached to the end of an infinitive (*buscármelo*) or gerund form (*comprándomelo*) of the verb. If you are combining two object pronouns, the same rules apply but you must also place them in the proper order with respect to each other. If you are not sure which order to put them in, don't stress out; "ME LO" out. That is to say that the direct-object pronoun goes second whether the first one is reflexive or indirect. Or you may prefer the acronym R.I.D. (reflexive, indirect, direct) to *rid* yourself of the confusion.

Unidad 19

Los verbos que implican o indican el futuro – Verbs That Imply or Indicate the Future

There are many tenses in the Spanish language and you have been exposed to three distinct ones (present, preterite, and imperfect), not counting progressive forms, but you also learned early on (p.90) how to talk about the future without using the future tense. With the verb *ir* plus the preposition *a* followed by the infinitive of another verb, you can talk about things that *are going to happen.*

> *Ej.* <u>Voy a jugar</u> al béisbol el próximo sábado.
>
> Mis papás y yo <u>vamos a visitar</u> a mis abuelos este verano.

This is done with the present tense of the conjugated verb (*ir*). The assumption is that you are proceeding with the plans now, in the present, to do something in the future. Although you may have never thought of them in this way, you already know other verbs that serve the same function: *querer, preferir, tener que, necesitar, deber,* etc.

> *Ej.* Quiero (ahora) viajar (en el futuro) a México durante las vacaciones.
>
> Necesitamos (ahora) comprar (en el futuro) un boleto de ida y vuelta.

In the above examples, we see a need or a want that is current, even though the action to be carried out is in the future.

Los tiempos progresivos – Progressive Tenses

You've been working with the progressive present for a while now (pp.94, 121), but you can use the progressive form with any verb tense. You can say what someone *was* doing, *will be* doing, *has been* doing, *would be* doing, *would have been* doing, etc. All you need is the correct tense and conjugation of the verb *estar* and the very same gerund forms (*-ando, -iendo*) you already know. Don't forget about the irregular forms (p.121).

> *Ej.* **Estoy** jugando al fútbol ahora. (present – shows what's happening at *this* moment)
> **Estuve** jugando al fútbol por cuatro horas. (preterite – shows duration of time)
> **Estaba** jugando al fútbol cuando me llamaste. (imperfect – shows background info.,
> what was happening at *that* moment)
>
> **Estamos** leyendo su novela. (present – shows what's happening at *this* momento)
> **Estuvimos** leyendo su novela toda la noche. (preterite – shows duration of time)
> **Estábamos** leyendo cuando nos llamaste. (imperfect – shows background info.,
> what was happening at *that* moment)

¡Ojo! The gerund forms, like infinitives, allow you to attach object pronouns (*le, la, se*) to the end.

> *Ej.* ¿Por qué estás haciendo <u>tu maleta</u>?
> <u>La</u> estoy haciendo porque hoy me voy.   or   Estoy haciéndo<u>la</u> porque hoy me voy.

Los mandatos / las órdenes (el imperativo) – Commands / Orders (imperative mood)

We have all been told what to do as well as told others what to do, so we are familiar with the concept of commands. How to conjugate them in Spanish is a different story. Let's take the following example for starters: your mom tells you, "Clean your room." What verb tense is the verb "clean"? Could she have meant, "Clean your room *last week*"? Of course not; a command cannot be given in the present for a past action. So, is it possibly present or near future? "Clean your room *right now / before I get home*"? Absolutely. So is this the present tense in Spanish? It would seem that commands are the present tense, but what happens if you tell your mom, "no," or you simply don't do it for any number of possible reasons? Does any *cleaning* end up getting done? As you can see, commands cannot be the present tense because it merely shows what someone *wants* to happen but it cannot be confirmed that the event actually takes place at the time indicated in the command. So, we can conclude that commands are similar to the present tense, but they are not identical.

The most important thing to remember about commands is that since we cannot confirm that an action will take place, much less *when* it will take place, they are not considered to be a verb tense (tense meaning time). This means that several rules we have learned so far are not valid with commands. We will cover these differences as we go.

This unit, as the concept of commands is quite new, we will focus on familiar, 2nd person commands (*tú*). There are two forms to understand: affirmative (do it) and negative (don't do it). And, as always, we must consider the ending of the verb in question.

comprar

affirmative (+) tú: compra (buy)   negative (–) tú: <u>no</u> compres (don't buy)

prender

affirmative (+) tú: prende (turn on)   negative (–) tú: <u>no</u> prendas (don't turn on)

compartir

affirmative (+) tú: comparte (share)   negative (–) tú: <u>no</u> compartas (don't share)

The first thing to note is that the affirmative command looks like the *él / ella* form in the present (-ar → -a, -er → -e, -ir → -e). The second thing to note is that the negative command requires the opposite ending of the *tú* form in the present (-ar → -es, -er → -as, -ir → -as).

Los mandatos irregulares – Irregular Commands

Although commands are not a verb tense, there are still irregular conjugations. Commands cannot be in the past, and although they are not quite fully present because of the possibility that the desired action won't be carried out, irregularities in the present are what determine whether a command is regular or irregular.

All stem-changing verbs in the present maintain the same change in the command forms. Since *tú* has a change in the present, all stem-changing verbs will be irregular in the *tú* command form whether it is affirmative or negative.

mostrar (o → ue)

presente:	muestro		mandato	(+) tú:	muestra
	muestras			(–) tú:	no muestres
	muestra	muestran			

volver (o → ue)

presente:	vuelvo		mandato	(+) tú:	vuelve
	vuelves			(–) tú:	no vuelvas
	vuelve	vuelven			

conseguir (e → i)

presente:	consigo		mandato	(+) tú:	consigue
	consigues			(–) tú:	no consigas
	consigue	consiguen			

As you know, stem-changing verbs are not the only irregular verbs in the present; sometimes the *yo* form has a unique ending. In these cases, the root of the command form looks like the root of either the infinitive (*tú*, affirmative commands) or the *yo* form (*tú*, negative commands).

salir	→	salgo	affirmative (+) tú: sal	negative (–) tú: no salgas
tener	→	tengo	affirmative (+) tú: ten	negative (–) tú: no tengas
poner	→	pongo	affirmative (+) tú: pon	negative (–) tú: no pongas
traer	→	traigo	affirmative (+) tú: trae	negative (–) tú: no traigas
hacer	→	hago	affirmative (+) tú: haz	negative (–) tú: no hagas
ver	→	veo	affirmative (+) tú: ve	negative (–) tú: no veas
ir	→	voy	affirmative (+) tú: ve	negative (–) tú: no vayas

Los mandatos reflexivos – Reflexive Commands

Another thing that is different about commands is that the placement of object pronouns is determined by whether the command is affirmative or negative. Notice that the pronoun in the affirmative command is attached to the end, forming one word. This may create the need for an accent mark that is not needed in the negative form. We will discuss this accent more next unit.

abrocharse	affirmative (+) tú: abróchate	negative (–) tú: no te abroches
sentarse (e → ie)	affirmative (+) tú: siéntate	negative (–) tú: no te sientes

Unidad 20

Los mandatos / las órdenes (el imperativo) – Commands / Orders (imperative mood)

You are now familiar with the concept of commands and the differences between their conjugation rules and the conjugation rules for verb tenses. But so far, you have only seen the *tú* forms. In reality, there are commands for 1st and 2nd person forms except for the *yo* form. If you found yourself giving yourself a command, you would probably use the *tú* form, unless of course you were worried about offending yourself; then you would obviously use the more formal *Ud.* form. And if you are talking to yourself, anything is possible. For *nosotros* and *vosotros* command forms, see pages 183-184.

¡Ojo! You must be talking *to* someone to give him or her a command, therefore there are no commands for 3rd person (*él / ella, ellos / ellas*), which are used to talk *about* someone.

In this unit, we will expand on what you already know by incorporating the *Ud.* and *Uds.* forms. Just as with any verb conjugation, the *tú* form is used in familiar settings (friends, family, children, etc.), whereas *Ud.* is used in formal settings (adults that you don't know very well). *Uds.*, on the other hand, can be used as the plural form of *tú* or *Ud.* in Latin America.

As with the *tú* forms, irregulars in the present are irregulars in the command form. Take a look at the following verbs and notice the patterns.

apoyar

(+) **tú:**   apoya
(–) **tú:** no apoyes

(+) **Ud.:**   apoye   (+) **Uds.:**   apoyen
(–) **Ud.:** no apoye   (–) **Uds.:** no apoyen

resolver (o → ue)

(+) **tú:**   resuelve
(–) **tú:** no resuelvas

(+) **Ud.:**   resuelva   (+) **Uds.:**   resuelvan
(–) **Ud.:** no resuelva   (–) **Uds.:** no resuelvan

influir (y)

(+) **tú:**   influye
(–) **tú:** no influyas

(+) **Ud.:**   influya   (+) **Uds.:**   influyan
(–) **Ud.:** no influya   (–) **Uds.:** no influyan

Notice that the *tú*, affirmative command is the *only* form here that maintains the present-tense endings; all others require the opposite ending of their respective present-tense conjugations.

Remember our list of irregulars where the *yo* form in the present had a unique conjugation (p.130)? Their patterns are similar to other commands when it comes to the *Ud.* and *Uds.* forms.

salir → salgo	(+) tú: sal	(–) tú: no salgas	(+/–) Ud.: salga	(+/–) Uds.: salgan
tener → tengo	(+) tú: ten	(–) tú: no tengas	(+/–) Ud.: tenga	(+/–) Uds.: tengan
poner → pongo	(+) tú: pon	(–) tú: no pongas	(+/–) Ud.: ponga	(+/–) Uds.: pongan
traer → traigo	(+) tú: trae	(–) tú: no traigas	(+/–) Ud.: traiga	(+/–) Uds.: traigan
hacer → hago	(+) tú: haz	(–) tú: no hagas	(+/–) Ud.: haga	(+/–) Uds.: hagan
ver → veo	(+) tú: ve	(–) tú: no veas	(+/–) Ud.: vea	(+/–) Uds.: vean
ir → voy	(+) tú: ve	(–) tú: no vayas	(+/–) Ud.: vaya	(+/–) Uds.: vayan
venir → vengo	(+) tú: ven	(–) tú: no vengas	(+/–) Ud.: venga	(+/–) Uds.: vengan
decir → digo	(+) tú: di	(–) tú: no digas	(+/–) Ud.: diga	(+/–) Uds.: digan
ser → soy	(+) tú: sé	(–) tú: no seas	(+/–) Ud.: sea	(+/–) Uds.: sean
dar → doy	(+) tú: da	(–) tú: no des	(+/–) Ud.: dé	(+/–) Uds.: den

Remember *abrocharse* and *sentarse* from last unit? They were the two examples of reflexive verbs in command form I gave you. This unit, we will study many reflexive verbs and we will add in the *Ud.* and *Uds.* forms. Notice the difference in reflexive pronouns as well as their placement.

quejarse

(+) tú: quéjate
(–) tú: no te quejes

(+) Ud.: quéjese   **(+) Uds.:** quéjense
(–) Ud.: no se queje   **(–) Uds.:** no se quejen

reírse (e → í)

(+) tú: ríete
(–) tú: no te rías

(+) Ud.: ríase   **(+) Uds.:** ríanse
(–) Ud.: no se ría   **(–) Uds.:** no se rían

All object pronouns (*me, te, se, le, lo / la, nos, os, se, les, los / las*) follow the same rules within a given conjugation form whether that is a verb tense or a command.

explicar

(+) tú: explícame
(–) tú: no me expliques

(+) Ud.: explíquelo   **(+) Uds.:** explíquenmelo
(–) Ud.: no lo explique   **(–) Uds.:** no me lo expliquen

Los acentos escritos – Written Accent Marks

You should now be aware of the importance of written accent marks, especially with verb conjugations (p.124), but you still do not know how to use them in every circumstance to maintain proper pronunciation. To better understand them, take a look at these basic rules:

➤ If the word ends in a vowel (*a, e, i, o, u*), *n* or *s*, the normal, unaccented stress falls on the second-to-last (penultimate) syllable.

ha·bl<u>o</u>	ha·bla·mo<u>s</u>	co·m<u>o</u>	co·me·mo<u>s</u>
ha·bla<u>s</u>		co·me<u>s</u>	
ha·bl<u>a</u>	ha·bla<u>n</u>	co·m<u>e</u>	co·me<u>n</u>

➤ If the word ends in a consonant other than *n* or *s*, the normal, unaccented stress falls on the last syllable.

ha·bla<u>r</u>   co·me<u>r</u>   vi·vi<u>r</u>

➤ If the word does not follow the above rules, a written accent must be used to show where the proper stress falls.

ha·bl<u>á</u>i<u>s</u>   co·m<u>é</u>i<u>s</u>   ha·bl<u>ó</u>   co·m<u>í</u>   ha·bl<u>á</u>·ba·mo<u>s</u>

You've learned *where* accent marks are required in the present, preterite and imperfect tenses (p.124), and now you know *why*.

Only by understanding *why* we need written accent marks can we possibly know *where* to put them since it is impossible to memorize every single word in the Spanish language. Last unit, I pointed out that affirmative reflexive commands have written accent marks, but negative reflexive commands do not. Applying the rules above, we should now be able to understand why.

a·bro·ch<u>a</u>   a·br<u>ó</u>·cha·t<u>e</u>   no te a·bro·che<u>s</u>

The stressed syllable in the above examples is *bro*. The first and third examples follow the first rule (second-to-last syllable stressed), whereas the second example followed the third rule (breaking the first rule). By attaching the pronoun *te* to the end of the word *abrocha*, we added a syllable. This would have changed the second-to-last syllable from *bro* to *cha*. In order to avoid this change and maintain the original stress, a written accent is required.

This accent mark is also required with infinitives and gerund forms when we attach a pronoun to the end. Take a look at the following examples and see if you can identify why some have accent marks and others do not.

comprar	lavar	regalando
comprarlo	lavarse	regalándolo
comprármelo	lavárselas	regalándonoslo

<u>**Los comparativos – Comparatives**</u>

Comparatives, you may remember (pp.92, 115), make comparisons between two nouns. You know they can be used with adjectives and adverbs, but they can also be used with verbs. In the case of verbs, the issue of which subject the verb is conjugated to arises, but easy enough, the solution is the same as it is for adjectives: you simply conjugate according to the first noun.

> *Ej.* <u>Pablito grita</u> *más.*   <u>Mis hermanos gritan</u> *más.*
> <u>Pablito grita</u> *más que* mis hermanos.   <u>Mis hermanos gritan</u> *más que* Pablito.
>
> <u>Pablito grita</u> *tanto como* mis hermanos. (<u>Pablito shouts</u> *as much as* my brothers do.)

Although, in English, we often confuse object pronouns (me, him, us, them, etc.) with subject pronouns (I, he, we, they, etc.), they are never confused by native speakers in Spanish. If you are comparing subjects in Spanish, use subject pronouns across the board. If you are comparing objects (direct or indirect), use object pronouns across the board.

> *Ej.* <u>Verenice</u> da *mejores* consejos *que* <u>yo</u>. (… *mejores* consejos *que* ~~mí~~.)
> <u>Yo</u> doy *mejores* consejos *que* <u>Verenice</u>.
>
> Magda te respeta <u>a ti</u> *más que* <u>a mí</u>.
> Yo te respeto <u>a ti</u> *más que* <u>a Magda</u>. (Notice the "personal *a*.")

What happens when we confuse our pronouns?

> *Ej.* Magda te respeta a ti *más que* <u>a mí</u>. (Magda respects you *more than* she respects <u>me</u>.)
> Magda te respeta a ti *más que* <u>yo</u>. (Magda respects you *more than* <u>I</u> respect you.)
>
> A ti te gusta correr *más que* a <u>mí</u>. (You like running *more than* <u>I</u> like running.)
>   (Literally: running pleases you *more than* it pleases <u>me</u>.)
> A ti te gusta correr *más que* <u>yo</u>. (You like running *more than* you like <u>me</u>.)
>   (Literally: running pleases you *more than* <u>I</u> please you.)

With this in mind, let's see a different type of comparative: "My teacher treats me *like* a child."

> *Ej.* Mi maestra me trata *como* <u>un niño</u>. (My teacher treats me *like* a child would.)
> Mi maestra me trata *como* <u>a un niño</u>. (My teacher treats me *like* she would a child.)

The only difference is the "personal *a*," which tells us *un niño* is an object, not a subject.

- **Common comparative pitfall**

Do you remember the common comparative pitfall of *de* vs. *que* (p.115)? Consider the following phrase: "You are taller than I thought." Is this a comparative? Is this a comparison between how tall "you" are and how tall "I thought" is? Of course not; that doesn't even make sense.

> *Ej.* "*Eres más alto* **que** *yo pensé.*" ??? Nope!
> "*Eres más alto* **de lo que** *yo pensé.*" ??? Now you're speakin' my language!

134

Los superlativos – Superlatives

Superlatives are similar to comparatives in structure, but what makes nouns "super" is that there *is* no comparison, or in other words, everything else pales in comparison. Since there is no comparison, there is no question as to which noun the adjectives modify.

> *Ej.* Maribel es <u>*la más*</u> talentos<u>a</u>. (Maribel is *the most* talented.)
> Alejandro es <u>*el más*</u> talentos<u>o</u>. (Alejandro is *the most* talented.)

Without making a direct comparison with anyone in particular, you can give context if you wish.

> *Ej.* Brenda es <u>*la menos*</u> vanidos<u>a</u> (de toda la clase).
> Joel es <u>*el menos*</u> egoísta (de todos los estudiantes).

When asking a question about a group of females, the adjectives are feminine. When asking about a group of males or a mixed group of males and females, the adjectives are masculine. The gender (and number) of the answer is independent of the gender (and number) in the question.

> *Ej.* ¿Quién es <u>*el más*</u> comprensiv<u>o</u> de todos los pasajeros?
> Irene es <u>*la más*</u> comprensiv<u>a</u> de todos los pasajeros.

The plural forms look as you probably expect.

> *Ej.* ¿Quiénes son <u>*los más*</u> considerad<u>os</u>?
> Las señoras son <u>*las más*</u> considerad<u>as</u>.

- *el (más), la (más), lo (más)* **and the nominalization (noun-ing) of adjectives**

You've learned that you can turn an adjective into a noun by using the noun's article and the adjective in question (p.115). This is what is happening in the examples above. When referring to a masculine noun, use *el/los*. When referring to a feminine noun, use *la/las*. This is like saying "the one(s)." But if what you are referring to is unspecified or abstract, use what some people call the neuter form, *lo*, and the masculine form of the adjective. This is like saying "the thing."

> *Ej.* <u>*lo*</u> *que* me gusta (más) es – *what* I like (most) is / *the thing* that I like (most) is
> <u>*lo*</u> (más) *chistos<u>o</u>* es su pelo – *the funny*(est) *thing* is her hair
> <u>*lo*</u> *peor* es que – *the worst thing* is that

- **Common superlative pitfall**

Although *más* means "more" and "most," for expressions like "<u>The more</u> Spanish I learn, <u>the more</u> confidence I have," do not use *lo más*. Instead, use *cuanto/a(s) más*, *mientras más*, or *entre más* for the first part, and *más* or *mejor* for the second part. *Menos* and *peor* can work in some cases.

> *Ej. Cuant<u>o</u> más* español aprendo, *más* confianza tengo. (*cuanto* modifies *español*)
> *Cuantas más* clases de español tomo, *mejor* lo hablo. (*cuantas* modifies *clases*)
> *Mientras más* español aprendo, *más* confianza tengo.
> *Entre más* clases de español tomo, *mejor* lo hablo.

Unidad 21

El participio pasado – Past Participle

The past participle is not a difficult concept to understand, but due to differences in Spanish and English, many students struggle with it. In English, you might know of it as the "ed" form of a verb. The problem with that understanding is that the regulars in the past tense (preterite) and the regulars in the past participle both end in "ed."

> *Ej.* The door is <u>closed</u>. (past participle)
> I <u>closed</u> the door. (past tense)

In the first example, the word *closed* is a description of the state of the door. In the second example, we have a description of an action but know nothing of the state of the door because we don't know whether or not someone opened it afterward. When either the past tense or the past participle is irregular, we can clearly see the difference.

> *Ej.* My essay is <u>written</u>. (past participle)
> I <u>wrote</u> my essay. (past tense)

In the first example, we learn of the state of the essay. In the second, we know how it got that way. What we don't know in the second example is whether it is still that way. In both cases, we have irregular forms and these would rarely be confused by a native speaker of English.

El participio pasado como adjetivo – Past Participle as an Adjective.

In the examples above, the past participle was used as an adjective; it served as a description of a noun. In Spanish, it serves the same function. The difference between Spanish and English, however, is that adjectives in Spanish have gender (masculine and feminine) and number (singular and plural). In English, these concepts do not exist for adjectives.

> *Ej.* Mi <u>papá</u> está enojad<u>o</u>.
> Mi <u>mamá</u> está aburrid<u>a</u>.
> Mis <u>papás</u> están divorciad<u>os</u>.

You have probably already used the above examples in context without knowing that these adjectives were past participles. The most important thing to understand is that the root of a past participle is a verb, but the past participle itself is not a verb; sometimes it is an adjective (modifying a noun), sometimes it is an adverb (modifying a verb).

> verb: cansar(se)   →   adjective: cansado/a
>   divertir(se)   →   divertido/a

¡Ojo! Verbs can be reflexive, but adjectives cannot.

Since past participles come from verbs, in order to understand how to form them, we must know whether the verb is an *-ar*, *-er*, or *-ir* verb. Notice that *-er* and *-ir* verbs have the same endings.

-ar	**-er**	**-ir**
-ado, -ados, -ada, -adas	-ido, -idos, -ida, -idas	-ido, -idos, -ida, -idas

Adjectives are used most frequently with the verbs *estar*, *ser*, and *parecer*, and past participles are no exception.

> *Ej.* El aire <u>está</u> contaminado.
> La vida urbana <u>es</u> muy animada.
> El campo <u>parece</u> muy aburrido.

In English as well as in Spanish, there are irregular forms of the past participle, but being irregular in one language does not make it irregular in another language. In contrast to the regular endings, these ones (among others) in Spanish end in *to*, *ta*, *tos*, or *tas*.

abrir	→ abierto	to open	→	open (not opened)
escribir	→ escrito	to write	→	written (not writed)
inscribir(se)	→ inscrito	to sign up	→	signed up (regular)
describir	→ descrito	to describe	→	described (regular)
poner(se)	→ puesto	to put (on)	→	on (not puted)
ver	→ visto	to see	→	seen (not seed)
resolver	→ resuelto	to resolve	→	resolved (regular)
volver	→ vuelto	to return	→	back (not returned)
morir(se)	→ muerto	to die	→	dead (not died)
freír	→ frito (also freído)	to fry	→	fried (not fryed)
romper	→ roto	to break	→	broken (not breaked)
		to tear	→	torn (not teared)

There are also a few that have a different irregular ending: *-cho*, *-cha*, *-chos*, or *-chas*

decir	→ dicho	to say	→	said (not sayed)
		to tell	→	told (not telled)
hacer	→ hecho	to do	→	done (not doed)
		to make	→	made (not maked)

You have seen a few of these irregulars without knowing that they were past participles of verbs.

> *Ej.* Mi bisabuela está <u>muerta</u>. (morir)
> Me gustan las papas <u>fritas</u>. (freír)
> La artesanía es <u>hecha</u> a mano. (hacer)

Los verbos (el presente perfecto) – Verbs (present-perfect tense)

You have already studied in depth the present, preterite, and imperfect tenses as well as commands (not a tense). Now you will see your fourth verb tense: the present perfect. The present-perfect tense, both in English and Spanish, is often interchangeable with the preterite tense; both describe past actions. The difference between the two is that the present perfect connects those past actions to the present, whereas the preterite does not. Consider the following examples in English.

> *Ej.* They <u>lived</u> in the city for 10 years. (They probably don't live there anymore.)
> They <u>have lived</u> in the city for 10 years. (They probably still live there.)

Take a look at some more examples of the present perfect in English.

> *Ej.* I <u>have walked</u> to school before.
> They <u>have written</u> six essays for that class.
> She <u>has done</u> her homework every day this year.

The present-perfect tense is called a *compound* tense because it has two components: a helping verb (to have) and the past participle of the verb you are conjugating. Above, you have a regular past participle (-ed), a common irregular (-en) and one that is completely irregular (done). In English, the helping verb is *to have*, but that is not the verb *tener* in Spanish. *Tener* is used to show possession, but in the case of the present perfect, we use the verb *haber* conjugated in the present tense followed by a past participle. The past participle here is an adverb (no gender or number).

haber – to have (not possession)		-ed
he	hemos	-ar → -ado (~~ados, ada, adas~~)
has	habéis	-er → -ido (~~idos, ida, idas~~)
ha	han	-ir → -ido (~~idos, ida, idas~~)

There are a few verbs, both in English and Spanish, where the form of the past participle changes depending on whether it is an adjective or part of the present-perfect tense. Take a look at a couple of examples in English.

> *Ej.* My grandfather is <u>dead</u>. (to die)   My grandfather has <u>died</u>. (to die)
> My brother is <u>asleep</u>. (to sleep)   My brother has <u>slept</u>. (to sleep)

Both of these examples would use the same word in Spanish:

> *Ej.* Mi abuelo está <u>muerto</u>. (morir)   Mi abuelo ha <u>muerto</u>. (morir)
> Mi hermano está <u>dormido</u>. (dormir)   Mi hermano ha <u>dormido</u>. (dormir)

Since this is an introduction to the concepts of past participles, let's focus on the verbs whose past participles are the same in adjective form as well as in the present-perfect tense, but know there are plenty of examples where they're different.

> *Ej.* está despierto, ha despertado (despertar)   está lleno, han llenado (llenar)
> está contento, han contentado (contentar)   está limpio, hemos limpiado (limpiar)

There is no apparent rhyme or reason to irregulars, so asking why verbs are irregular is pointless. In order to properly use *regular* past participles or any *regular* verb in a given verb tense, we must simply learn a set of rules and apply them to every regular verb. Irregulars are a little more difficult. The first thing we must understand is that irregulars are not optionally irregular; we must accept that they just are. Although we are able to categorize most of them, we must understand the nature of each category and all of its changes. Sometimes, we must learn the irregulars individually because they are unique and do not fit into any category. Take a look at some examples in Spanish.

- **Regulares:**

    Ej. Yo <u>he vivido</u> en Colorado por 6 años.   I have lived in Colorado for 6 years.
          ¿<u>Ha caminado</u> alguna vez a la escuela?   Has she ever walked to school?
          El tráfico <u>ha contribuido</u> al ruido.   Traffic has contributed to the noise.
          <u>Hemos intentado</u> sacar buenas notas.   We have tried to get good grades.
          ¿Cómo <u>has estado</u>?   How have you been?
          Ella <u>ha sido</u> muy responsable este año.   She has been very responsible this year.

- **Irregulares:**

    Ej. <u>He hecho</u> mi tarea.   I have done my homework.
          <u>Hemos escrito</u> muchos ensayos.   We have written a lot of essays.
          No <u>ha dicho</u> la verdad en su vida.   She hasn't told the truth in her life.
          Mis papás <u>han resuelto</u> su bronca.   My parents have resolved their problem.

- **Reflexivos:**

    Ej. <u>Se han inscrito</u> en sus clases.   They have signed up for their classes.
          <u>Me he roto</u> la pierna.   I have broken my leg.
          Mi abuelo ya <u>se ha muerto</u>.   My grandpa has already died.
          <u>Nos hemos puesto</u> los zapatos.   We have put on our shoes.
          <u>Se ha abrochado</u> su propio cinturón.   He has buckled his own seatbelt

Notice the placement of the reflexive pronouns (*me, te, se, nos, os, se*) in the above examples. You know from previous verb tenses (not commands) that object pronouns, whether reflexive, direct, or indirect, are placed immediately before a conjugated verb. In the case of the present-perfect tense, that conjugated verb is the verb *haber*. Take a look at some more complicated examples and notice the placement of the object pronouns. Notice that in the last two examples, the infinitive is used because the verb follows a preposition, and therefore the pronouns are attached to the end.

    Ej. Me los he puesto.   I have put them on.
          Te lo ha dicho mil veces.   He has told you a thousand times.
          …después de haberlo hecho.   …after having done it.
          …por habérmelas explicado.   …for having explained them to me.

¡Ojo! In all perfect tenses (*haber* + past participle), the past participle is an adverb and, therefore, does not have gender or number. This means that it always ends in *o*.

Unidad 22

Los verbos (el pluscuamperfecto) – Verbs (pluperfect tense)

The present-perfect tense (pp.138-139) is used to describe past actions or events that are still relevant to the present. The pluperfect tense is used to describe past actions or events that are prior to—and relevant to—another action or event in the past.

> *Ej.* I didn't go to the restaurant with them because I <u>had</u> (already) <u>eaten</u>.
> They <u>had washed</u> their hands before eating.

Take a look at some more examples of the pluperfect in English.

> *Ej.* I didn't buy the DVD when it came out because I <u>had</u> (already) <u>seen</u> the movie twice.
> She <u>had turned</u> in her report before her colleagues even started theirs.

The pluperfect, like the present perfect, is a compound tense because it has two components: a helping verb (to have) and the past participle of the verb you are conjugating. Whereas the present perfect uses the verb *haber* in the present tense, the pluperfect uses the verb *haber* in the imperfect tense. Remember, the past participle here is an adverb (no gender or number).

haber – to have (not possession)		-ed
había	habíamos	-ar → -ado
habías	habíais	-er → -ido
había	habían	-ir → -ido

Compare the examples above with their Spanish translations below:

> *Ej.* No fui al restaurante con ellos porque yo (ya) <u>había comido</u>.
> Ellos <u>se habían lavado</u> las manos antes de comer.
>
> Yo no compré el DVD cuando salió porque yo (ya) <u>había visto</u> la película dos veces.
> Ella <u>había entregado</u> su reportaje antes de que sus colegas aun empezaran los suyos.

See pages 136-139 for rules and examples concerning regular and irregular past participles as well as pronoun placement for perfect tenses. Below is a quick-reference summary. Notice the patterns of irregular past participles with the same verb roots.

- **Regulares: -ado** (jugado), **-ido** (bebido, vivido)

- **Irregulares: -to** (abierto, cubierto, escrito, inscrito, descrito, puesto, compuesto, impuesto, supuesto, visto, previsto, resuelto, vuelto, devuelto, envuelto, muerto, frito, roto), **-cho** (dicho, hecho, deshecho, satisfecho), **-so** (impreso, also imprimido)

¡Ojo! In perfect tenses, in Spanish, nothing can come between *haber* and the past participle, unlike in English: "I <u>had</u> already <u>seen</u> …" – *Yo <u>había</u> ~~ya~~ <u>visto</u> … → Yo ya <u>había</u> <u>visto</u> …*

Unidad 23

Los verbos (el futuro) – Verbs (future tense)

You've already learned how to talk about the future (pp.90, 128). *Ir* (in the present tense) + *a* + infinitive is a common way to talk about the future.

> *Ej.* <u>Voy a jugar</u> al golf mañana. – <u>I am going to play</u> golf tomorrow.
> ¿A qué hora <u>vas a cenar</u>? – What time <u>are you going to eat</u> dinner?

This is the compound form (multiple verbs). There is also a simple form (one verb) that is equally common. Unlike the other verb tenses you've studied so far, the endings in the future tense are the same whether the verb is *-ar*, *-er* or *-ir*. Also unlike the other verb tenses you've studied so far, regular verbs in the future tense are conjugated by adding the ending to the infinitive. Take a look at the following regular verbs in the future tense.

comprar – to buy		volver – to return	
compraré	compraremos	volveré	volveremos
comprarás	compraréis	volverás	volveréis
comprará	comprarán	volverá	volverán

> *Ej.* Mi tía <u>comprará</u> pronto un carro nuevo. – My aunt <u>will buy</u> a new car soon.
> No <u>volveremos</u> hasta medianoche. – We <u>won't return</u> until the middle of the night.

You can see in the examples above that the future tense is used to say what someone will or won't do. As with all verb tenses, there are irregular verbs and many of the irregulars in the future are the usual suspects from most other verb tenses. Although their endings are the same as the regulars, irregulars do not use the infinitive as a base. Below are the most common irregulars.

hacer (har) – to do / to make		poner (pondr) – to put / to set	
haré	haremos	pondré	pondremos
harás	haréis	pondrás	pondréis
hará	harán	pondrá	pondrán

poder (podr) – to be able		venir (vendr) – to come	
podré	podremos	vendré	vendremos
podrás	podréis	vendrás	vendréis
podrá	podrán	vendrá	vendrán

querer (querr) – to want		tener (tendr) – to have	
querré	querremos	tendré	tendremos
querrás	querréis	tendrás	tendréis
querrá	querrán	tendrá	tendrán

saber (sabr) – to know (info.)		decir (dir) – to say / to tell	
sabré	sabremos	diré	diremos
sabrás	sabréis	dirás	diréis
sabrá	sabrán	dirá	dirán

valer (valdr) – to be worth		salir (saldr) – to go out	
valdré	valdremos	saldré	saldremos
valdrás	valdréis	saldrás	saldréis
valdrá	valdrán	saldrá	saldrán

Los verbos (el futuro perfecto) – Verbs (future-perfect tense)

Now that you've seen two perfect tenses (present perfect and pluperfect), it should be easy to add the future perfect to your repertoire. This tense is used to talk about future events or actions that will have happened prior to—and relevant to—another future event or action. Try not to get bogged down by the timeline of these perfect tenses; your brain already knows what to do with them.

> *Ej.* After my shift on Saturday night, I <u>will have worked</u> 60 hours this week.
>
> If you take too long, you <u>will have missed</u> your chance.

As with all other perfect tenses, all you need for the future perfect is our ever-so-helpful "helping" verb, *haber*, conjugated in the future tense, and our now-familiar past participle. Notice that its conjugations are irregular like *saber*.

haber – to have (not possession)		-ed
habré	habremos	-ar → -ado
habrás	habréis	-er → -ido
habrá	habrán	-ir → -ido

Compare the examples above with their Spanish translations below:

> *Ej.* Después de mi turno el sábado por la noche, <u>habré trabajado</u> 60 horas esta semana.
>
> Si tardas demasiado, <u>habrás perdido</u> tu oportunidad.

Use this space to take a deep breath before the plunge ahead.

Or use it to draw a picture of your head exploding from imminent information overload.

Los verbos (el subjuntivo) – Verbs (subjunctive mood)

Do you remember commands (pp.129-132)? Of course you do! You may also remember them as the imperative mood. There are many verb tenses in Spanish, but there are also moods – three to be exact: the indicative, the imperative, and the subjunctive.

The **indicative mood** encompasses the majority of your understanding of verbs so far. It "indicates" when an action or event takes place: past, present, future, past of the past, past of the future, future of the past, etc. There are **nine verb tenses** in the indicative mood.

The **imperative mood**, or commands, is used to tell someone what to do. You may remember that since the one being ordered to carry out the action can refuse, forget, etc., the *when* of the action cannot be confirmed at the time of the command. This means that the imperative mood does not have verb tenses.

That leaves us with the **subjunctive mood**, which has cross-over with the above two moods. It is used to express doubt and uncertainty about whether or not an event or action will happen, fear and other emotions about an event or situation, hypothetical situations, as well as to indicate what one subject wants another subject to do. There are **four verb tenses** in the subjunctive mood, giving us **thirteen total verb tenses** to navigate in order to be fluent in Spanish.

The indicative and imperative moods are commonly used in English, but the subjunctive mood is all but dead, leaving us with very little to relate to when learning it in Spanish. While you can get by without using it yourself, I can assure you it is alive and well in Spanish and the better you understand it, the better you'll be able to communicate with native speakers. There is a huge learning curve with the subjunctive for native speakers of English, so be patient with yourself and get ready to shed a few tears.

The subjunctive mood is predominately used after the word *que*, indicating the introduction of a subordinate clause, so let's start there. In most cases, this *que* does not translate well into English, and in the cases in which it does translate, it is often omitted in English but cannot be omitted in Spanish. Enough lead-up; let's get to it.

How would you translate the following phrase: *Te quiero leer*?

Did you say, "I want you to read" (*Te quiero* – I want you, *leer* – to read)?

What about: *Quiero leerte*?

Did you say, "I want to read to you" (*Quiero* – I want, *leerte* – to read to you)?

Given what you've learned about the placement of object pronouns relative to verbs, whether conjugated or not (pp.85, 93, 96, 98-101, 110-117, 125-127), you have the prior knowledge to recognize that *te quiero leer* and *quiero leerte* are both grammatically correct ways to say the same thing. So, now you have to ask yourself which is the correct translation. Well, what else do you know that you can reference? What does *quiero leer* mean? "I want to read," right? So, no matter where we place the *te*, our phrase means, "I want to read to you."

The subjunctive mood is how "I want you to read" can be translated into Spanish. I cannot emphasize this enough: translating the subjunctive literally will not help you understand it. This is a great point in your studies to start thinking in Spanish, letting go of any dependence on thinking in English you may still have.

The imperative mood is used to tell someone what to do (*Lee.* – "Read."), but that can come off as a little harsh. An alternative is to express to someone what you want them to do without telling them directly to do it. Let's break down our sentence: "I want you to read."

"I want" is the indicative mood, present tense. That's easy – *Quiero*.

Next, *que* (literally "that," but I'm telling you it's going to sound stupid)

Then, finally, the subjunctive mood of the present tense (in this case) of the verb "to read," conjugated for the person we want to do it: *tú*. Similar to the imperative mood (commands), the person who wants the action to take place has no control over the outcome (grammatically speaking, that is), so the verb endings are the opposite of the indicative pattern, just like the imperative pattern (p.129).

Indicative pattern in the **present** tense: **-ar** (habl<u>ar</u>) → **-a** (habl<u>a</u>)

-er (le<u>er</u>) → -e (le<u>e</u>)

-ir (viv<u>ir</u>) → -e (viv<u>e</u>)

Subjunctive pattern in the **present** tense: -ar → -e (habl<u>e</u>)

-er → -a (le<u>a</u>)

-ir → -a (viv<u>a</u>)

Drum roll, please … (*Yo*) *quiero que* (*tú*) *le<u>as</u>*. (Don't make me translate it literally!)

Regardless of its translation, learn to think *que* when using the subjunctive and you'll be less likely to use it in the wrong context. Below are **regular** verbs, in the **present** of the **subjunctive** mood.

	habl<u>ar</u>		**com<u>er</u>**		**viv<u>ir</u>**
que	**habl<u>e</u>**	que	**com<u>a</u>**	que	**viv<u>a</u>**
que	**habl<u>es</u>**	que	**com<u>as</u>**	que	**viv<u>as</u>**
que	**habl<u>e</u>**	que	**com<u>a</u>**	que	**viv<u>a</u>**
que	**habl<u>emos</u>**	que	**com<u>amos</u>**	que	**viv<u>amos</u>**
que	**habl<u>éis</u>**	que	**com<u>áis</u>**	que	**viv<u>áis</u>**
que	**habl<u>en</u>**	que	**com<u>an</u>**	que	**viv<u>an</u>**

¡Ojo! The *yo* and *él/ella/Ud.* forms are always the same as each other in the subjunctive mood.

> *Ej.* **Dese<u>an</u>** (indicative, not in dispute) *que* **limpi<u>emos</u>** los platos (subjunctive, in doubt).
> **Necesit<u>a</u>** (indicative, fact) *que* **escrib<u>as</u>** la carta (subjunctive, you may not comply).
> **Prefer<u>imos</u>** (indicative) *que* **habl<u>en</u>** con el jefe (subjunctive, they may or may not).
> **Esper<u>o</u>** (I hope) *que* **comprend<u>as</u>** un poco del subjuntivo (I won't hold my breath).
> **Pid<u>o</u>** (I ask) *que* **estudi<u>es</u>** un poco cada día (pretty please).

Unidad 24

Los verbos (el subjuntivo) – Verbs (subjunctive mood)

It's normal to over apply a rule or concept shortly after learning it. One example is being tempted to make every verb reflexive soon after learning the concept of reflexive pronouns. Another example is forgetting about the indicative mood and using the subjunctive mood for simple sentences. Be careful to not throw out what you already knew about showing desire.

When talking about what a subject wants to have happen, follow these two general rules:

➤ If one subject desires that another subject do something, use the subjunctive to show that the first subject has no grammatical control over the outcome.

> *Ej.* Los padres (subject #1) quieren **que** →
> sus hijos (subject #2) **coman** muchos vegetales.

¡Ojo! The above sentence does not indicate whether the parents' children eat a lot of vegetables or not. It doesn't indicate what their children do at all; it merely indicates what the parents want.

➤ If one subject desires to do the action, use the infinitive.

> *Ej.* Los padres (subject #1) quieren →
> **comer** (still same subject) muchos vegetales.

Showing what one subject wants another subject to do is only one use of the subjunctive. Expressing the speaker's doubt about whether something is real or whether something will happen is another use. Take a look at the two following statements. See if you can figure out why one uses the indicative and the other uses the subjunctive.

> *Ej.* Creo **que** →
> **va** (indicative) a llover hoy. – I believe (that) it is going to rain today.
>
> No creo **que** →
> **vaya** (subjunctive) a llover hoy. – I don't believe (that) it is going to rain today.

Would you agree that if we removed "I believe (that)" from the first example, the sentence, for all intents and purposes, would have the same meaning?

Would you agree that if we removed "I don't believe (that)" from the second example, the sentence would have the exact opposite meaning?

The speaker uses the subjunctive to negate or deny "it is going to rain." In English, we do not make this type of distinction, but in Spanish, it sounds pretty weird to deny something by saying, *no creo que*, and then immediately affirm what was just denied by stating, *va a llover*.

¡Ojo! Whether or not it rains does not matter grammatically. What matters is what the speaker believes or doesn't believe. The subjunctive here is all about the speaker's perspective.

When you're talking about what you believe, think, doubt, etc., put your statement to this test by deleting the main clause. If the meaning remains the same, you need the indicative. If it means the opposite of what you intended, you need the subjunctive.

> *Ej.* Pienso que eres inteligente. → ~~Pienso que~~ eres inteligente. (same)
>
> No creo que el bus viene a tiempo. → ~~No creo que~~ el bus viene a tiempo. (opposite)

The first example checks out, so *eres* (indicative) works. The second one, however, does not check out, so *viene* does **not** work. This is what the second example should look like:

> No creo **que** el bus **venga** a tiempo.

Dudar means to doubt, so it will work like *no creer* or *no pensar*, whereas *no dudar* works like *creer* and *pensar*.

> *Ej.* <u>Dudo</u> **que** el bus **venga** a tiempo. – I doubt the bus will arrive on time.
> ~~I doubt~~ the bus will arrive on time. (opposite)
>
> <u>No dudo</u> **que eres** inteligente. – I don't doubt you are intelligent.
> ~~I don't doubt~~ you are intelligent. (same)

The subjunctive mood shares characteristics with both the indicative mood and the imperative mood. Here are a few things to keep in mind when conjugating the subjunctive.

➤ The placement of object pronouns is the same as the indicative: before the conjugated verb, attached to an infinitive, etc. (pp.85, 93, 96, 98-101, 110-117, 125-127).

> *Ej.* No creo que **te vayas a acostar** temprano durante tus vacaciones.
> No creo que **vayas a acostarte** temprano durante tus vacaciones.

➤ **Irregulars** in the subjunctive, like irregulars in the imperative, are based on the *yo* form in the present tense of the indicative (pp.130-132).

salir → <u>salgo</u>	Mi papá quiere **que yo salga** de la casa.
tener → <u>tengo</u>	Yo deseo **que tú tengas** tiempo para estudiar.
poner → <u>pongo</u>	No creo **que te pongas** una corbata para ir al gimnasio.
traer → <u>traigo</u>	Espero **que Estrella traiga** suficiente comida a la fiesta.
hacer → <u>hago</u>	Dudo **que Jorge y Tomás hagan** mucho ejercicio.
ver → <u>veo</u>	El maestro quiere **que tú y yo veamos** películas en español.
ir → voy	No quieres **que yo vaya** a México sin ti, ¿verdad?
venir → <u>vengo</u>	Esperamos **que tú vengas** a la fiesta este viernes.
decir → <u>digo</u>	Necesito **que Uds. me digan** la verdad.
ser → soy	La mamá de Penélope quiere **que sea** médica.
saber → <u>sé</u>	Quiero **que tú sepas** que no estoy enojado contigo.

¡Ojo! The *yo* and *él/ella/Ud.* forms, are always the same as each other in the subjunctive mood, so it's much more important that you use subject pronouns to maintain clarity.

Los verbos irregulares (el subjuntivo del presente)

The following are complete charts of some of the irregular verbs on the previous page so that you can better see their patterns.

salir	tener	ver	ir	decir	ser
que salga	que tenga	que vea	que vaya	que diga	que sea
que salgas	que tengas	que veas	que vayas	que digas	que seas
que salga	que tenga	que vea	que vaya	que diga	que sea
que salgamos	que tengamos	que veamos	que vayamos	que digamos	que seamos
que salgáis	que tengáis	que veáis	que vayáis	que digáis	que seáis
que salgan	que tengan	que vean	que vayan	que digan	que sean

In addition to the irregulars mentioned above and on the previous page, there are stem-changing verbs in the present tense of the subjunctive, which are irregular like stem-changing verbs in the indicative, but with a twist for -ir verbs.

mostrar (o → ue) – to show

indicativo:	muestro	mostramos	**subjuntivo:**	que muestre	que mostremos
	muestras	mostráis		que muestres	que mostréis
	muestra	muestran		que muestre	que muestren

volver (o → ue) – to return / to go back

indicativo:	vuelvo	volvemos	**subjuntivo:**	que vuelva	que volvamos
	vuelves	volvéis		que vuelvas	que volváis
	vuelve	vuelven		que vuelva	que vuelvan

Just like in the indicative, the subjunctive forms of -ar and -er verbs are stem-changing in all forms except the *nosotros* and *vosotros* forms; -ir verbs, on the other hand, have a twist. In addition to the normal stem changes, the *nosotros* and *vosotros* forms *do* have a stem change, but it isn't the same as the present-tense change; it is the same stem change used in the preterite tense for -ir verbs (p.109) and the gerund (-iendo form) (p.121).

dormir (o → ue) (o → u) – to sleep

indicativo:	duermo	dormimos	**subjuntivo:**	que duerma	que durmamos
	duermes	dormís		que duermas	que durmáis
	duerme	duermen		que duerma	que duerman

conseguir (e → i) (e → i) – to get – to acquire

indicativo:	consigo	conseguimos	**subjuntivo:**	que consiga	que consigamos
	consigues	conseguís		que consigas	que consigáis
	consigue	consiguen		que consiga	que consigan

convertir (e → ie) (e → i) – to convert

indicativo:	convierto	convertimos	**subjuntivo:**	que convierta	que convirtamos
	conviertes	convertís		que conviertas	que convirtáis
	convierte	convierten		que convierta	que conviertan

Los verbos (el subjuntivo o el indicativo) – Verbs (subjunctive or indicative mood)

In addition to the standard *que*, there are a few other words that introduce the subjunctive. Words like *posiblemente* (possibly), *probablemente* (probably), *quizá(s)* (maybe) and *tal vez* (perhaps), by definition, express a certain level of doubt. In these cases, when used before the verb, either the indicative or the subjunctive can be used. Some cultures use the subjunctive and indicative interchangeably with these words, whereas other cultures make a slight distinction based on the level of doubt. The phrase *no saber si* (to not know if/whether) can go either way, as well.

> *Ej.* Posiblemente viene este sábado. (said somewhat optimistically)
> Posiblemente venga este sábado. (said somewhat pessimistically)
>
> Probablemente tenemos tiempo después de clases. (90% chance)
> Probablemente tengamos tiempo después de clases. (70% chance)
>
> Quizá voy al cine con Uds. (Save me a spot.)
> Quizá vaya al cine con Uds. (Don't hold your breath.)
>
> Tal vez tomamos un cafecito el lunes que viene. (I'd like to.)
> Tal vez tomemos un cafecito el lunes que viene. (I'm not sure if you'd like to.)
>
> No sé si mi amiga viene/venga hoy. (The difference is more cultural than semantic).

¡Ojo! If the verb is used first, the indicative is obligatory.

> *Ej.* Viene posiblemente este sábado.
> ~~Venga posiblemente este sábado.~~ (Would be interpreted as an Ud. command.)

Another fun word is *aunque*. There is definitely more doubt when used with the subjunctive.

> *Ej.* No querré ir al cine el próximo viernes, aunque (*even if*) tenga bastante dinero.
> No quiero ir al cine el próximo viernes, aunque (*even though*) tengo bastante dinero.

Los verbos (el subjuntivo del presente perfecto)

The present-perfect tense in the subjunctive mood, as it is in the indicative mood, is used to talk about past actions or events that are relevant to the present moment. The difference, then, is the same difference we see in the present tense between the two moods: subordinate clause, preceded by *que*, expressing desire, preference, doubt, etc.

haber – to have (not possession)		-ed
que haya	que hayamos	-ar → -ado
que hayas	que hayáis	-er → -ido
que haya	que hayan	-ir → -ido

> *Ej.* No creo que <u>hayan ganado</u> la lotería.
> Prefieren que <u>hayamos comprado</u> los regalos antes de la fiesta.

148

Los verbos (el subjuntivo o el indicativo) – Verbs (subjunctive or indicative mood)

To say that learning the subjunctive mood is difficult would be an understatement. It is complicated, subtle, and, in some cases, subjective. Its subjectivity, in particular, makes it especially hard to master, even for native Spanish speakers. Most textbooks only give you 1st person examples of the subjunctive.

> *Ej.* <u>Creo</u> que los extraterrestres nos <u>han visitado</u>. (indicativo)
> <u>No creo</u> que los fantasmas <u>existan</u>. (subjuntivo)

The use of the subjunctive here is straightforward because the subject (*yo*) is the speaker. But what happens when the subject of the sentence is different from the speaker? Whose belief or doubt is expressed: the subject's or speaker's?

> *Ej.* Mi hermana cree que los extraterrestres nos <u>han visitado</u>. (indicativo)
> Mi hermana cree que los extraterrestres nos <u>hayan visitado</u>. (subjuntivo)

Both of the above examples are grammatically correct, although the second one may sound strange even to some native speakers. In the first one, the speaker probably has no contrary belief worth mentioning. In the second, the speaker believes his/her sister is crazy.

> *Ej.* Mi amigo no cree que los fantasmas <u>existan</u>. (subjuntivo)
> Mi amigo no cree que los fantasmas <u>existen</u>. (indicativo)

The examples above are grammatically correct. In the first one, the speaker probably has the same belief as the friend. In the second, the speaker cannot believe his/her friend is so skeptical.

> *Ej.* ¿Crees que los extraterrestres <u>existen</u>? (The speaker hasn't made up his/her mind.)
> ¿Crees que los extraterrestres <u>existan</u>? (The speaker obviously doesn't believe it.)
> No creas/pienses que <u>soy</u> tonta. (To tell someone what not to think, use the indicative.)

Another way the subjunctive is used is to show interest in something or someone that the speaker acknowledges may or may not exist, and may even fantasize about.

> *Ej.* ¿Tienes un lápiz que me <u>prestes</u>? (prestar – to lend)
> Quiero un trabajo que me <u>pague</u> mucho dinero y me <u>dé</u> seis semanas de vacaciones.
> Necesito unos amigos a quienes les <u>encante</u> viajar.
> Busco una novia que <u>sea</u> muy bonita y <u>tenga</u> un buen sentido de humor.
> ¿Hay alguien que <u>lea</u> poesía? (No hay nadie que <u>lea</u> poesía.)

In these examples above, the speaker doesn't have any particular pencil, job, friends, girlfriend, or "someone" in mind. For "no hay nadie" (or "no hay nada"), the subjunctive is used to show that the speaker acknowledges that there is no way to verify such a bold statement.

¡Ojo! The "personal *a*" (p.126) does not apply to the above examples since they are impersonal, however, two exceptions are the words *nadie* (no one/anyone) and *alguien* (someone).

> *Ej.* No conozco **a** nadie que <u>sepa</u> (saber) japonés.
> Busco **a** alguien que <u>hable</u> alemán.

Unidad 25

Los verbos (el subjuntivo o el indicativo) – Verbs (subjunctive or indicative mood)

You've now seen two very different uses of the subjunctive. The first one was to show desire (pp.143-145) and the second one was to show doubt or lack of belief (pp.145-146). Instead of trying to memorize every type of example, let's proceed by breaking the subjunctive down into two categories: **head** and **heart**.

- **Head**

Understanding – creer, pensar, comprender, entender, reconocer, opinar, considerar, suponer, imaginar(se), figurarse, comprobar, saber, deducir, recordar, acordarse (de), averiguar, descubrir, adivinar, soñar, intuir, estar seguro (de), estar convencido (de), etc. + *que*

Senses – ver, oír, notar, observar, comprobar, darse cuenta (de), descubrir, sentir, etc. + *que*

Language – decir, admitir, contar, afirmar, narrar, escribir, comunicar, referir, confesar, murmurar, susurrar, explicar, manifestar, contestar, revelar, jurar, prometer, sostener, indicar, responder, comentar, declarar, relatar, señalar, leer, mencionar, etc. + *que*

Basic Rules:

➢ If verb 1 is affirmative, then <u>verb 2</u> requires the indicative.
   Ej. Creo que <u>es</u> buena idea.
   Veo que <u>tienes</u> un carro nuevo.

➢ If verb 1 is negative, then <u>verb 2</u> requires the subjunctive.
   Ej. No creo que <u>sea</u> buena idea.
   No admito que <u>tengas</u> mejor carro que yo.

Impersonal Statements – ser, ser evidente, ser cierto, ser indudable, ser indiscutible, ser obvio, ser verdad, ser seguro, estar claro, estar visto, estar demostrado, dar la impresión (de), verse, notarse, resultar, pasar, suceder, etc. + *que*

   Ej. Es evidente que tú <u>has</u> aprendido mucho.
   Es verdad que <u>es</u> difícil aprender el subjuntivo.

   No está claro que <u>hayas</u> aprendido el subjuntivo.
   No es obvio que <u>sea</u> fácil aprender el subjuntivo.

   ¿Es que no te <u>gusta</u> el ajo?
   No, no es que el ajo no me <u>guste</u>, sino que siempre <u>ponen</u> demasiado.

- **Heart**

Emotions – gustar, encantar, avergonzarse, molestar, fastidiar, dar pena, contentarse con, conformarse con, cansarse de, hartarse de, resignarse a, sufrir, aguantar, soportar, extrañar, admirar, consolar, doler, aburrir, divertir, entusiasmar, alegrar, alegrarse (de), entristecer, apenar, lamentar, quejarse de, temer, tener miedo de, sentir, estar temeroso de, estar asombrado de, estar sorprendido (de), estar satisfecho (de), tener interés en … + *que*

Will or Desire – esperar, querer, desear, preferir, aspirar a, pretender, intentar, apetecer, oponerse a, conseguir, lograr, hacer (lograr) … + *que*

Commands, Advice, Pleas, Prohibition – decir (ordenar), ordenar, mandar, decretar, aconsejar, desaconsejar, recomendar, animar a, invitar a, incitar a, pedir, rogar, suplicar, solicitar, procurar, permitir, consentir, dejar, acceder a, prohibir, impedir, obligar a, hacer (obligar), exigir … + *que*

Other Verbs – interesar, ayudar a, esperar a, tolerar, contribuir a, aventurarse a, exponerse a, criticar, aprobar, estar decidido a, estar acostumbrado a, estar dispuesto a … + *que*

Basic Rules:

➤ Whether verb 1 is affirmative or negative, <u>verb 2</u> requires the subjunctive.
   Ej. Quiero que <u>salgas</u>.
       No quiero que <u>salgas</u>.

➤ If verb 1 and verb 2 refer to the same person, then <u>verb 2</u> usually requires the infinitive, particularly if the subject has control over the outcome of verb 2.
   Ej. Quiero <u>salir</u>.
       No quieren <u>salir</u>.

Impersonal Statements – (no) ser bueno, ser malo, ser mejor, ser peor, ser fácil, ser difícil, ser raro, ser necesario, ser curioso, ser extraño, estar bien, estar mal, ser (in)útil, ser (im)probable, poder, ser (im)posible, ser estupendo, ser maravilloso, ser esencial, ser sorprendente, ser natural, ser (in)justo, ser estúpido, ser ridículo, ser terrible, ser horroroso, ser (i)lógico, ser una pena, ser imprescindible, ser indispensable, ser una (des)ventaja, ser una locura, ser una barbaridad, ser una coincidencia, ser una tontería, ser una lástima, parecer mentira, ser hora de, ser tiempo de, no haber (la menor) posibilidad (esperanza, oportunidad, etc.) de, bastar, hacer falta, convenir, tener derecho a, poder ser, dar pena (rabia, gusto, alegría, tristeza, vergüenza …), valer más … + *que*

   Ej. Es bueno que estudies español.
       No es bueno que te frustres.

   Ej. Es bueno estudiar español. (universal statement)
       No es bueno frustrarse. (universal statement)

Additional Expressions: para, con el fin de, a menos, a no ser, con tal de, acaso, sin … + *que*

¡Ojo! In certain cases, verb 1 can be omitted, often when no one has control of the outcome.
   Ej. Que te mejores pronto. Que les vaya bien. Que tengan un bonito día.

Los verbos (el subjuntivo o el indicativo) – Verbs (subjunctive or indicative mood)

You might have noticed that a few verbs appear on both lists (head/heart). This is not a mistake. The distinction between the two hangs solely on the use of the subjunctive or indicative.

Sentir – You can feel with your heart as well as with your physical senses.

> *Ej.* Siento que tengas frío. (corazón – empatía) – I'm sorry you are cold.
> Siento que tienes frío. (cabeza – percepción) – I sense/perceive/see that you are cold.

Decir – You can relate what someone tells you to do, which shows desire in the form of an indirect command, but you can also relate what someone's physical senses perceive.

> *Ej.* "Me dice que corra rápidamente." (corazón – indirect command/desire) – subjunctive
> ("Me dice, 'Corre rápidamente.'") – imperativo (mandato)
>
> "Me dice que corro rápidamente." (cabeza – información/belief) – indicative
> ("Me dice, 'Corres rápidamente.'") – indicativo (presente)

- **Routine vs. Future**

Although most conjugations in the subjunctive mood follow the word *que*, it isn't always the case. The words *cuando* (when), *en cuanto/tan pronto como* (as soon as) can either indicate a routine action/event or a future action/event. When used to talk about **routine** actions/events, the **indicative** is required. When used to talk about **future** action, the **subjunctive** is required, no matter how certain you are that the event will occur.

> *Ej.* <u>When</u> I travel abroad, I usually prefer Latin America. (routine)
> I always brush my teeth <u>as soon as</u> I get up in the morning. (routine)
>
> She's going to go out for a run <u>as soon as</u> the sun comes up tomorrow. (future)
> I'll buy a new car <u>when</u> I win the lottery next week. (future)

The first two are examples of routine, and you already know how to narrate your daily routine fairly well. The second two examples are both future. The sun will come up tomorrow and that is a fact of science. It is not a fact, however, that I will win the lottery next week. Grammatically, though, these are the same concept. It may not be a question of *if* but rather a question of exactly *when*. That uncertainty is the reason for the subjunctive. Let's see the translations.

> *Ej.* <u>Cuando</u> viajo (indicativo) al extranjero, normalmente prefiero Latinoamérica.
> Siempre me cepillo los dientes <u>en cuanto</u> me levanto (indicativo) en la mañana.
>
> Ella va a salir a correr <u>tan pronto como</u> salga (subjuntivo) el sol mañana.
> Compraré un carro nuevo <u>cuando</u> gane (subjuntivo) la lotería la próxima semana.

¡Ojo! ***Después de que*** requires the subjunctive when referring to the future and the indicative when referring to a routine or past sequence. ***Antes de que*** always requires the subjunctive.

152

Unidad 26

Los verbos (el subjuntivo) – Verbs (subjunctive mood)

Although mastering the subjunctive mood may (*definitely will*) take you years, hopefully you are starting to get a feel for its subtle and sometimes subjective nature.

You know the subjunctive usually follows the word *que*, and can follow the word *cuando* (p.152), but it can also follow the words *donde, como, quien(es)*, and *cuanto/a(s)*. Often these words are followed by the subjunctive form of the verb *ser* (*sea/sean*). This structure is used to express indifference to a choice and/or to defer to another person to make a decision.

> *Ej. lo que sea* – whatever (it may be)
> *cuando sea* – whenever (it may be)
> *cuanto/a sea / cuantos/as sean* – however much/many (it/they may be)
> *donde sea* – wherever (it may be)
> *como sea* – however (it may be)
> *quien sea / quienes sean* – whoever (it/they may be)

While it's one of the most common verbs to use in this context, *ser* isn't the only verb that can be used. The verb *querer* is also very common.

> *Ej. lo que (ella) quiera* – whatever she wants (what she wants remains to be seen)
> *cuando quieran* – whenever you (all) want
> *cuanto queramos* – however much we want
> *donde (yo) quiera* – wherever I want
> *como queráis* – however you (all) want
> *a quien quieras* – to whomever you want

In certain contexts, the words *cuando, cuanto, donde, como, cual(es)*, and *quien(es)* can be combined with the word *quiera* (the subjunctive of *querer*).

> *Ej. cuandoquiera* – whenever   *dondequiera* – wherever
> *cuantoquiera* – however much   *quienquiera / quienesquiera* – whoever
> *comoquiera* – however   *cualquiera / cualesquiera* – whichever

Cualquiera serves as a pronoun (by itself) or as an adjective (with a noun). When used before a noun, the final *a* is dropped: *cualquier cosa, cualesquier coches*. You have surely seen words whose endings are dropped before nouns: *grande → gran hombre, primero → primer piso*.

The following are similar expressions using the subjunctive:

> *Ej. Pase lo que pase, ...* – Whatever happens, ...
> *Sea quien sea, ...* – Whoever it is, ...
> *Hagas lo que hagas, ...* – Whatever you do, ...
>
> *Por mucho que intentes, ...* – No matter how much you try, ...
> *Por más lejos que vayamos, ...* – No matter how far (away) we go, ...

Los verbos (el pretérito vs. el imperfecto)

Unlike in English, Spanish has two simple past tenses: the preterite (pp.102-103) and the imperfect (pp.122-123). As with *por/para*, *ser/estar/haber*, and *saber/conocer*, thinking in English will not help you understand their differences. Mastering their uses takes a lot of exposure and a keen ear. There are certain words and contexts that require one or the other, but sometimes it's a subjective choice. The more control you have over these tenses, the more precisely you'll be able to convey what you mean to convey and the greater the subtleties you'll be able to perceive.

- **Use the preterite:**
  - ➤ to tell what events/actions took place.
    - *Fui al club y me divertí bailando.*
  - ➤ to inform that an event/action happened a definite number of times.
    - *Salió a correr seis veces la semana pasada.*
  - ➤ to talk about the duration of an event/action (even if it wasn't an action).
    - *Estuvimos en el centro comercial por tres horas.*
  - ➤ to tell of an event or action that had a definitive start and stop.
    - *Viste la tele de las 19:00 a las 23:30 anoche.*
  - ➤ to talk about a series of events that can be grouped together as one.
    - *Nuestro equipo de fútbol jugó muy mal el año pasado (varios partidos).*
  - ➤ to convey a causal relationship between events/actions.
    - *Ella salió corriendo cuando vio al ladrón.*

- **Use the imperfect:**
  - ➤ to paint an image of the background or scene surrounding the events or actions.
    - *Era una noche lluviosa y oscura. El viento silbaba y el cielo tronaba.*
  - ➤ to describe habitual actions or actions that happened an indefinite number of times.
    - *De niña, ella jugaba en el parque todos los fines de semana.*
  - ➤ to describe action that was in progress when an event occurred.
    - *Yo nadaba (estaba nadando) en la piscina cuando oí la alarma.*
  - ➤ to reference what a printed text said (the text doesn't cease to inform once you read it).
    - *El artículo decía que los supervivientes fueron trasladados al refugio.*
  - ➤ to blur the clarity of an event/action that would conventionally require the use of the preterite. This is a technique used in journalism to remove the focus from an event/action to create contrast with and focus on events deemed more important to the story. For their vague and blurry nature, dreams are often narrated in the imperfect.

The preterite takes the reader forward in time from one event to another. The imperfect pauses the action and allows the reader to stop, look around, and imagine. When narrating a story, there is always a balance to be struck between the preterite and the imperfect. If you give too much background information with the imperfect, your reader may lose interest before the events/actions of the story take place. If you don't give enough background information and go straight to the exciting events of the story, your reader will fail to picture the scene and, consequently, have a hard time empathizing with the characters and/or struggle to understand their motivations.

¡Ojo! Although common in English, the conditional tense in Spanish (p.155) cannot be used to talk about past routine. Instead, the imperfect is used.

Ej. As a kid, <u>I would often play</u> all day. – De niño, <u>yo a menudo</u> ~~jugaría~~ jugaba todo el día.

Unidad 27

Los verbos (el condicional) – Verbs (conditional tense)

You've already seen the future tense (p.141), which is obviously used to talk about the future of the present, but what about the future of the past? Although you might not have considered this concept previously, you've certainly applied it perfectly thousands of times before. Consider this exchange between two co-workers on a random Monday morning:

> *Ej.* María: When do you think <u>you'll (you will) hand in</u> your report?
> Esteban: Don't worry; <u>I'll (I will) hand it in</u> by Wednesday morning.

Since Wednesday is still in the future as of this exchange, it makes sense to use the future tense. Now let's flash forward to Thursday and see what happens to the verb tense.

> *Ej.* María: You told me <u>you'd (you would) hand in</u> your report by yesterday morning.
> Esteban: I'm sorry; I really thought <u>I'd (I would) be able to</u> …

Now that the once future is the past, we have to adjust our verb tense to correspond. Not coincidentally, given their relation, the conditional tense follows the same rules and exceptions as the future tense; only its endings are different.

comprar – to buy		volver – to return	
compraría	compraríamos	volvería	volveríamos
comprarías	compraríais	volverías	volveríais
compraría	comprarían	volvería	volverían

Let's look again at that exchange, this time in Spanish.

> *Ej.* María: ¿Para cuándo piensas que <u>entregarás</u> tu reportaje? (futuro)
> Esteban: No te preocupes; lo <u>entregaré</u> para el miércoles por la mañana. (futuro)
>
> María: Me dijiste que <u>entregarías</u> tu reportaje para ayer. (condicional)
> Esteban: Disculpa; de verdad pensé que <u>podría</u> … (condicional)

All irregulars in the future tense have the same irregular roots in the conditional tense. Here's a review with conditional endings.

hacer (har) – to do / to make		poner (pondr) – to put / to set	
haría	haríamos	pondría	pondríamos
harías	haríais	pondrías	pondríais
haría	harían	pondría	pondrían

poder (podr) – to be able		
querer (querr) – to want	-ía	-íamos
tener (tendr) – to have	-ías	-íais
venir (vendr) – to come	-ia	-ían
saber (sabr) – to know (information)		
salir (saldr) – to go out		

Los verbos (el subjuntivo del imperfecto)

Remember, the subjunctive isn't a verb tense, but rather a mood. We have studied the subjunctive of the present tense, but there is also a subjunctive of the past (imperfect) tense, too. Its rules and uses are the same as in the present (head/heart), but its conjugations are obviously different.

	hablar		**comer**		**vivir**
que	**habl**ara	que	**com**iera	que	**viv**iera
que	**habl**aras	que	**com**ieras	que	**viv**ieras
que	**habl**ara	que	**com**iera	que	**viv**iera
que	**habl**áramos	que	**com**iéramos	que	**viv**iéramos
que	**habl**arais	que	**com**ierais	que	**viv**ierais
que	**habl**aran	que	**com**ieran	que	**viv**ieran

Remember, the *nosotros* form in the imperfect always has an accent mark whether the verb is regular, irregular, *-ar*, *-er*, or *-ir*.

Los verbos irregulares (el subjuntivo del imperfecto)

By now, you are no stranger to the concept of irregular verbs. Verb tenses (*voy, fui, iba, querrá*), commands (*pon, haz*), past participles (*visto, dicho*), and even the gerund (*durmiendo, pidiendo*) have irregular forms. The subjunctive of the imperfect is no exception. The good thing is that its irregular forms are not new; you've seen them in multiple contexts already: *durmió, durmiendo, que durmamos*. Let the *ellos/ellas/Uds.* form in the preterite be your guide.

ir/ser (fueron)	**querer (quisieron)**	**decir (dijeron)**	**dormir (durmieron)**
que fuera	que quisiera	que dijera	que durmiera
que fueras	que quisieras	que dijeras	que durmieras
que fuera	que quisiera	que dijera	que durmiera
que fuéramos	que quisiéramos	que dijéramos	que durmiéramos
que fuerais	que quisierais	que dijerais	que durmierais
que fueran	que quisieran	que dijeran	que durmieran

estar (estuvieron)	**saber (supieron)**	**dar (dieron)**	**pedir (pidieron)**
que estuviera	que supiera	que diera	que pidiera
que estuvieras	que supieras	que dieras	que pidieras
que estuviera	que supiera	que diera	que pidiera
que estuviéramos	que supiéramos	que diéramos	que pidiéramos
que estuvierais	que supierais	que dierais	que pidierais
que estuvieran	que supieran	que dieran	que pidieran

These are just a few of the many irregular verbs you've studied in the preterite. As I hope you can appreciate, this guide cannot possibly cover everything there is to know in the Spanish language. That said, I invite you to explore the *Real Academia Española* (www.rae.es) as it is, undoubtedly, the most highly regarded Spanish-language resource in existence. It gives you access to the most comprehensive dictionaries, which will hopefully be of great future use to you. In addition, it has a complete verb conjugator (search the verb in the dictionary and click the blue "*conjugar*" button).

Los verbos (el infinitivo o el subjuntivo)

As you already know (pp.143-144), *quiero leerte*, and *quiero que leas* are significantly different. They need to be so that you know who is expected to read. There are a few verbs, however, that, although the subjunctive may be used, the infinitive can also be used and the meaning remains the same. This is due to the nature of the verbs. While it is common to want to do something to someone else, it's not common to allow yourself, advise yourself, help yourself, teach yourself, prohibit yourself, etc, therefore there is no confusion as to who is to do the action.

> *Ej.* Déjame leer. / Deja(me) que (yo) lea. – Let me read. (dejar)
> Nos permitió salir. / (Nos) permitió que saliéramos. (permitir)
> Te aconsejo estudiar. / (Te) aconsejo que estudies. (aconsejar)
> Me hizo correr. / (Me) hizo que (yo) corriera. (hacer)

Other verbs commonly used both ways are: *recomendar*, *sugerir*, and *prohibir*.
Some verbs, like *ir*, require the preposition *a* regardless of which construction you use.

> *Ej.* Me obligó a buscarte. / (Me) obligó a que (yo) te buscara. (obligar)
> Nos pone a trabajar. / (Nos) pone a que trabajemos. (poner)
> Te voy a ayudar a estudiar. / (Te) voy a ayudar a que estudies. (ayudar)

Other verbs commonly used both ways that require an *a*, are: *invitar a*, *mandar a*, *incitar a*, and *enseñar a*. There is no limit to how many verbs you can string together. Don't forget your *a* if it's required.

> *Ej.* Pepa va a obligarme a permirtirte ayudar a Pedro a enseñarle a Paco a nadar.
> Pepa va a obligar a que yo permita que ayudes a que Pedro le enseñe a que Paco nade.

The syntax (word order) of the above phrases is correct either way you word it. Their meaning: "Pepa is going to make me allow you to help Pedro teach Paco to swim." Twice, in the first example above, you see an *a* that is not underlined. These are the "personal *a.*"

Los verbos (el infinitivo o el indicativo)

With verbs of perception: *ver, mirar, oír, escuchar, sentir, observar*, etc., you can use either the infinitive or the indicative. The meaning is slightly different, but both work grammatically.

> *Ej.* Te vi entrar por la puerta trasera. – I saw you come in through the back door.
> Vi que entraste por la puerta trasera. – I saw (that) you came in through the back door.
> Te vi cuando entraste por … – I saw you when you came in through the back door.
>
> Me oyeron gritar. – They heard me shout.
> Oyeron que grité. – They heard (that) I shouted.
> Me oyeron cuando grité. – They heard me when I shouted.
>
> Te sentí tocarme el pelo. – I felt you touch my hair.
> Sentí que me tocaste el pelo. – I felt (that) you touched my hair.
> Te sentí cuando me tocaste el pelo. – I felt you when you touched my hair.

Unidad 28

Los verbos (las situaciones hipotéticas) – Verbs (hypothetical situations)

As you've seen (p.155), the conditional tense can be used as the future of the past, but that isn't its only use. It can also be used to hypothesize what *would* happen under certain "conditions."

> *Ej.* What <u>would you do</u> with a million dollars?
> Where <u>would you like</u> to go on vacation?
> <u>I could eat</u> ten hotdogs in ten minutes.

These examples require the conditional tense because, in its most literal sense, certain conditions are required to carry out the action. Take a look at the translations of the above examples.

> *Ej.* ¿Qué <u>harías</u> con un millón de dólares?
> ¿Adónde te <u>gustaría</u> ir de vacaciones?
> (Yo) <u>podría</u> comer diez salchichas en diez minutos.

These statements above are simple, but many hypothetical statements include an "**if**" clause.

> *Ej.* <u>If I had</u> a million dollars (I don't), I'd buy a new house.
> I'd love to play golf <u>if my back didn't hurt</u> so much (but it does).

Even though these statements use the past tense in English, you instinctively know they are statements about the present. It is the same in Spanish, although the past tense is subjunctive of the imperfect.

> *Ej.* <u>Si tuviera</u> un millón de dólares (no lo tengo), compraría una casa nueva.
> Me encantaría jugar al golf <u>si la espalda no me doliera</u> tanto (pero sí me duele).

If the hypothetical is **present**, use the formula: *si* + **imperfect subjunctive** and **conditional**. But what if the hypothetical is past? That's where the final two perfect tenses come in handy.

condicional perfecto		subjuntivo del pluscuamperfecto	
habría	habríamos	que hubiera	que hubiéramos
habrías	habríais	que hubieras	que hubierais
habría	habrían	que hubiera	que hubieran

If the hypothetical is **past**, use: *si* + **pluperfect subjunctive** and **conditional perfect**.

> *Ej.* <u>If I had won</u> the lottery drawing (I didn't), I would have bought a new house.
> I would have played golf <u>if I hadn't hurt</u> my back (but I did).

These statements use perfect tenses to show their past nature. Check them out in Spanish.

> *Ej.* <u>Si hubiera ganado</u> la lotería (no la gané), habría comprado una casa nueva.
> Habría jugado al golf <u>si no me hubiera lastimado</u> la espalda (pero sí me la lastimé).

Los verbos (el subjuntivo del imperfecto)

Although they are much less common, it's worth mentioning that there are alternate endings for the subjunctive in the imperfect. You should focus on mastering the conjugations you've already seen (p.156), but don't be surprised if you hear one of the conjugations below from time to time.

	hablar		**com**er		**viv**ir
que	**habl**ase	que	**com**iese	que	**viv**iese
que	**habl**ases	que	**com**ieses	que	**viv**ieses
que	**habl**ase	que	**com**iese	que	**viv**iese
que	**habl**ásemos	que	**com**iésemos	que	**viv**iésemos
que	**habl**aseis	que	**com**ieseis	que	**viv**ieseis
que	**habl**asen	que	**com**iesen	que	**viv**iesen

Of course, don't forget your irregulars.

ir/ser (fueron)	**querer (quisieron)**	**decir (dijeron)**	**dormir (durmieron)**
que fuese	que quisiese	que dijese	que durmiese
que fueses	que quisieses	que dijeses	que durmieses
que fuese	que quisiese	que dijese	que durmiese
que fuésemos	que quisiésemos	que dijésemos	que durmiésemos
que fueseis	que quisieseis	que dijeseis	que durmieseis
que fuesen	que quisiesen	que dijesen	que durmiesen

estar (estuvieron)	**saber (supieron)**	**dar (dieron)**	**pedir (pidieron)**
que estuviese	que supiese	que diese	que pidiese
que estuvieses	que supieses	que dieses	que pidieses
que estuviese	que supiese	que diese	que pidiese
que estuviésemos	que supiésemos	que diésemos	que pidiésemos
que estuvieseis	que supieseis	que dieseis	que pidieseis
que estuviesen	que supiesen	que diesen	que pidiesen

And the alternate pluperfect subjunctive forms must be:

que hubiese, hubieses, hubiese, hubiésemos, hubieseis, hubiesen + past participle

In English, the phrase "as if" followed by the subjunctive is commonly replaced with "like" followed by the indicative. Perhaps this is due to the demise of the subjunctive in English.

> *Ej.* He's goofing around *as if* I had all day to wait.
> He's goofing around *like* I have all day to wait.

Since the subjunctive is alive and well in Spanish, these phrases use *como si* followed by the subjunctive of the imperfect to show that the statement is not true.

> *Ej.* Está haciendo monerías *como si* yo tuviera/tuviese todo el día para esperar.
> Está haciendo monerías ~~como yo tengo~~ todo el día para esperar.

Los verbos (el subjuntivo – presente y pasado)

As previously stated, the rules and uses of the subjunctive are not tense specific; they apply the same for the present as they do for the past. As with the indicative, you can mix and match your verb tenses based on what you are trying to communicate. Mind your "head" and "heart" verbs.

> *Ej.* <u>Creo</u> que mi tío <u>fue</u> al banco ayer. (presente/pasado)
> <u>No creo</u> que mi tío <u>fuera</u> al banco ayer.
>
> <u>Parece</u> que mi tío <u>ha ido</u> al banco (porque no está aquí ahora).
> <u>No parece</u> que mi tío <u>haya ido</u> al banco (porque todavía está aquí).
>
> <u>Era obvio</u> cuando te conocí que <u>tenías</u> un buen sentido de humor. (pasado/pasado)
> <u>No me sorprendió</u> cuando te conocí que <u>fueras</u> comediante profesional.

Likewise, you can mix and match your tenses when talking about hypothetical situations.

> *Ej.* Si estudiara más (este semestre),
> estaría sacando una buena nota en clase (ahora).
> Si hubiera estudiado más (el semestre pasado),
> habría sacado una buena nota en clase (el semestre pasado).
> Si hubiera estudiado más (anoche),
> no estaría teniendo tantos problemas con este examen (ahora).

Los verbos (el subjuntivo o el indicativo) – Verbs (subjunctive or indicative mood)

As you might remember, when it comes to expressing belief and doubt, the use of the subjunctive is dependent on the speaker's doubt, not the subject's within the sentence. (p.149) What may look like a breaking of the "basic rules" of "head" verbs (p.150) is really a matter of perspective. In that same vein, when talking about the past, we can break from the rules when the speaker presently believes or knows something that he/she previously did not.

> *Ej.* Pepe: Hoy es mi cumpleaños.
> Marta: Ay, Pepe, siento no haberte comprado nada. <u>No sabía</u> *que* <u>era</u> tu cumple.

What Marta is saying with the use of the indicative is that although she didn't know before, she does now, thus there is no need for the subjunctive, even though the "head" verb is negative.

> *Ej.* Pepe: ¡Sabías que ayer cumplí 18 años!
> Marta: No, yo <u>no sabía</u> *que* <u>cumplieras</u> 18 años.

What Marta is saying with the use of the subjunctive is that she not only didn't know, but that she's not too sure about it even now. Whether it was or wasn't Pepe's birthday yesterday is not grammatically relevant. What *is* relevant is Marta's perspective now and, in this case, she rejects Pepe's claim that she knew yesterday was his birthday.

Los verbos (el indicativo y el subjuntivo)

As previously stated (p.143), there are nine verb tenses in the indicative mood and four (*) in the subjunctive mood. That means there is not a unique corresponding tense in the subjunctive mood for every unique tense in the indicative mood; they have to share. The following chart shows the corresponding tenses.

Indicativo:

   1. **presente** →
   2. **futuro** →

Ej. Creo que <u>es</u> alto. (presente) →
No dudo que <u>hará</u> sol mañana. (futuro) →

   3. **presente perfecto** →
   4. **futuro perfecto** →

Ej. Es cierto que <u>han ganado</u>. (pres. perfecto) →
Es indudable que <u>habrá comido</u>. (fut. perf.) →

   5. **pretérito** →
   6. **imperfecto** →
   7. **condicional** →

Ej. Es evidente que les <u>gustó</u>. (pretérito) →
Es obvio que <u>estaba</u> feliz. (imperfecto) →
Estaba claro que <u>querrían</u>. (condicional) →

   8. **pluscuamperfecto** →
   9. **condicional perfecto** →

Ej. Quizá lo <u>había visto</u>. (pluscuamperfecto) →
Probablemente <u>habría ido</u>. (cond. perfecto) →

Subjuntivo:

1. **presente**

No creo que Miguel <u>sea</u> alto. (presente)
Dudo que <u>haga</u> sol mañana. (presente)

2. **presente perfecto**

No es cierto que <u>hayan ganado</u>. (pres. perf.)
Es dudable que <u>haya comido</u>. (pres. perf.)

3. **imperfecto**

Es absurdo que les <u>gustara</u>. (imperfecto)
Es curioso que <u>estuviera</u> feliz. (imperfecto)
No estaba claro que <u>quisieran</u>. (imperfecto)

4. **pluscuamperfecto**

Quizá lo <u>hubiera visto</u>. (pluscuamperfecto)
Posiblemente <u>hubiera ido</u>. (pluscuamperfecto)

* There is actually a fifth subjunctive form (future subjunctive), but it is virtually obsolete (like the subjunctive in English). It is used today only in legal documents and traditional sayings, but you might come across it some day in classic literature.

   Ej. Allá donde <u>fueres</u>, haz lo que <u>vieres</u>. ("When in Rome, do as the Romans do.")

Unidad 29

La descripción avanzada

Gender and number, adjective-noun agreement, and adjective placement are essential and fundamental pieces of the Spanish language. You already have the tools to understand their basic applications (pp.81, 92), but between the breaking of basic rules and the faithful application of advanced rules, there are plenty of subtleties to be learned in the name of linguistic mastery.

- **Nouns and their gender**

You already know that many nouns end in *e* or a consonant and that learning their definite articles (*el, la*) helps you learn the gender of these nouns. You also know that most nouns that end in *o* are masculine and most that end in *a* are feminine. I say "most," of course, because there are exceptions. Let's look at a few different types of rule breakers.

> *Ej.* el planeta, el mapa, la mano, el día, el sofá, el papá, el yoga, la libido, etc.

The above examples break the rules for different reasons. Some words ending in ***ma*** are masculine (due to their non-Latin origins), while others are feminine (of Latin origin).

> **Masculine**: el sistema, fantasma, problema, drama, idioma, tema, clima, poema, etc.
> **Feminine**: la forma, plataforma, pluma, paloma, goma, gama, fama, dama, mamá, etc.

In some cases, the masculine form means one thing and the feminine form means another.

> *Ej.* **el** cometa – comet, **el** coma – coma, **el** papa – pope, **el** capital – capital (money), etc.
> **la** cometa – kite, **la** coma – comma, **la** papa – potato, **la** capital – capital (city), etc.

Some nouns have ambiguous gender; some people use them as masculine and others as feminine.

> *Ej.* el/la azúcar, el/la mar, el/la sartén, el/la margen, el/la sauna, el/la radio, etc.

For some nouns that describe people, the difference in grammatical gender depends on the gender of the person. With professions traditionally reserved for men, the Spanish language hasn't fully caught up with the progressive shift in gender roles, leaving questions about the correct usage.

> *Ej.* el atleta (alto), el deportista (guapo), el modelo (viejo), el indígena, el psiquiatra, etc.
> la atleta (alta), la deportista (guapa), la modelo (vieja), la indígena, la psiquiatra, etc.
> Ella es el piloto? Ella es la piloto? Ella es la pilota? Ella es la juez? Ella es la jueza?

In the case of animal names, some have both masculine and feminine forms, based on the sex of the individual animal, and some are either masculine or feminine regardless of the animal's sex. In the latter cases, the words *macho* (male) and *hembra* (female) are used to distinguish its sex. Lastly, there are animals that have unique names for their respective sexes.

> *Ej.* el gato/la gata, el perro/la perra, el elefante/la elefanta, el león/la leona, etc.
> la jirafa (macho, hembra), el puma (macho, hembra), la ballena (macho, hembra), etc.
> el toro/la vaca, el gallo/la gallina, el tigre/la tigresa, el caballo/la yegua, etc.

Some nouns appear to break the rules because their colloquial (informal) form is actually short for a longer form, where the gender of the word is more obvious.

> *Ej.* la foto(grafía), la moto(cicleta), la expo(sición), la disco(teca), etc.

The following nouns are feminine, but since they start with a *stressed* (tonic) *a*, the masculine article (definite – *el/la* or indefinite – *un/una*) is used. This is to avoid the double *a* sound, but, remember, only if the first syllable is stressed. Note that adjectives still agree with the gender of the noun, not the article. Also note that there is no double *a* problem if the noun is plural.

> *Ej.* el/un alma (hermosa), el/un ave (muerta), el/un agua (fría), el/un área (pequeña), etc.
>   las almas (hermosas), unas aves (muertas), las aguas (frías), unas áreas (pequeñas), etc.

Lastly, the peculiar case of the word *arte*, whose singular form is masculine and plural form is feminine, as evidenced by the adjectives that modify them.

> *Ej.* el arte romano, las bellas artes

- **Nouns and their number**

You've already seen the basic rules for making nouns plural from their singular form (p.81), but there are a few curious types of nouns that don't follow these rules. Take a look.

> *Ej.* el robot/los robots (not robotes), el club/los clubs, el póster/los pósters, etc.

These words are taken directly from English and therefore usually use the plural form in English. The same is done in English with Spanish words: taco/tacos (not tacoes, like potatoes/tomatoes). Other plurals that are unique like their English counterparts are nouns ending in *is*. In these cases, the plural forms are the same as the singular forms. In English, the -is becomes -es.

> *Ej.* la crisis → las crisis – crisis → crises, la tesis → las tesis – thesis → theses, etc.

There are other singular nouns ending in *s* that don't have separate plural forms (*el/los bíceps, virus, clímax, lunes, martes, miércoles, jueves, viernes*, etc.) and most compound nouns (*el/los abrelatas, paraguas, sacapuntas, sujetapapeles*, etc.). Many singular nouns that end in *í* or *ú* (with an accent mark) have two acceptable plural forms, one following the rules and one breaking them.

> *Ej.* el colibrí → los colibríes/colibrís, el tabú → los tabúes/tabús, etc.

- **Adjectives also used as nouns**

You've learned about the nominalization (nouning) of adjectives (p.115), but some adjectives have been nominalized so frequently that they are now considered true nouns.

> *Ej.* La chica (niña/muchacha) compró una camisa muy chica (pequeña).
>   El optimista tiene perspectivas optimistas.
>   La giganta vieja es más giganta que todos los demás gigantes.

163

- **Adjective placement**

You should know by now that adjectives most often follow the nouns they modify (p.81). This provides descriptive contrast.

> *Ej.* la casa <u>grande</u> (as opposed to the small house)
> los ojos <u>verdes</u> (as opposed to brown or blue eyes)

The purpose of adjectives, however, is not always to show contrast. This is the case of inherent characteristics. Often these characteristics are inherent to an individual or specific noun, or are inherent given a certain situation or circumstance. In these cases, the adjective comes first.

> *Ej.* las <u>grandes</u> Montañas Rocosas (there are no small Rocky Mountains)
> los <u>fríos</u> inviernos de Alaska (there are no warm Alaskan winters)
> los <u>verdes</u> ojos de mi hermano (he doesn't have any other color eyes)
> los <u>altos</u> rascacielos de Nueva York (all skyscrapers, by definition, are tall)

Other types of adjectives almost always precede the noun.

> ➢ Adjectives indicating quantity, specific or general
>   *Ej.* <u>docientas</u> personas, <u>muchos</u> problemas, <u>otra</u> cosa, <u>primera</u> vez, <u>tanta</u> gente
> ➢ Short-form possessive adjectives
>   *Ej.* <u>nuestras</u> amigas, <u>tu</u> bici, <u>sus</u> mascotas
> ➢ mejor, peor, más, menos (with quantities, *más* and *menos* usually come after)
>   *Ej.* tu <u>mejor</u> amigo, su <u>peor</u> pesadilla, <u>menos</u> tiempo, <u>más</u> tacos, (tres tacos <u>más</u>)

Some adjectives have a different meaning based on where they are placed.

> *Ej.* carro <u>nuevo</u> (latest model), <u>nuevo</u> carro (new to the owner, synonymous with *otro*)
> color <u>diferente</u> (unusual: chartreuse), <u>diferente</u> color (synonymous with *otro*)
> amigo <u>viejo</u> (refers to friend's age), <u>viejo</u> amigo (refers to the age of the friendship)
> <u>pura</u> agua (only water), agua <u>pura</u> (free of contaminants)
> la <u>misma</u> presidenta (the same as before), la presidenta <u>misma</u> (the president herself)

- **A word (or several) about *mismo***

The word *mismo* means "same" in some contexts, but it is also used to add emphasis either in examples like the one above or in reflexive like constructions meaning "oneself."

> *Ej.* Mario me dio regalos a mí. (*a mí* adds emphasis)
> Yo me di regalos a mí <u>mismo</u>. (*mismo* is added when the verb is reflexive)

¡Ojo! Above, *mism<u>o</u>* is masculine. This means that the person speaking is masculine. If the person speaking were female, *mism<u>a</u>* would be used. For plural pronouns, use *mism<u>os</u>/<u>as</u>*.

> *Ej.* Yo me di regalos a mí <u>misma</u>. (female speaking)
> Marta y yo nos dimos regalos a nosotras <u>mismas</u>. (Marta and speaker are both female)

o **Common *mismo* pitfall**

Many English speakers try to translate "myself" as "my" – *mi* "self" – *mismo* as though *mismo* were a noun to be possessed. In the previous example, *mí* has an accent mark, which means it is a pronoun, and *mismo* is an adjective modifying that pronoun, not the other way around. So, "ourselves" would be <u>*nosotros mismos*</u>, not <u>*nuestros mismos*</u>.

Indirect-object pronouns:

me (a mí)
te (a ti)
le (a él/ella/Ud.)
nos (a nosotros/as)
os (a vosotros/as)
les (a ellos/ellas/Uds.)

Reflexive pronouns:

me (a mí mismo/a)
te (a ti mismo/a)
se (a sí mismo/a)
nos (a nosotros/as mismos/as)
os (a vosotros/as mismos/as)
se (a sí mismos/as)

Ej. Mario nos dio regalos a mí y a mis hermanos. (he gave us)
Mario se dio regalos a sí mismo. (he gave himself)
Nosotros nos dimos regalos los unos a los otros. (we gave each other)
Nosotros nos dimos regalos a nosotros mismos. (we gave ourselves)

Now that you have a handle on reflexive pronouns, which use the preposition *a*, let's look at examples of prepositional phrases with a couple other prepositions. The same concepts apply.

conmigo (with me)
contigo (with you)
con él/ella/Ud. (with him/her/you)
con nosotros/as (with us)
con vosotros/as (with you)
con ellos/ellas/Uds. (with them/you)

conmigo mismo/a (with myself)
contigo mismo/a (with yourself)
consigo / con él/ella/Ud. mismo/a
con nosotros/as mismos/as (with ourselves)
con vosotros/as mismos/as (with yourselves)
consigo / con ellos/ellas/Uds. mismos/as

¡Ojo! Con is a unique preposition (-*migo*, -*tigo*, -*sigo*); all others follow the pattern below. Also, like the pronoun *yo, conmigo, contigo,* and *consigo* end in *o*, but are not masculine. There's no separate feminine *yo* (*ya?*); there's no *conmig<u>a</u>, contig<u>a</u>,* or *consig<u>a</u>*.

para mí (for me)
para ti (for you)
para él/ella/Ud. (for him/her/you)
para nosotros/as (for us)
para vosotros/as (for you)
para ellos/ellas/Uds. (for them/you)

para mí mismo/a (for myself)
para ti mismo/a (for yourself)
para sí mismo/a (for himself/herself/yourself)
para nosotros/as mismos/as (for ourselves)
para vosotros/as mismos/as (for yourselves)
para sí mismos/as (for themselves/yourselves)

The word *mismo* is not limited to object pronouns; it can be used to emphasize subjects, too.

Ej. Yo mismo/a voy a preparar la cena. (I myself …)
Tú mismo/a puedes aprender español. (You yourself …)
Mario mismo quiere hacerlo. (Mario himself …)
Ellas mismas dieron la fiesta. (They themselves …)

- **Adjectives also used as adverbs**

Adjectives modify nouns and, in Spanish, agree with them in gender and number. Adverbs, on the other hand, modify verbs, adjectives, and other adverbs, and have no agreement with anything. Hopefully these concepts are not foreign to you any more, but there are always difficult cases. Navigating adverbs that double as adjectives, especially when modifying an adjective, is not exactly intuitive. Here are some of these adjectives, in their adjective forms.

> *Ej.* medio litro – half a liter   demasiado tiempo – too much time
> media hora – half an hour   demasiadas casas – too many houses
> pocos cambios – few changes   bastante viento – quite a bit of wind
> poca comida – little (not much) food   bastantes herramientas – enough tools

The masculine, singular forms of the adjectives above double as adverbs. Remember, regardless of the noun being modified, adverbs do not modify nouns, so gender and number are nonexistent.

> *Ej.* Los muchachos son *demasiado* perezosos. – The youngsters are *too* lazy.
> La gente está *demasiado* enojada. – The people are *too* angry.
> Nosotros estamos *medio* locos. – We are *kind of* crazy.
> Ellas son *medio* hermanas. – They are *half* sisters.
> Los panes son *poco* saludables. – Breads are *not very* healthful.
> La casa está *un poco* sucia. – The house is *a bit* dirty.
> Juanita es *bastante* talentosa. – She is *quite* talented.
> Mis tíos son *bastante* viejos. – My aunt and uncle are *quite* old.

- **Consecutive adjectives and adverbs**

In Spanish, you can use multiple adjectives to describe the same noun or string multiple adverbs together. In the case of adjectives, when not specifically distinguishing between two or more similar objects, you use *y* to separate the last two adjectives, and commas to separate the rest.

> *Ej.* La casa es grande, lujosa y muy cara.
> Los empleados son honestos y sinceros.

When specifically distinguishing between two or more similar objects, you may eliminate the commas and the *y*, the first adjectives being the ones the objects have in common and the last ones being the ones that differentiate them. In most cases, you'll limit it to two adjectives.

> *Ej.* No me gusta la casa grande <u>amarilla</u>, sino la casa grande <u>blanca</u>.

Stringing multiple adverbs together is fairly intuitive. Remember, you can add *-mente* to the end of the feminine, singular form of many adjectives to make them adverbs (p.92). If you have consecutive adverbs with the ending *-mente*, reserve the *-mente* for the final adverb.

> *Ej.* El candidato habla *bien mal.* (muy mal)
> ¡Los novios están *completamente* y *locamente* enamorados!
> Los socios presentaron el presupuesto *clara, concisa* y *eficazmente*.

166

- **Diminutives, superlatives, and other fun effects**

There are three common suffixes to form the diminutive of a word: *-ito/a*, *-illo/a*, and *-ico/a*. The difference between these suffixes is mostly regional, but *-ito/a* is the most universal. The purpose of a diminutive form is to describe something physically smaller than one might expect, make something seem less imposing or less direct, and/or to make something sound cute.

Ej. la mesa – the table　　　　　　la mesita – the little table
　　　　　　　　　　　　　　　　　la mesica – the little table
　　una pregunta – a question　　　una preguntita – a quick question
　　　　　　　　　　　　　　　　　una preguntilla – a quick question
　　los gatos – the cats　　　　　　los gatitos – the kittens / the tiny cats
　　Miguel – Michael　　　　　　　Miguelito – Mikey

Sometimes the suffix requires a *c*, which makes it easier to pronounce, but the rules governing this are speculative and are not universal; some people may use the *c*, whereas others may not.

Ej. un café – a coffee　　　　　un cafecito – a cup of coffee
　　un pueblo – a town　　　　　un pueblito – a small town
　　　　　　　　　　　　　　　un pueblecito – a small town
　　una vieja – an old woman　　una viejita – a little old lady
　　　　　　　　　　　　　　　una viejecita – a little old lady
　　pobre – poor　　　　　　　　pobrecito – (you) poor thing
　　　　　　　　　　　　　　　pobrecillo – (you) poor thing
　　un favor – a favor　　　　　un favorcito – a small favor

Diminutives are not limited to nouns; they can be adjectives or adverbs as well.

Ej. por favor – please　　　　　por favorcito – pretty please
　　perdón – I'm sorry　　　　　perdoncito – I'm so sorry
　　más o menos – okay / fine　　más o menitos – okay / fine (cuter)
　　adiós – bye　　　　　　　　adiosito – bye bye
　　pequeña – small　　　　　　pequeñita – really small
　　gordo – fat　　　　　　　　gordito – "kinda" fat / a "li'l fatty"

The smaller and cuter and less direct you want to be, the more *-it*'s you can add; there's no limit.

Ej. chiquitas – really small　　　chiquititas – really super small
　　rapidito – really quickly　　　rapiditito – really really quickly
　　un besito – a little kiss　　　un besitito – a li'l itty bitty kiss

A few diminutives are formed with *i*.

Ej. mamá → mami, papá → papi, chulo/a → chuli, Yolanda → Yoli, etc.

¡Ojo! Some nouns look like diminutives, but they have their own separate meanings.

> *Ej.* manzana – apple   manzanilla – chamomile
>   mesa – table   mesilla – nightstand

To have the opposite effect of the diminutive form, use the suffix *-ote/a*. This is called the augmentative and makes something seem bigger, more imposing, and/or more offensive. Notice the masculine form ends in *e*. For some words, adding *-ón* has this same effect.

> *Ej.* una palabra – a word   una palab<u>rota</u> – a swear word
>   una gorda – a fat woman   una gord<u>ota</u> – a big ol' fat woman
>   un abrazo – a hug   un abraz<u>ote</u> – a giant hug
>   un burrito – a burrito   un burr<u>ote</u> – a big burrito
>   un favor – a favor   un favorz<u>ote</u> – a huge favor
>   un problema – a problem   un problem<u>ón</u> – a big problem

The bigger, more imposing you want the word to be, the more *-ot*'s you can add.

> *Ej.* un burr<u>otote</u> – a big, fat burrito   un burr<u>ototote</u> – a big fat "honkin'" burrito
>   grand<u>ota</u> – huge   grand<u>otota</u> – crazy huge
>   un gat<u>ote</u> – a giant cat   un gat<u>otote</u> – an enormous cat

You can add these endings to adjectives and the nouns they modify for maximum effect. If you throw in the word *pero*, followed by a long pause, like you're struggling to believe it yourself, it's like saying, "and I mean *really* …"

> *Ej.* una casita pequeñita – a teeny, tiny house
>   Es una casita, pero pequeñita. – It's a tiny house, and I mean *really* tiny.
>   Es fuerte, ¡pero fuertote! – He's strong, and I mean *really* strong!

The prefix *requete-* or *re-*, for short, adds intensity to an adjective.

> *Ej.* ¡Ese gato es <u>requete</u>feo! – That cat is ugly as hell!
>   Estaba <u>re</u>cansada cuando llegué a casa. – I was super tired when I got home.
>   ¡Los modelos son <u>re</u>guapos! – The models are crazy good looking!

You've seen how to use one superlative form (p.135), but there is also a suffix that is considered another form of the superlative: *-ísimo/a*. Notice the accent mark on the antepenultimate (third-to-last) syllable. This superlative form is like adding "really" to an adjective.

> *Ej.* grande – big   grand<u>ísimo</u>/a – really big
>   buenas – good   buen<u>ísimas</u> – really good

As you might suspect, you can add "really" as many times as you want by adding more and more *is*'s. Feel free to go wild with this for comical effect, but remember your accent mark on the antepenultimate syllable.

> *Ej.* famos<u>ísima</u> – really famous   famosisis<u>ísima</u> – really, really, really famous
>   tont<u>ísimo</u> – really stupid   tontis<u>ísimo</u> – really, really stupid

Ser vs. estar

You've been working with *ser* and *estar* since the first couple units (pp.83, 97). You've seen several rules and many more examples, yet there is still more to understand. Both mean "to be," yet they are not interchangeable (of course there are a few exceptions). Let's review and expand.

- **Use *ser:***

  - to describe origin. (<u>Soy</u> de Nevada.)
  - to describe physical characteristics. (El carro <u>era</u> verde.)
  - to describe time. (<u>Eran</u> las 11:30 de la noche.)
  - to describe days. (Ayer <u>fue</u> jueves.)
  - to describe dates. (Mi cumpleaños <u>es</u> el 1 de abril.)
  - to describe character traits. (Alejandro <u>es</u> inteligente.)
  - to describe professions. (Itzel siempre <u>ha sido</u> profesora.)
  - to describe relationships. (Ellas <u>son</u> medio hermanas.)
  - to describe what something is made of. (El anillo <u>es</u> de platino.)
  - to describe events in the passive voice. (La casa <u>fue</u> destruida por la tormenta.)
  - to describe when or where an event takes place. (La fiesta <u>será</u> en mi casa.)

- **Use *estar*:**

  - to describe physical location. (<u>Estamos</u> en Colorado.)
  - to describe physical position. (<u>Estuvieron</u> acostadas.)
  - to describe ongoing action. (<u>Estaba</u> corriendo.)
  - to describe mental states of being. (<u>Estamos</u> locas.)
  - to describe emotional states of being. (<u>Estaban</u> deprimidos.)
  - to describe physical states of being. (La comida <u>está</u> caliente.)
  - to describe the result of an action. (La casa <u>está</u> destruida gracias al tornado.)
  - to describe what something is made of. (El rascacielos <u>está</u> *hecho* de acero y cemento.)
  - to describe what something looks like. (<u>Estás</u> guapa hoy.)
  - to describe a characteristic in contrast to expectations. (¡Guau, qué alto <u>está</u> tu hijo!)
  - to describe a temporary job. (Manuel <u>está</u> *de* mesero.)

¡Ojo! Thinking *ser* is permanent and *estar* is temporary is an oversimplified approach to understanding this breakdown that will lead you astray.

  Ej. Mi abuelo <u>está</u> muerto. (and not coming back) La casa <u>es</u> azul. (but could be painted)

Many adjectives change meaning depending on whether *ser* or *estar* is used. Here are a few.

	ser – to be	estar – to be
libre	free (a right / not jailed)	free (not busy or occupied)
aburrido/a	boring	bored
entretenido/a	entertaining	entertained
cansado/a	tiring	tired (worn out)
molesto/a	annoying (*molestoso*)	annoyed
vivo/a	a living being	alive
rico/a	rich (not poor)	delicious (food or experience, etc.)
verde	green	unripe
bueno/a	good	good (food – tasty, person – good looking)
malo/a	bad	sick
preparado/a	educated (schooling)	prepared (ready)
listo/a	clever / witty / smart	ready
seguro/a	safe (not dangerous)	sure / certain (person), safe (not in danger)
orgulloso/a	prideful	proud
loco/a	scatter-brained	crazy
atento/a	attentive / courteous	aware
consciente	conscientious	awake / conscious (not unconscious)

The following are a few adjectives that permit *ser* or *estar* without changing meanings.

> *Ej.* casado/a, soltero/a, viudo/a, ciego/a, manco/a, sordo/a,
> cojo/a (ser/estar cojo – disability, estar cojo – injury)

Haber – To Be (sort of)

You've been studying *haber* as an auxiliary (helping) verb in perfect tenses, but you first saw it in a completely different contex (p.95). Although it is the same verb in both cases, for all intents and purposes, it is different.

¡Ojo! In the following contexts, *haber* has no subject, therefore there is only one conjugation per tense. The thing that *is* is the direct object. Think of it as *tener*, without a subject.

> *Ej.* ¿Por qué buscar <u>problemas</u> donde no <u>los</u> hay? (hay/tengo una cosa – la hay / la tengo)

Indicativo:

presente – hay (there is/are)
pretérito – hubo (there was/were)
imperfect – había (there was/were, there used to be)
futuro – habrá (there will be)
condicional – habría (there would be)
presente perfecto – ha habido (there has/have been)
pluscuamperfecto – había habido (there had been)
futuro perfecto – habrá habido (there will have been)
condicional perfecto – habría habido (there would have been)

Subjuntivo:

presente – que haya (that there be)

imperfecto – que hubiera (that there be)

presente perfecto – que haya habido
pluscuamperfecto – que hubiera habido

Lo de "lo" – The Thing About "lo"

The word *lo* has multiple uses. You know it best as a direct-object pronoun and you may remember it as what some call the neuter form (p.135). There is another way you have used it hundreds of times by now, but probably don't fully grasp why. I'm referring to *lo siento*. This *lo* is an anaphoric reference, which is a word that refers to an idea previously stated in the conversation.

> *Ej.* Eugenio: <u>Mi gato ha muerto hoy</u>.
> Carmen: ¡Ay, no! <u>Lo</u> siento mucho.

- **Common *lo siento* pitfall**

The *lo* of *lo siento* refers to whatever was mentioned that you feel bad for, so if Carmen in the above example found out from someone else that Eugenio's cat had died, she wouldn't call up Eugenio out of the blue and say, "*Lo siento mucho.*" She would need to specify what she felt bad about, and she couldn't use *lo* ("*Lo siento mucho que tu gato haya muerto.*") because the cat's death would have not yet been mentioned in that conversation. Carmen, therefore, would say, "*Siento mucho que tu gato haya muerto.*"

The anaphoric *lo* is also commonly used with the verbs *ser* and *estar*. Notice that, in English, no word is necessary; the concept is simply omitted.

> *Ej.* Marta: Pepa, ¡eres <u>maleducada y molestosa</u>!
> Pepa: ¡No <u>lo</u> soy; <u>lo</u> eres tú! – No I'm not; you are!
>
> Arturo: ¿<u>Lista</u>, María?
> María: Sí, <u>lo</u> estoy. – Yes, I am (ready).

Knowing that the meanings of some adjectives depend on whether you use *ser* or *estar*, you could have some fun with the last example. The joke would be on the person who asked the question without specifying the intended (assumed) verb.

> *Ej.* Arturo: ¿<u>Lista</u>, María?
> María: Sí, <u>lo</u> soy. – Yes, I am *witty*.

Saber is another verb that, in theory, requires an anaphoric *lo*, but it is frequently omitted.

> *Ej.* Rigoberto: <u>¿A qué hora empieza el partido</u>?
> Catrina: No <u>lo</u> sé. (No sé.) – I don't know.

¡Ojo! The anaphoric *lo* has no gender or number as it is not a direct-object pronoun; it's always *lo*.

The *lo* in phrases like *lo chistoso es* (p.135) is, for all intents and purposes, the same as the anaphoric *lo*, but there needn't be any previous idea stated in that very conversation. Like in the title of this lesson, "*lo de*" is a very common phrase and means "the thing" or "the thing about."

> *Ej.* Estoy pensando en <u>lo de</u> ayer. No te preocupes de <u>lo de</u> tu jefe.

Unidad 30

La acentuación y la entonación – Accentuation and Intonation

➢ If the word **ends** in a **vowel**, *n*, or *s*, the stressed syllable (*sílaba tónica*) is the second-to-last. All other syllables in the word are unstressed (*sílabas átonas*).

ca<u>mi</u>na	
<u>co</u>rre	*palabras **llanas*** – words stressed on the **penultimate** syllable
ca<u>mi</u>nan	
<u>co</u>rres	no accent mark needed
calce<u>ti</u>nes	
vis<u>tie</u>ndo	
entrena<u>do</u>ra	

➢ If the word **ends** in **any other consonant**, the stressed syllable (*sílaba tónica*) is the last. All other syllables in the word are unstressed (*sílabas átonas*).

cami<u>nar</u>	
pa<u>red</u>	*palabras **agudas*** – words stressed on the **final** syllable
entrena<u>dor</u>	
su<u>til</u>	no accent mark needed

➢ If the word does not follow the first two rules, a written accent mark is needed to show which syllable is stressed (sílaba tónica).

<u>lá</u>piz	*palabra llana*: penultimate syllable stressed with accent mark; breaks 2nd rule
<u>cés</u>ped	*palabra llana*: penultimate syllable stressed with accent mark; breaks 2nd rule
televi<u>sión</u>	*palabra aguda*: final syllable stressed with accent mark; breaks 1st rule
so<u>fá</u>	*palabra aguda*: final syllable stressed with accent mark; breaks 1st rule
calce<u>tín</u>	*palabra aguda*: final syllable stressed with accent mark; breaks 1st rule
vis<u>tién</u>dome	*palabra **esdrújula***: antepenultimate syllable stressed w/accent mark; breaks 1st rule
<u>ú</u>til	*palabra llana*: penultimate syllable stressed with accent mark; breaks 2nd rule
cami<u>ná</u>bamos	*palabra **esdrújula***: antepenultimate syllable stressed w/accent mark; breaks 1st rule

las vocales fuertes/abiertas (strong/open vowels): **a, e, o, á, é, í, ó, ú**

las vocales débiles/cerradas (weak/closed vowels): **i, u, ü**

diptongo (two vowels pronounced in one syllable): vocal fuerte + vocal débil
                                                    vocal débil + vocal débil

c**ai**go	s**ei**s	c**iu**dad	contin**uo**	g**ua**nte	c**au**sar
c**ie**ncia	d**eu**da	c**ui**dado	peri**ó**dico	a**hu**mado (the *h* is not a factor)

el hiato/adiptongo (two vowels pronounced in different syllables): vocal fuerte + vocal fuerte

ca**e**r	v**e**o	ten**í**amos	contin**ú**o	c**ao**s	**oa**sis
oc**é**ano	**oe**ste	ca**í**da	le**í**do	almo**ho**a (the *h* is not a factor)

el triptongo (three vowels pronounced in a single syllable): vocal fuerte + dos vocales débiles

averig**üéi**s	g**uau**	limp**iau**ñas	sem**iau**tomático

- **Common intonation pitfalls**

When it comes to cognates or words that share their roots with a word in English, a common mistake is to stress the syllable that is stressed in the English word instead of following the rules.

Ej. ¿Qué sig·ni·fi·ca?   vs.   sig·ni·fi·cance → ¿Qué sig·ni·fi·ca?
Yo par·ti·ci·po …   vs.   par·ti·ci·pate   → Yo par·ti·ci·po …
Tú co·or·di·nas …   vs.   co·or·di·nate   → Tú co·or·di·nas …

In any given word, there can only be one tonic (stressed) syllable, the rest are atonic (unstressed). Adverbs with the suffix *-mente* are the unofficial exception to the rule. The syllable that would be stressed in the adjective form, before adding the suffix *-mente*, stays stressed and the penultimate (second-to-last) syllable of *-mente* is also stressed, following the rules on the previous page. If the adjective form has an accent mark, the corresponding adverb form retains that accent mark.

Ej. pro·ba·ble → pro·ba·ble·men·te
rá·pi·da   → rá·pi·da·men·te
fre·cuen·te → fre·cuen·te·men·te

Be careful not to assume the stressed and unstressed syllables alternate rhythmically. The following examples have back-to-back stressed syllables.

Ej. nor·mal → nor·mal·men·te (nor·mal·men·te)
co·mún → co·mún·men·te (co·mun·men·te)

A *clitic* is a single-syllable, unstressed word that is intonated as though it were attached to the word that either precedes it or follows it. This sounds ridiculous in English as we are accustomed to stressing any word or syllable that we want to add emphasis to. Spanish does not allow such freedom.

Ej. Mi ca·sa es su ca·sa. – In this common phrase, only the *ca* is stressed. Fight the urge to stress the contrast between possessive adjectives,
"Mi casa es su casa."

¿Pre·fie·res tu ca·fé con le·che o sin le·che? – I know you want to stress *con* and *sin*, as you probably did just now in your head, but native speakers would not stress these clitics in Spanish.

There is no hard and fast rule that I have ever come across for this, so you must listen intently to native Spanish speakers from around the world if you want to master this native intonation.

Ej. ¿Es pa·ra mí o pa·ra ti? – In this case, you should stress the *mí* and the *ti*.
Yo no lo quie·ro. – The *yo* could be stressed here, or not.
No lo quie·ro yo. – *Yo*, here, is placed at the end to be emphasized.

La pronunciación

As you can imagine, it's tough to teach pronunciation on paper. In the first unit (p.80), I gave you some rough basics to get you started, but mastery can only come through listening. Every country or region has a unique dialect, including pronunciation of certain letters. The biggest difference between accents in English is the way people pronounce vowels. In Spanish, vowel sounds are universal, but some consonants vary quite a bit. If you study phonetics in Spanish, you'll learn that some consonants have several unique sounds, like *n*, depending on the letters on either side of them. It isn't necessary—or practical—for the average person to learn phonetics to master pronunciation, so here are some advanced observations you can try to tune your ear to when listening to native speakers.

➢ There is no *schwa* /ə/ sound in Spanish. When pronouncing your vowels, try to open your mouth to an exaggerated, almost comical extent. This will keep *schwa* at bay.
  Ej. el<u>e</u>ph<u>a</u>nt (the underlined vowels here are the *schwa* sound in English, like "uh")
    <u>e</u>l<u>e</u>fant<u>e</u> (all three sound the same, like *ten* in Spanish)

➢ Vowels have only one sound each in Spanish.
  Ej. *a* is always *a* as in <u>agua</u>
    e is always *e* as in <u>eres</u> (*tres* and *seis* do not rhyme)
    i is always *i* as in <u>mi</u> (*idea* is a tricky one; give it a shot)
    o is always *o* as in <u>tomo</u>
    u is always *u* as in <u>uno</u> (never "yu" like "<u>u</u>se" in English)

➢ The *h* is silent, except in foreign words (*hockey*, *sushi*) and when preceded by *c* (*ch*). Pronounce words with *h* as though the *h* weren't there at all.
  Ej. "onor" (<u>h</u>onor), "carboidrato" (carbo<u>h</u>idrato), "desacer" (des<u>h</u>acer), etc.

➢ The *ch* sound in Spanish is almost universally like the "ch" sound in English in the word "change," but in northern Mexico, the *ch* sound is more like the "sh" sound in the English word "<u>sh</u>elf." "*Son las osho de la noshe.*" In Spain and Chile, there's a subtle "ts" sound to it.

➢ The *k* sound in *co*, *ca*, *cu*, *que*, and *qui*, is much softer than it is in English. It borders on an English "g" sound.

➢ The soft *g* sound and the *j* sound are identical to each other in Spanish, but there is quite a difference between countries in how harsh of a sound it makes. In Mexico, for example, it is very soft, like an English "h" in the word "hope." In Spain, on the other hand, it has a very harsh, scratchy, throaty sound.

➢ The hard *g* sound in Spanish ranges from a little more subtle than the English "g" sound to an almost silent sound, particularly when followed by *u*.

➢ The *y* and the *ll* sounds are identical to each other in many countries and range in sound from the English "y" in "yoyo," like in Mexico, to the English "j" in Joe, like in Colombia, and even the French "g" like in the word *bourgeoise*, like in Argentina. Some countries, however, distinguish between the two, like in Paraguay, where the *y* is like the Mexican *y* but the *ll* is pronounced like *ly* – "calye" (*calle*).

➢ The *t* in Spanish is much softer than the "t" in English.

➢ The *d* is also much softer, close to the "th" in the English "those."

➢ The *b* and *v* sounds in Spanish are identical to each other. The possible confusion leads people to give them nicknames "*b grande*" or "*b alta*" because it is the largest/tallest of the two, and "*v chica*" or "*v corta*" because it is the smallest/shortest of the two. Some even say, "*b de burro*" o "*v de vaca*." Their sound varies by dialect, but often lies somewhere between the "b" and "v" in English.

➢ The *p* so soft that it is often mistaken for *b* by native English speakers. A deliberate ear and increased literacy will help resolve this issue.

➢ The letter *n* in Spanish has at least six different pronunciations. The easiest one to teach on paper is the *m* sound it makes when followed by *p*, *b/v*, or *m*.
    Ej. "um poco" (un poco), "um bistec" (un bistec), "emviar" (enviar)

➢ The phonetic symbol *theta* /θ/ represents the *z* and soft *c* sounds. In central and northern Spain, these letters sound like the "th" in the English word "think." In southern Spain and the rest of the Spanish-speaking world, *z* and *c* are pronounced like *s*, which is known as "*el seseo*."
    Ej. "diethiséis" vs. "diesiséis" (dieciséis), "thapatos" vs. "sapatos" (zapatos)

➢ The letter *x* most often sounds like *ks*, – "ekstra" (extra), but in parts of Spain it sounds like *s* – "estra" (extra). In indigenous words in Mexico, it has an *s* sound (Xochimilco), a *j* sound (México), or an English "sh" sound (mexica).

➢ The *s* in Spain has a very soft hissing quality to it, whereas in Latin America, it is pronounced like an English "s." The exception to this is when it's followed by *b/v*, *d*, *g*, *m*, or *n*. In these cases, you may detect a subtle English "z" quality to it.
    Ej. "dezde" (desde), "muzgo" (musgo), "ezmeralda" (esmeralda)

➢ The non-rolling *r* sound is very similar to the English "d" sound. This non-rolling *r* is only found directly between vowels within the same word.
    Ej. pero, cara, güero, ira, gurú, para, arena, aro, etc.

➢ The rolling *r* sound comes from a double *r* (*rr*) between vowels, or a single *r* not between two vowels of the same word. The action of rolling the *r* is "*ronronear*."
    Ej. perro, carro, guerra, Raúl, risa, contra, enrollamos, lacra, coordina, etc.

    If the *r* is at the end of a word, it rolls, but without voice, whispered, like a cat's purr.
    Ej. bailar, escoger, salir, por, flor, etc.

➢ The *words* **y** and **o** become **e** and **u** when followed by *i* and *o* sounds respectively. These are formal, written changes but stem from pronunciation issues.
    Ej. español y̶ **e** inglés, oxígeno y̶ **e** hidrógeno
        uno o̶ **u** otro, siete o̶ **u** ocho, adiós o̶ **u** hola

Remember that *c* and *g* have hard and soft sounds and that *z*, *qu* and *j* share phonetic spellings with them respectively (p.108). Adding *u* or *ü* to *g* rounds out the list.

> *Ej.* ga (ponga), go (digo), gu (gurú), gue (guerra), gui (guía)
> gua (agua), guo (contiguo), ~~guu~~, güe (bilingüe), güi (pingüino)
> ja (naranja), jo (José), ju (jugo), ge (general) / je (jerarquía), gi (gigante) / ji (jirafa)
> ca (casa), co (color), cu (culebra), que (queso), qui (quiero)
> cua (cualidad), cuo (inocuo), ~~cuu~~, cue (cuero), cui (cuidado)
> za (zapato), zo (comienzo), zu (azúcar), ce (celebrar), ci (cierro)

In just about every case, the goal is to maintain the same sound, not the same letter, when going back and forth from one form of a word to another.

> *Ej.* jue**go** → jue**gue**   averi**gua** → averi**güe**
> esco**ge** → esco**jo**   alo**ja** → alo**je** (no reason to change to *g*)
> ata**ca** → ata**que**   Puerto Rico → puertorri**que**ño
> ven**ce** → ven**zo**   comien**za** → comien**ces** (see note below about *ze*)

¡Ojo! Ze and zi are used in foreign words and archaic spellings (*zigzaguear, zebra, enzima*, etc.).

El alfabeto / el abecedario

There are 27 letters in the Spanish alphabet: the 26 English letters and *ñ*; *k* and *w* are used only for foreign words (*kilo, whisky*, etc.). There used to be 30, but *ch, ll*, and *rr* were eliminated in 1994. The only impact this change had on the language was alphabetical order (*cara, chino, coche* was *cara, coche, chino*). Unnecessary accent marks on monosyllabic words were also eliminated at the same time (*sóis, váis, véis, dáis, vé, fué, fuí, ví, vió, dí, dió, ó*, etc.) These changes were made to simplify the language. Note: *sé, él, tú, sí, té, dé, más*, etc. kept their accent marks for contrast with other words: *se, el, tu, si, te, de, mas*, etc.

a – *a*	**ñ** – *eñe*	**á** – *a con acento*
b – *be*	**o** – *o*	**é** – *e con acento*
c – *ce*	**p** – *pe*	**í** – *i con acento*
d – *de*	**q** – *cu*	**ó** – *o con acento*
e – *e*	**r** – *ere / erre*	**ú** – *u con acento*
f – *efe*	**s** – *ese*	
g – *ge*	**t** – *te*	**ü** – *u con crema* (or *con diéresis*)
h – *hache*	**u** – *u*	
i – *i* (*latina / romana*)	**v** – *ve / uve* (España)	
j – *jota*	**w** – *doble ve / ve doble / uve doble* (España) / *doble u*	
k – *ka*	**x** – *equis*	
l – *ele*	**y** – *i griega / ye*	**ch** – *ce hache* (formerly *che*)
m – *eme*	**z** – *zeta*	**ll** – *doble ele* (formerly *elle*)
n – *ene*		**rr** – *doble ere* (formerly *erre*)

la letra – letter	la sílaba – syllable	la palabra – word
la vocal – vowel	la hache – the letter h	la letra minúscula – lowercase letter
la consonante – consonant	la jota – the letter j	la letra mayúscula – capital letter

Irregular Conjugations That Stem From Pronunciation Issues

You've seen some irregular gerund forms (p.121) that require a *y* to break up the otherwise weak pronunciation of *aiendo* and *eiendo*. This ($i \rightarrow y$) change makes these words easier to pronounce.

> *Ej.* traer → trayendo, leer → leyendo, ir → yendo, etc.

Although some words, like *compañia*, have *ñ* followed by *í* (*i* with accent mark) and a vowel, verbs ending in *ñir* lose their *i* (*i* without accent mark) for the preterite *ió/ieron*, the gerund *iendo*, and the imperfect subjunctive *iera, ieras, iéramos*, etc. to avoid the weak pronunciation of *ñ* followed by *i* (*i* without accent mark) and a vowel.

teñir (e → i) – to dye

preterite

teñí	teñimos
teñiste	teñisteis
tiñó	tiñeron

gerund

tiñendo

imperfect subjunctive

tiñera	tiñéramos
tiñeras	tiñerais
tiñera	tiñeran

gruñir – to grunt / to growl

preterite

gruñí	gruñimos
gruñiste	gruñisteis
gruñó	gruñeron

gerund

gruñendo

imperfect subjunctive (alternate)

gruñese	gruñésemos
gruñeses	gruñeseis
gruñese	gruñesen

The verb *yacer* has three acceptable conjugations for the *yo* form: *yazco, yazgo, yago* due to pronunciation doubts. The verb *erguir* has two acceptable conjugations for the same reason.

erguir (e → i) – to straighten up / to put upright

present indicative

yergo / irgo	erguimos
yergues / irgues	erguís
yergue / irgue	yerguen / irguen

present subjunctive

yerga / irga	yergamos / irgamos
yergas / irgas	yergáis / irgáis
yerga / irga	yergan / irgan

The **imperative** follows the same patterns above. See p.183 for more on *nosotros* and *vosotros*.

(+) yo: ------------	**(+) nosotros:** yergamos / irgamos (basically subjunctive)
(–) yo: ------------	**(–) nosotros:** no yergamos / irgamos (basically subjunctive)
(+) tú: yergue / irgue	**(+) vosotros:** erguid (as with *tú*, not simply subjunctive)
(–) tú: no yergas / irgas	**(–) vosotros:** no yergáis / irgáis (basically subjunctive)
(+) Ud.: yerga / irga	**(+) Uds.:** yergan / irgan
(–) Ud.: no yerga / irga	**(–) Uds.:** no yergan / irgan

Querid@ estudiante,

 ¡Felicidades! ¡Lo has hecho: has cumplido con todo y lo sabes todo! Ahora, eres capaz de hablar de cualquier tema de interés, sin error alguno ni malentendido, con todos los hablantes nativos de español de todo el mundo, incluso a pesar de la jerga, de su acento, de su formación, y de las expresiones idiomáticas que usen de todas las épocas de la historia del mundo.

 ¡No te creas! Apenas has comenzado. Ahora tienes la base para seguir aprendiendo sin guía. Has leído mucho y has aprendido un montón, la verdad, pero siempre habrá más para aprender. Siempre. Es imposible poner todo lo que haya para aprender en un solo libro. Te dejo con unas últimas lecciones a continuación, pero sigue repasando todas las lecciones y listas de vocabulario de este libro mismo. El resto es responsabilidad tuya. Échale ganas al mundo. Viaja. Explora el idioma. Ve a conocer mucha gente. Toma más clases de español. Lee revistas en español, escucha la radio en español, estudia la música en español, mira la tele y muchas películas en español, escribe en español, lee literatura y poesía en español y aun piensa en español. Nunca dejes de avanzar porque todo lo que has adquirido se te puede perder. No te olvides: allá donde fueres, haz lo que vieres.

       Abrazotes,

       David

Unidad X

Los múltiples usos del "se"

The pronoun *se* may not seem complicated, but it is one of the most versatile words in the Spanish language and, therefore, one of the most difficult to master. You've seen it many times over as a reflexive pronoun (pp.99-101, 110-112), often translated as "oneself" (*llamarse, acostarse*) but frequently impossible to translate (*morirse, reírse*), but that's just one of its uses. In addition to the reflexive *se*, there is also the passive *se* and the impersonal *se*.

- ### El "se" pasivo y la voz pasiva (ser + participio pasado)

You've seen the past participle as an adjective (pp.136-137) but, so far, only with the verb *estar* to show a state of being or the result of an action. With few exceptions, the same past participle can also be used with the verb *ser*, but, in this context, it creates a passive voice for the action itself. The passive voice is a way of describing an action without needing to reference—or even know— the one who did the action. In the passive voice, the subject of the verb is what would otherwise be the direct object of the active voice.

> *Ej.* The house was built in 1964. (passive voice)
> My dad built the house in 1964. (active voice)

In the passive voice, the house is the subject; in the active voice, the house is the direct object.

> *Ej.* La casa fue construida en 1964. (voz pasiva)
> Mi papá construyó la casa en 1964. (voz activa)

It's important to note that the past participle (adjective) must agree with the subject in gender and number and the verb *ser* must be conjugated, likewise, according to that subject. If you do want to reference the person/thing responsible for the action, use *por* (by).

> *Ej.* Nosotras fuimos lesionadas anoche *por* el granizo.
> Los idiomas han sido estudiados *por* los lingüistas durante siglos.

The passive *se* can often be substituted for the passive construction above but not in every case, and you cannot assign responsibility with the passive *se* due to the nature of its agreement with the subject. Although it isn't reflexive semantically, grammatically it acts as though it were. As with the reflexive *se*, the passive *se* encompasses all six pronouns: *me, te, se, nos, os, se*.

> *Ej.* Nosotras nos lesionamos anoche.
> (~~We injured ourselves last night.~~ We were injured last night.)
>
> Los idiomas se han estudiado durante siglos.
> (~~Languages have studied themselves ....~~ Languages have been studied for centuries.)

- **El "se" impersonal**

Surely you've asked, "*¿Cómo se dice …?*" and seen a sign that says, "*Se habla español.*" Are you asking how something says itself? Does the sign mean that Spanish speaks itself? Of course not, so the use of *se* in these examples is certainly not reflexive. Do they mean that something gets said or that Spanish gets spoken? Perhaps. Prescriptive linguists (those whose mission it is to tell people how to speak) might argue that the impersonal *se* doesn't exist, that it is simply the passive *se*. Descriptive linguists (those whose mission is to describe how people speak) would argue that the impersonal *se* most definitely exists as evidenced by the verb's lack of agreement with the subject in signs around the Spanish-speaking world.

Signs like "*Se vende bicicletas*" and "*Se busca empleados*" are commonplace around the Spanish-speaking world. Could it be that all of them are grammatically incorrect because "*vende/bicicletas*" and "*busca/empleados*" don't agree? I'll let you decide.

If you don't accept the existence of the impersonal *se*, then you would argue that the signs *should* say "*Se vende̲n bicicletas*" and "*Se busca̲n empleados.*"

If you accept the existence of the impersonal *se* as grammatically correct simply because hundreds of millions of Spanish speakers couldn't all be wrong, then let's simply describe it.

If you substitute *se* with *uno*, you get:

"~~Se~~ Uno dice …"	"~~Se~~ Uno habla español"
"~~Se~~ Uno vende bicicletas"	"~~Se~~ Uno busca empleados"

Boom! Now there's no problem grammatically because *uno* is your subject and all your verbs are 3rd person, singular. So there you have it: the impersonal *se* is a 3rd person, singular subject that means *uno*. We don't know who, but we do know it is some*one* impersonal.

Not so fast: does this answer hold up under scrutiny? Can we test it against any other grammatical conventions? What happens if we were to make these statements negative? Would our syntax (word order) hold up?

"*Uno no̲ dice …*" → "*Se no̲ dice …*" ??? Nope!
"*Uno no̲ habla español*" → "*Se no̲ habla español*" ??? No way!
"*Uno no̲ vende bicicletas*" → "*Se no̲ vende bicicletas*" ??? You're kidding, right?
"*Uno no̲ busca empleados*" → "*Se no̲ busca empleados*" ??? What?! NO!

And what happens if our verb is also reflexive? We obviously *have* to use *uno*, not *se*.

"*Cuando uno̲ se levanta temprano …*" → "*Cuando se se levanta temprano …*" ??? 'fraid not!
"*Si uno̲ se siente mal …*" → "*Si se se siente mal …*" ??? C'mon, stop messin' around!!

So, is the impersonal *se* just an internationally rampant grammatical error or a curious grammatical phenomenon? You're the expert now; it's time to decide for yourself!

- **Los accidentes – ¿culpable o víctima?**

In English, especially as children, we say things like, "it fell" and "it broke." Maybe the wind blew it over and it broke, but maybe it broke because I wasn't being careful with it. We turn the object into the subject to avoid blame, express that it was an accident, or illustrate that we were somehow the victim of the incident. This linguistic technique is much more common in Spanish than it is in English. The action verbs are reflexive and our part in it is as the indirect object (the victim of the accident). Common verbs include: olvidarse, caerse, perderse, romperse, ocurrirse, hacerse, and dificultarse. Don't forget R.I.D. (pp.117, 127).

> *Ej.* El vaso se cayó. – The glass fell. (no one had anything to do with it)
> El vaso se me cayó. – I had something to do with its falling. Maybe I bumped it by
> accident or maybe it landed on me.
> Dejé caer el vaso. – I held it out and let it go on purpose.
>
> Las ventanas se rompieron. – The windows broke (got broken).
> Las ventanas se le rompieron a Abel. – Abel had something to do with it. Maybe he
> was carrying them or maybe he fell onto them.
> Abel rompió las ventanas. – Abel threw a rock at them or kicked them on purpose.
>
> Se nos olvidó el pastel. – We forgot the cake (but please don't be angry with us).
> Olvidamos el pastel. – This could imply we intended to forget it, which would be rare.
> Olvídalo. – Forget it. (someone telling you to forget about it intentionally)
>
> Se les perdieron las llaves. – They lost their keys and we feel bad for them.
> Perdieron sus llaves. – It may be the same as above, but maybe they lost them in a bet.

¡Ojo! The noun that fell, got broken, forgotten, or lost is the subject of the reflexive verb: *La llave se perdió* or *las llaves se perdieron.* Also, like with most verbs, the subject can be placed before or after the verb: *Se me olvidó el regalo* or *El regalo se me olvidó.* This technique can be done in all tenses and moods.

> *Ej.* No se te olviden los regalos. – Don't forget the presents. (modo imperativo)
> No creo que se te olviden. – I don't think you'll forget them. (subjuntivo del presente)
> Se me ha ocurrido que … – It has occurred to me that … (indicativo, presente perfecto)
> ¿Se os dificulta correr tanto? – Is it difficult for you guys to run so much?
> Se nos hace cada vez más tonto. – It seems/gets more and more stupid to us.

You don't have to be talking about accidents to combine reflexive verbs with indirect objects.

> *Ej.* Se me acercó. – She approached me. (acercarse – to approach)
> Me le acerqué. – I approached her.

Some people may perceive a subtle difference between some verbs and their reflexive form.

> *Ej.* caer – to fall (towards the ground), caerse – to fall (accidentally, like to slip or to trip)
> morir – to die (general), morirse – to die (of natural causes)

Los verbos (el futuro como especulación)

You've seen the simple future tense and its most common use: the future of the present, just like in English (p.141). Another common use of the simple future tense is to speculate or wonder. The phrase "I wonder" could be translated as *me pregunto*, and to say, "I ask myself" would also make sense in English, but that is not the only way to speculate or wonder in Spanish. That's where the simple future tense comes in.

Imagine this scenario: you and your friends are out at the park playing soccer. No one has a wristwatch anymore and no one brought their cellphone to the game. After seemingly hours of playing, one player turns to the other players and says, "I wonder what time it is." The person making that statement is making the assumption that no one knows exactly, but invites the speculation from the group. In Spanish, the simple future tense is used and phrased in the form of a question. If you want to respond with speculation, saying, "I bet," just make it a statement.

> *Ej.* I wonder what time it is.   (Me pregunto) ¿Qué hora será?
> Could it be after 8:00?   (Me pregunto) ¿Serán las ocho pasadas?
> I bet it's around 7:30.   Serán las siete y media.

No one knows for sure, but that doesn't stop anyone from speculating. Certainly, they could say, "*No lo sé, que no tengo reloj conmigo,*" but where is the fun in that?

Imagine another scenario: you and a friend are hanging out at your house, watching a movie late at night. Suddenly, you both hear a knock at the door. You aren't expecting company and it's too late for it to be a political canvasser. You don't ask your friend, "*¿Quién es?*" because you know your friend has less of a clue than you; it's your house, after all. So, naturally, you speculate.

> *Ej.* Who could that be?   (Me pregunto) ¿Quién será?
> Maybe it's the neighbor.   (Me pregunto) ¿Será un vecino?

This speculation works for any verb, not just *ser*.

> *Ej.* I wonder how old they are.   (Me pregunto) ¿Cuántos años tendrán?
> I wonder what's for dinner.   (Me pregunto) ¿Qué habrá de cenar?
> I bet he comes here every day.   Vendrá acá todos los días.

What if you want to speculate about the past? You got it: you use the conditional tense.

> *Ej.* I wonder what she did for a living.   (Me pregunto) ¿A qué se dedicaría?
> I wonder why it was closed.   (Me pregunto) ¿Por qué estaría cerrado?

This works for the future and conditional perfect tenses, too.

> *Ej.* I bet he's sold his car.   Habrá vendido su carro.
> I wonder if he'd already seen it.   (Me pregunto) ¿Lo habría visto ya?

Los verbos (el imperativo) – nosotros y vosotros

By now, you are quite familiar with commands (pp.129-132) and how they compare to and contrast with the indicative and subjunctive moods. You are now ready to learn the last two pieces of the puzzle: *nosotros* and *vosotros*. Whereas the *vosotros* form is a true command, the *nosotros* form is more of a suggestion to a group that includes the speaker (exhortative). The best translation is "Let's ____." That said, *let's* fill in the gaps from a previous chart (p.131).

apoy*ar*

(+) **yo:** ------------   (+) **nosotros:**   apoy*emos* (basically subjunctive)
(–) **yo:** ------------   (–) **nosotros:** <u>no</u> apoy*emos* (basically subjunctive)

(+) **tú:**   apoy*a*   (+) **vosotros:**   apoy*ad* (as with *tú*, not simply subjunctive)
(–) **tú:** <u>no</u> apoy*es*   (–) **vosotros:** <u>no</u> apoy*éis* (basically subjunctive)

resolv*er* (o → ue)

(+) **yo:** ------------   (+) **nosotros:**   resolv*amos* (basically subjunctive)
(–) **yo:** ------------   (–) **nosotros:** <u>no</u> resolv*amos* (basically subjunctive)

(+) **tú:**   resuelv*e*   (+) **vosotros:**   resolv*ed* (as with *tú*, not simply subjunctive)
(–) **tú:** <u>no</u> resuelv*as*   (–) **vosotros:** <u>no</u> resolv*áis* (basically subjunctive)

influ*ir* (y)

(+) **yo:** ------------   (+) **nosotros:**   influy*amos* (basically subjunctive)
(–) **yo:** ------------   (–) **nosotros:** <u>no</u> influy*amos* (basically subjunctive)

(+) **tú:**   influy*e*   (+) **vosotros:**   influ*id* (as with *tú*, not simply subjunctive)
(–) **tú:** <u>no</u> influy*as*   (–) **vosotros:** <u>no</u> influy*áis* (basically subjunctive)

Some argue that the only "true" command forms are *tú* and *vosotros*, affirmative forms, all the rest being simply the subjunctive. While that is a legitimate way to look at it, that argument breaks down with the placement of object pronouns in the affirmative command forms.

imperativo: (nosotros) apoyémos<u>lo</u>   **subjuntivo:** (nosotras) que <u>lo</u> apoyemos
             (vosotros) apoyad<u>lo</u>   (vosotras) que <u>lo</u> apoyéis
             (ustedes) apóyen<u>lo</u>   (ustedes) que <u>lo</u> apoyen

imperativo: (nosotros) resolvámos<u>la</u>   **subjuntivo:** (nosotras) que <u>la</u> resolvamos
             (vosotros) resolved<u>la</u>   (vosotras) que <u>la</u> resolváis
             (ustedes) resuélvan<u>la</u>   (ustedes) que <u>la</u> resuelvan

When the pronouns attached to the *nosotros* command form begin with *se* (pp.117, 127), the first *s* is dropped.

             conseguir (e → i) (e → i)   comprar

(+)   consigámo<u>se</u>las (consigamos<u>se</u>las)   (+)   comprémo<u>se</u>lo (compremos<u>se</u>lo)
(–) no <u>se</u> las consigamos   (–) no <u>se</u> lo compremos

Although the double *s* is not permitted, there is no problem with double *n*, which you encounter when combining *nos* with the *Uds.* command form.

conseguir (e → i) (e → i)   **comprar**

(+)   consígan<u>nos</u>la   (+)   cómpren<u>nos</u>los
(–) no <u>nos</u> la consigan   (–) no <u>nos</u> <u>los</u> compren

Similar to the cases of double *s* on the previous page, watch what happens to affirmative commands of reflexive verbs for *nosotros* and *vosotros*: the *s* and *d*, respectively, are dropped.

dormirse (o → ue) (o → u)   **sentarse (e → ie)**

(+)   durmámo<u>nos</u> (durmámo~~s~~<u>nos</u>)   (+)   sentémo<u>nos</u> (sentémo~~s~~nos)
(–) no <u>nos</u> durmamos   (–) no nos sentemos

(+)   dormí<u>os</u> (dormi~~d~~os)   (+)   senta<u>os</u> (senta~~d~~os)
(–) no <u>os</u> durmáis   (–) no <u>os</u> sentéis

There is one exception to the rule above for reflexive verbs in the *vosotros* form: *irse*. Instead of dropping the *d*, the correct affirmative form is *idos*.

You've noticed that the affirmative *vosotros* commands are formed by replacing the *r* of the infinitive with a *d. apoyar → apoyad, resolver → resolved, influir → influid,* etc. The coolest thing about this is that there are no exceptions. *ser → sed, ver → ved, ir → id*

Remember our list of irregulars whose *yo* forms in the present had a unique conjugation (p.132)? With the affirmative forms of *vosotros* being all regular, and the rest being, with the exception of pronoun placement, the same as the subjunctive, the gaps in our chart are easy to fill in.

salir	(+) vosotros: salid	(–) no salgáis	(+/–) nosotras: salgamos
tener	(+) vosotros: tened	(–) no tengáis	(+/–) nosotros: tengamos
poner	(+) vosotras: poned	(–) no pongáis	(+/–) nosotros: pongamos
traer	(+) vosotras: traed	(–) no traigáis	(+/–) nosotros: traigamos
hacer	(+) vosotras: haced	(–) no hagáis	(+/–) nosotros: hagamos
ver	(+) vosotros: ved	(–) no veáis	(+/–) nosotros: veamos
venir	(+) vosotros: venid	(–) no vengáis	(+/–) nosotros: vengamos
decir	(+) vosotras: decid	(–) no digáis	(+/–) nosotros: digamos
ser	(+) vosotras: sed	(–) no seáis	(+/–) nosotros: seamos
dar	(+) vosotros: dad	(–) no deis	(+/–) nosotras: demos

Although predictable in the *vosotras* forms, the *nosotras* forms of *ir* and *irse* have alternatives.

ir	(+) vosotras: id	(–) no vayáis	(+/–) nosotros: vayamos / vamos
irse	(+) vosotras: idos	(–) no os vayáis	(+/–) nosotros: vayámo<u>nos</u> / vámo<u>nos</u>

With all the dropped letters and exceptions, you see why I separated these two from the rest.

184

Los verbos (el voseo) – Verbs (the use of *vos*)

Vosotros, used in the Castilian dialect (central and northern Spain), is an alternative to the 2nd person, plural form *ustedes*. Likewise, in many countries, there is an alternative to the 2nd person, singular form *tú*. While not universal, this alternative is called *vos* and is used in at least one region of almost every country in Central and South America. According to the *Real Academia Española*, these countries are Argentina, Bolivia, Chile, Colombia, Costa Rica, Ecuador, El Salvador, Guatemala, Honduras, Nicaragua, Paraguay, Uruguay, and Venezuela.

The conjugations for *vos* are the same as those for *tú*, with the exception of the indicative of the present tense and affirmative commands. Even though Spain uses *vosotros*, but not *vos*, and the countries that use *vos* do not use *vosotros*, their conjugations share morphological origins, as do the words themselves: *vosotros* (*vos* + *otros*).

	vosotros (present / [+] command)		**vos (present / [+] command)**
caminar	camináis / caminad	→ (drop the *i* and *d*) →	caminás / caminá
comer	coméis / comed	→ (drop the *i* and *d*) →	comés / comé
vivir	vivís / vivid	→ (no change, drop the *d*) →	vivís / viví
pensar	pensáis / pensad	→ (drop the *i* and *d*) →	pensás / pensá
volver	volvéis / volved	→ (drop the *i* and *d*) →	volvés / volvé
pedir	pedís / pedid	→ (no change, drop the *d*) →	pedís / pedí
estar	estáis / estad	→ (drop the *i* and *d*) →	estás / está
dar	dais / dad	→ (drop the *i* and *d*) →	das / da
tener	tenéis / tened	→ (drop the *i* and *d*) →	tenés / tené
poner	ponéis / poned	→ (drop the *i* and *d*) →	ponés / poné
traer	traéis / traed	→ (drop the *i* and *d*) →	traés / traé
hacer	hacéis / haced	→ (drop the *i* and *d*) →	hacés / hacé
ver	veis / ved	→ (drop the *i* and *d*) →	ves / ve
ser	sois / sed	→ (drop the *i* and *d*) →	sos / sé
venir	venís / venid	→ (no change, drop the *d*) →	venís / vení
decir	decís / decid	→ (no change, drop the *d*) →	decís / decí
salir	salís / salid	→ (no change, drop the *d*) →	salís / salí
ir	vais / id	→ (drop the i, change the verb) →	vas / andá (just like *andar*)

¡Ojo! Neither *vosotros* nor *vos* observes stem changes. The written accent marks on the *vos* forms are necessary to maintain the emphasis on the same syllables as those of *vosotros*.

Finally, let's look at reflexive verbs.

sentarse	os sentáis / sentaos	→ (drop the *i* and *d*) →	te sentás / sentate
ponerse	os ponéis / poneos	→ (drop the *i* and *d*) →	te ponés / ponete
vestirse	os vestís / vestíos	→ (no change, drop the *d*) →	te vestís / vestite

Los tiempos verbales y sus funciones

We have seen how the indicative mood corresponds to the subjunctive mood across all tenses (p.161), but *why* and *how* we choose to use a given tense in the first place may still warrant some additional clarification and summary. The following chart shows each verb tense in its corresponding mood and the temporal (time) function it serves.

Mood	el indicativo	Function (it's used to talk about …)	el subjuntivo	el imperativo
				(mandatos)
	el presente	the PRESENT of the PRESENT	el presente	------------
Simple	el pretérito	the PAST of the PRESENT	------------	------------
Verb	el imperfecto	the PRESENT of the PAST	el imperfecto	------------
Tenses	el futuro	the FUTURE of the PRESENT	------------	------------
	el condicional	the FUTURE of the PAST	------------	------------
Compound	el presente perfecto	the PAST of the PRESENT	el presente perfecto	------------
Verb	el pluscuamperfecto	the PAST of the PAST	el pluscuamperfecto	------------
Tenses	el futuro perfecto	the PAST of the FUTURE	------------	------------
(*haber*)	el condicional perfecto	the PAST of the FUTURE of the PAST	------------	------------

Las citas directas e indirectas (indicativo) – Direct & Indirect Quotes

A direct quote is someone's exact words, whereas an indirect quote is a paraphrasing of those words, making all necessary and relevant changes to verb tenses and person (1st, 2nd, 3rd). I've given you a handful of examples of how indirect quotes work (pp.152, 155), but let's look at the full gamut across all thirteen tenses, starting with the indicative mood.

Cita directa: Cita indirecta:

el presente   **el imperfecto**
    Ej. "Yo no lo quiero hacer".   →   Dijo que él no lo quería hacer.
    "¿Te gusta o no?"   →   Preguntó que si me gustaba o no.

el futuro   **el condicional**
    Ej. "Iré el sábado".   →   Dijo que ella iría el sábado.
    "¿Estaréis cansados?"   →   Preguntó que si estaríamos cansados.

el presente perfecto / el pretérito   **el pluscuamperfecto**
    Ej. "Te hemos llamado 5 veces".   →   Dijeron que me habían llamado 5 veces.
    "Uds. salieron antes que yo.   →   Dijo que habíamos salido antes que él.

el futuro perfecto   **el condicional perfecto**
    Ej. "Yo ya me habré graduado".   →   Dijiste que ya te habrías graduado.
    "¿Habrás comido?"   →   Pregunté que si habrías comido.

Note that all nine verb tenses in the indicative are covered above. If you were to paraphrase the words of someone using the tenses in the right column, the verb tenses would remain the same.
    Ej. "Yo no lo quería hacer".   →   Dijo que él no lo quería hacer.

Las citas directas e indirectas (imperativo → subjuntivo) – Direct & Indirect Quotes

We've seen how the imperative (Unidades 19-20) and subjunctive (Unidades 23-28) resemble each other in their conjugations (*hable*, *escriba*, *ponga*, *sea*, *vaya*, etc.) as well as whether, by their nature, the verbs in question will ever find their way to our timeline or forever go undone. Let's see their relation to each other through the lens of direct and indirect quotes. When the direct quote is a command (the imperative), the resulting indirect quote must be the subjunctive. While the command (the words that were uttered) may be in the past, the verb tense you choose is a matter of whether the command is seen as a standing order until it is carried out (*presente*) or the window of time to comply has come and gone (*imperfecto*).

Cita directa:		Cita indirecta:
tú, vos, Ud. (2ª persona, singular)		**yo (1ª persona, singular)**
Ej. "Habla más". (tú)	→	Me dice que hable más. (standing order)
"Hablá más". (vos)	→	Me dijo que hablara más. (over and done)
"Hable más". (Ud.)		
Ej. "¡Hazlo!" (tú)	→	Me dice que lo haga. (standing order)
"¡Hacelo!" (vos)	→	Me dijo que lo hiciera. (over and done)
"¡Hágalo!". (Ud.)		
Ej. "Siéntate, por favor". (tú)	→	Me dice que me siente. (standing order - *jaja*)
"Sentate, por favor". (vos)	→	Me dijo que me sentara. (over and done)
"Siéntese, por favor". (Ud.)		
vosotros/as, Uds. (2ª persona, plural)		**nosotros/as (1ª persona, plural)**
Ej. "Paraos". (vosotros/as)	→	Nos dice que nos paremos. (standing order)
"Párense". (Uds.)	→	Nos dijo que nos paráramos. (over and done)
Ej. "No vayáis". (vosotros/as)	→	Nos dice que no vayamos. (standing order)
"No vayan". (Uds.)	→	Nos dijo que no fuéramos. (over and done)
Ej. "Esperadme". (vosotros/as)	→	Nos dice que la esperemos. (standing order)
"Espérenme". (Uds.)	→	Nos dijo que la esperáramos. (over and done)

The above examples are simple sentences (one subject and verb) to focus on the lesson at hand, but you can imagine how complicated things could get with compound sentences (more than one subject and verb), which means you might need a dash of indicative with a splash of subjunctive.

Ej. Ale – Pídele a tu amiga que me llame si quiere una entrevista.
Marisol – Sale pues, lo haré.

Dos semanas más tarde ...

Ale – Te dije que le pidieras a tu amiga que me llamara si quería una entrevista, ¿verdad?
Marisol – Sí, y te dije que lo haría. ¿Por qué me preguntas? ¿Es que no te ha llamado?

Los verbos con preposición

Mastering prepositions in another language is a tall task. Between English and Spanish, you can't simply learn a single translation for each preposition and call it a day unless you want to sound like a foreigner forever. In one context, one translation may work, but in another context, it may betray you. I recommend you learn prepositions in relation to the verbs that require them. As with every list in this guide, this list is not all-inclusive, but it is a good start.

acceder (a)
acostumbrarse (a)
asomarse (a)
atreverse a + *inf.*
animar a + *inf.*
asistir (a)
aprender a + *inf.*
ayudar a + *inf.* – to help to __
comenzar a + *inf.*
conducir (a)
contribuir (a)
dirigirse (a)
dedicarse (a)
decidirse a + *inf.*
echarse a + *inf.*
enseñar a + *inf.*
empezar a + *inf.*
esperar (a) – to wait (to)
enfrentarse (a / con)
faltar (a)
forzar a + *inf.*
ir a + *inf.*
impulsar a + *inf.*
incitar a + *inf.*
limitarse (a)
llegar a + *inf.*
oler (a) – to smell (like)
obligar a + *inf.*
ponerse a + *inf.*
parecerse (a) – to look (like)
prepararse a / para + *inf.*
resignarse (a)
renunciar (a)
recurrir (a)
saber (a) – to taste (like)
sonar (a) – to sound (like)
tender a + *inf.*
mandar a + *inf.*
unirse (a) – to join
volver a + *inf.* – to _____ again
abusar (de)
acordarse (de)

acabar de + *inf.* – to have just + *past participle*
alegrarse (de)
apoderarse (de)
aprovecharse (de)
arrepentirse (de)
avergonzarse (de)
asegurarse (de)
burlarse (de)
contagiarse (de)
convencer (de)
cubrir (de) – to cover (in)
cambiar (de)
carecer (de)
cansarse (de)
depender (de) – to depend (on)
disfrutar (de)
divorciarse (de)
darse cuenta (de)
dejar de + *inf.* – to quit/stop _____ing
dudar (de) – to doubt
despedirse (de)
enamorarse (de) – to fall in love (with)
embarazarse (de) – to become pregnant (with)
emocionarse (de)
encargarse (de)
enterarse (de)
hartarse (de)
irse (de)
llenar (de / con)
ocuparse (de)
olvidarse (de)
pensar (de) – to think / have an opinión (about)
preocuparse (de)
quejarse (de)
reírse (de)
separarse (de)
servir (de) – to serve (as)

salir (de)
vestirse (de)
acabar (con)
contar (con) – to count (on)
compartir (con)
comprometerse (con / a) – to commit (to)
comenzar (con / por)
cumplir (con)
casarse (con) – to get married (to)
encontrarse (con)
empezar (con / por)
enojarse (con / de)
llevarse (con)
pelearse (con)
relacionarse (con)
reunirse (con)
soñar (con) – to dream (about / of)
tener que ver (con)
tropezarse (con)
ayudar (en / con) – to help (with)
consistir (en) – to consist (of)
confiar (en)
convertirse (en)
dudar (en) – to hesitate
entrar (en / a)
especializarse (en)
fijarse (en)
frustrarse (con / de)
influir (en / sobre)
interesarse (en)
insistir (en)
involucrarse (en)
meterse (en)
molestarse en + *inf.* – to bother _____ing
pensar (en) – to be thinking (about, in the moment)
sentarse (en / a)
tardar (en)

Por vs. para

You've seen examples of *por* and *para* in context, but maybe you've never seen any rules describing their usage. As with *el pretérito/el imperfecto*, *ser/estar/haber*, and *saber/conocer*, the English translation will not help you distinguish *por* from *para*. Both mean "for" in multiple cases. The key is to learn their uses in context. You could substitute with the phrases in parentheses.

- **Use *por* in the following contexts:**

  - in favor of (*a/en favor de*)   (Luchamos *por* la libertad. Votó *por* el demócrata.)
  - in search of (*en busca de*)   (Voy [a] *por* agua. Vinieron [a] *por* mí.)
  - instead of (*en lugar de*)   (Trabajé *por* Joel porque él estaba enfermo.)
  - on someone else's behalf   (Tengo vergüenza *por* él; ¡qué tonto es!)
  - cause or reason (*a causa de*)   (No jugamos *por* el viento. Chilló *por* miedo.)
  - in exchange for (*a cambio de*)   (Pagaron $10 *por* la camisa. Le di eso *por* esto.)
  - duration of time (*durante*)   (Camina *por* 30 minutos. Fue doctor *por* 30 años.)
  - general time frame (*en*)   (Me baño *por* la noche. Tomo café *por* la mañana.)
  - means of transportation (*en*)   (No les gusta viajar *por* autobús. Viajaré *por* tren.)
  - means of communication   (Habla *por* teléfono. Me comunico *por* WhatsApp.)
  - through (*a través de*)   (Anduvimos *por* Cusco. Corrí *por* los pasillos.)
  - along or by (location)   (Juegan *por* el río. El parque queda *por* la librería.)
  - multiplication and division   (5 *por* 5 son 25. 12 dividido *por* 3 son 4.)
  - velocity   (Corrimos 10 millas *por* hora.)
  - frequency (*al/a la, cada*)   (Trabajo 8 horas *por* día. Ganan 30.000 € *por* año.)
  - gratitude   (Gracias *por* tus sugerencias. Gracias *por* todo.)
  - congratulations   (Felicidades *por* tu premio.)
  - apology   (Discúlpame *por* molestarte. Perdón *por* el ruido.)
  - passive voice with *ser*   (El poema fue escrito *por* Octavio Paz.)
  - the future   (Estoy emocionado *por* el concierto este viernes.)
       (Tengo miedo al huracán que está *por* venir.)

- **Use *para* in the following contexts:**

  - destination or direction (*a, hacia*)   (Nos vamos *para* Puerto Rico. Salió *para* la playa.)
  - intended recipient of something   (El regalo es *para* mi tío. La compré *para* Nohemi.)
  - use or purpose of something   (La cama es *para* dormir. La leche es *para* mi té.)
  - deadline   (Tengo que entregar el reportaje *para* el lunes.)
  - in contrast to a norm or expectation   (Habla mucho *para* una niña de dieciocho meses.)
  - in order to + *inf.*   (Fuimos al parque *para* jugar al fútbol.)

As you can plainly see, there are far more distinct uses for *por* than for *para*, so if you are in doubt, and have to wager a random guess, the odds are on the side of *por*. For some expressions, like *por favor*, it may be a stretch to find its guiding rule. When you say it, are you asking someone to do something "in exchange for" your favor? Perhaps. Is your *favor* the "cause" or the "reason" for someone's action? Maybe. Some expressions are common enough that they are worth memorizing, regardless of the rule you might apply to it. Memorizing the following idiomatic expressions will help you use *por* and *para* correctly.

- **Idiomatic expressions using *por***

por lo general – in general / generally
por lo menos (al menos) – at least
por supuesto – of course
por (de) casualidad – by chance
por un lado (por una parte) – on the one hand
por otro lado (por otra parte) – on the other hand
palabra por palabra – word for word
por primera vez – for the first time
por último – lastly
por fin – finally
por ahora – for now
por ejemplo – for example
por ningún lado – nowhere
por todas partes (por todos lados) – everywhere
la razón por (la que/cual) – the reason for (which)
por accidente – by accident
seguido por (seguido de) – followed by
por (de) nada – it was nothing / you're welcome

por separado/a – separately
por cierto (a propósito) – by the way
por eso – for that / that's why
por lo tanto – therefore
por consiguiente – consequently
por ende – thus
por desgracia – unfortunately
por suerte – luckily / fortunately
por si acaso – (just) in case
por favor – please
por ciento / por cien – percent
por adelantado – in advance
por completo – completely
por el amor de dios – for the love of god
¡Ay, por dios! – Good lord!
por medio de – by way of
por lo visto – apparently
por poco – barely / narrowly / just

- **Subtleties between *por* and *para***

¿por qué? – why? / because of what?
¿para qué? – in order to what? for what purpose?

por arriba – (from) (up) above
para arriba (hacia arriba) – upward

por fuera (afuera) – (on the) outside
para afuera (hacia afuera) – (to the) outside

por abajo – (from) underneath / down below
para abajo (hacia abajo) – downward

por dentro (adentro) – (on the) inside
para adentro (hacia adentro) – (to the) inside

por aquí – this way / over here
para acá – over here / in this direction

para siempre – forever (more common)
por siempre – forever (less common)

por allí – that way / over there
para allá – over there / in that direction

hay muchas cosas para hacer – there are a lot of things to do
hay muchas cosas por hacer – there are a lot of things that remain to be done
hay muchas cosas que hacer (hay que hacer muchas cosas) – … a lot of things that have to be done

- **Idiomatic expressions using *para***

para colmo – to top it all off
ser elegible para – to be eligible for
para más información – for more información
cambio para un billete de $20 – change for a $20 bill
tener problemas para + *inf.* – to have problems (with) _____ing

aplicar para (solicitar) – to apply for
cualificar / calificar para – to qualify for

El español mal hablado

In graduate school, I took a course on discourse analysis. We had a guest professor one day who asked the class, "*¿Qué es el español?*" One by one, we shouted out completely valid answers, but none of them was what he was looking for. Finally, we relented, and he indulged us. "*El español,*" he said, "*es el latín mal hablado.*" Throughout my bachelor's and master's programs, there wasn't a single utterance more impactful on the way I approached the Spanish language—or language in general—than that one. Language is living, ever changing, pitting each generation against all previous ones.

In 1492, Spanish was officially declared a language as the regional kingdoms were unified into one single Spanish kingdom. For centuries prior, there was the educated class, which spoke Latin, and the uneducated class, which spoke a progressively more bastardized form of Latin (street Latin, if you will). This street Latin, no longer intelligible by citizens of other countries that supposedly also spoke Latin, was, by virtue of its unintelligibility, a new language. Thus, *Español*—or *Castellano*, as it is known in some Spanish-speaking countries—was born. From *El cantar del mío Cid* to *El ingenioso hidalgo don Quixote de la Mancha* to the Spanish taught in schools across the globe today, the Spanish language has evolved and will continue to evolve until it is no longer spoken by anyone on the planet.

One of the stated goals of the *Real Academia Española* is the preservation of the Spanish language. While this is commendable, it is inherently a losing fight. The reality is that even the prestigious *RAE* is aware that the Spanish language is evolving, and they continually update their dictionaries to reflect modern linguistic trends. In the same discourse analysis class I mentioned earlier, we went on to discuss "prescriptive" vs. "descriptive" grammar. Prescriptive grammar is that which attempts to teach people the correct way to speak (write, etc.), whereas descriptive grammar attempts to identify and document the way people speak. Both are completely valid points of view. The more fluidly you can move from one to the other, the better communicator you'll be.

If the point of language is to communicate, then the most effective form of communication is to speak the other person's language, literally and figuratively. Sometimes asking "How are things, my brother?" will resonate with someone on a deeply human level, and other times it will draw laughs and mockery. In contrast, "Sup, brah?" may make the connection you are looking for, and other times it may get you uninvited to the next academic conference.

If you are like me, your curiosity is insatiable and you want to know every detail of the Spanish language. I encourage you to indulge that passion, keeping in mind that not everyone shares our passion for detail and that there are factors beyond the academic side of language that play into effective communication. I've had to learn to relax and go with the flow when I hear native Spanish speakers make grammatical errors. Even when my interest is just to understand why they chose to say what they said, I've had to bite my tongue for the sake of the interaction. If you are talking to your college professor or your local Spanish tutor, ask away. If you are talking to a client or trying to navigate your way through a foreign country, take it in stride and focus on the connection with the person in front of you, not on their word choices. If you are not like me, and you don't get caught up in the "why" of everything, well, then, disregard this paragraph.

My last lesson to you—given what you know about my take on the Spanish language—is obviously tongue-in-cheek: "*El español mal hablado.*" Every language has its idiosyncrasies and oddities; some people label them as errors and some label them as regionalisms. The beauty of it all is that you get to decide how you interpret them.

- **"*Laísmo*," "*loísmo*," and "*leísmo*"**

Laísmo and *loísmo* are the improper use of direct-object pronouns (*lo, la, los, las*) in place of indirect objects.

Ej. "La di un beso" (Le di un beso)   "No la dije nada" (No le dije nada)

Un beso is the direct object since it is the "what" you gave. That means what is missing is the "to whom" you gave the *beso*. This is the indirect object that should be represented by the pronoun *le*. *Nada* is the direct object, therefore the person should be the indirect object (*le*).

Leísmo is the improper use of indirect-object pronouns (*le, les*) in place of direct objects.

Ej. "Le vi ayer" – "*le*" representing a woman (La vi ayer)

The "what" you saw is the woman, and although it is a person, not an inanimate object, it still is the direct object.

These linguistic phenomena can be found in regional pockets all over the Spanish-speaking world. One interesting oddity is that in Spain, *le* substitutes for *lo* only when referring to a human direct object (masculine, singular). Although not universal, it is academically accepted.

Ej. le abracé (a mi tío)   los abracé (a mis tíos)
      la abracé (a mi tía)   las abracé (a mis tías)

Although "*lo abracé*" (*a mi tío*) is academically accepted and prevalent in Latin America, it sounds odd to many Spaniards, as though "*mi tío*" were being treated as less than human.

The *Real Academia Española* (www.rae.es) has a *Diccionario panhispánico de dudas* (drop-down menu from their home page), which tackles the trickiest, most highly debated topics in the Spanish language. If you search "*leísmo*," you will find everything you could want to know on the matter. The *RAE* is both prescriptive and descriptive in its approach, telling you the academically accepted norms without shying away from giving examples in literature that deviate from the recommended usage. Search individual verbs if you're not sure if they need a direct or indirect-object pronoun.

Ej. servir*le* or servir*la*? molestar*le* or molestar*la*? llamar*le* o llamar*la*? etc.

Regardless of what the *RAE* recommends, for every expert in one country who says "*ayudarle*" is a clear example of *leísmo*, there is another expert in another country who says "*ayudarla*" is a clear example of *laísmo*. Perhaps the best advice I ever heard regarding this dilemma was from a Colombian classmate of mine in graduate school: "*a cada quien, según su propia realidad*."

- **Borrowed words**

Spanish, like every other language, has incorporated many words borrowed from English. Some are exactly as they look in English: *jeans, hockey, parking, mall, hall,* etc. Some require a little brainwork to decipher: *guachimán* (watchman), *barman* (bartender), *living* (living room), etc.

- **Mispronunciations, malapropisms, and other linguistic oddities**

Surely you are guilty of at least one of the following mispronunciations in English, most likely without knowing it:

> *Ej.* "ignowledge" (acknowledge), "spinage" (spinach), "ostridge" (ostrich), "perserverance" (perseverance), "fermiliar" (familiar), "expecially" (especially), "expresso" (espresso), "pundant" (pundit), "infinant" (infinite), "architectual" (architectural), "jewlery" (jewelry), "nucular" (nuclear), "acrost" (across), etc.

Do you know other people who mispronounce these words? Do you cringe when you hear them or do you take it in stride? Do you judge them? What about when people use the wrong word (malapropism) or butcher an idiomatic expression or erroneously and unintentionally mash up words? We all do it from time to time. Sometimes it leads to laughter and sometimes we coin a new word that we later can't imagine not having at our disposal, like "brunch" or "webinar."

> *Ej.* lay (laid, have laid) vs. lie (lay, have lain), accept vs. except, "lip sing" (lip sync), hunger "pains" (pangs), "tow the line" (toe the line), "for all intensive purposes" (for all intents and purposes), "I could care less" (I couldn't care less), "it begs the question" (it raises the question), "refudiate" (repudiate + refute), etc.

There is a psycholinguistic basis for these "misspeaks." Sometimes we misapply or over apply a rule. Sometimes we don't understand the origin of a phrase, so we make up what we think the person must've ("must of") said. This is often subconscious, and I'm sure there are quite a few psycholinguistic studies on the matter. The following are common errors you'll hear from native Spanish speakers from time to time. Don't let them rattle your faith in what you've learned, but feel free to embrace them as cultural oddities without passing judgment. I would also encourage you not to adopt them for yourself, as the more standard your Spanish is, the more universally understood and accepted your communication will be.

> *Ej.* "muncho" (mucho), "haiga" (haya – confused with *haga*?), "fuistes, hablastes, comistes," etc. (fuiste, hablaste, comiste, etc. – over applying the "*s*" associated with the *tú* form), "dijieron, trajieron," etc. (dijeron, trajeron, etc. – misapplying the regular ending *-ieron*), "nadien" (nadie – supposed plural form?), "habían dos carros" (había dos carros – treating the direct object as the subject of *haber*, which doesn't exist), "siéntensen" (siéntense – over applying the "*n*" associated with the *Uds.* form), "detrás mío" (detrás de mí – treating the adverb *detrás* as a noun), "cercas" (cerca), "a voz de pronto" (a bote pronto – not understanding the origin of the phrase), etc.

Sometimes *a* gets erroneously attached to another word due to its prevalence in other structures.

> *Ej.* "qué a̲gusto" (qué gusto – a̲ mi gusto, estoy a̲ gusto, etc.)
> "quiere a̲verte" (quiere verte – a̲ ver, vamos a̲ ver, etc.)

Sometimes irregular verbs are taken as regular verbs.

> *Ej.* tostar (o → ue) "tosta" (tuesta), degollar (o → üe) "degolla" (degüella), plegar (e → ie) "plega" (pliega), cocer (o → ue) "coce" (cuece)

Some errors are very consistent, some deliberate for ease of pronunciation, and others for reasons that are beyond my powers of perception and intuition.

> *Ej.* e → i: "voltiar" (voltear), "airopuerto" (aeropuerto), "pior" (peor), etc.
> s → j before k sound: "ej que" (es que), "ejcuela" (escuela), "ejquina" (esquina), etc.
> f → j: "juimos" (fuimos), "jueron" (fueron), "jumar" (fumar), etc.
> ue → uo: "fuogo" (fuego), "juogo" (juego), "luogo" (luego), "puodo" (puedo), etc.
> the dropping of *ll*: "tortía" (tortilla), "cae" (calle), "se ama" (se llama), etc.
> the dropping of *d* in words ending in *ado*: "lao" (lado), "pescao" (pescado), etc.

If American English is your first language, you'd probably understand, "I am going to the store," if you heard someone say, "Ama go the store." Why ask, "do you want to?" when you can say, "wanna?" Perhaps you're from Scotland or New Zealand and can teach me a thing or two about *your* colloquial English that I wouldn't otherwise understand. Think about non-native English speakers; what do you think their chances are of understanding the meaning when they hear this kind of nonsense? Slim to none, and Slim just left town, as my dad would say. It's not that it's spoken too quickly, it's that it isn't spoken clearly. As you travel the Spanish-speaking world, you're going to have to adapt to how others speak because, chances are, they won't adapt to you. So, when you hear a Mexican ask, "*¿Quihúbole?*" or a Colombian exclaim, "*¡Hijue!*" or a Chilean ask, "*¿Comestái?*" etc., cut yourself some slack. In every country, you'll find some people who speak clearly and some who decidedly do not. Just do your best and forget the rest.

- **Americanisms and other regionalisms**

There are probably more than a dozen ways to say *bueno* in Spanish when you not only consider different eras, but also every tiny pocket and corner of the Spanish-speaking world. How many can you name in English? Cool, neat, sweet, fresh, rad, bad, legit, dope, righteous, boss, sick, wicked, def, gnarly, dank, bitchin, tight, hip, groovy, tubular, wizard, etc.

> *Ej.* chévere, chido, suave, padre, genial, a todo dar, buena onda, guay, bacán, chulo, etc.

If you want to say you like something, don't limit yourself to *me gusta* and *me encanta* when you can throw out a Mexican "*me late*" or a Spanish "*me (súper) mola.*"

Why say, *sí* in the U.S. when you could say, "*simón*" or *no* when you could say, "*chale*"?

Don't let the name *Real Academia Española* fool you; it's not just for Spain. Check out their *Diccionario de americanismos*: http://lema.rae.es/damer. Here you'll find words that their *Diccionario de la lengua española* does not have registered.

> *Ej.* monitorear, troca, agendar, etc. (don't let anyone tell you these are not words)

It also has *calcos*, which are words that already had one or more meanings in Spanish, but because of their similarities to foreign words or some other foreign influence, they've taken on new meanings colloquially.

> *Ej.* carpeta – file folder (now carpet), ratón – mouse (now mouse for a computer), etc.

Some common words or phrases in one country sound silly in another and may not be understood or even accepted. So, if you learn a phrase in one country, or from this guide, then a native Spanish speaker says that's not how you say it and tries to correct you, don't let it shake your faith in what you know to be true; simply ask them how they would say it and add it to your repertoire.

> *Ej.* When fruit goes bad, you'll hear "*se echó a perder*" in Mexico, but in Spain, they say, "*se estropeó*." Each sounds ridiculous to the other culture. If you say "*según yo*," in Mexico, you won't raise an eyebrow; if you say it in Spain, brace for laughter.

Some words or phrases have different meanings in different countries, leading to frequent miscommunications between native Spanish speakers.

> *Ej.* In many countries, *chillar* means "to scream," wheareas in others, it means "to cry." In some countries, *qué pena* means "how sad," in others, "how embarrassing."

Some words or phrases have a normal, everyday meaning in some countries, but in others, they are vulgar and offensive. I don't mean to be vulgar or offensive here, just informative, so you don't get yourself into trouble.

> *Ej. Fregar* means "to scrub" or "to wash," but in some countries, it means "to screw over." *Coger* means "to grab" or "to take," but in some countries, it means "to f**k."

So, when a Spaniard tells a Mexican that she is going to *coger un taxi*, it's met with either laughter or indignation. In the Caribbean, *la guagua* means "the bus" and they *cogen la guagua* all the time. In some countries in South America, *la guagua* means "the baby." You see how easily you could get into trouble!! A similar case in English is the word "bugger." In the U.S., it describes children when they are naughty, and you might even hear a little old lady say it as an exclamation. Outside of the U.S. (and maybe Canada), it absolutely does not mean a naughty child!

- **Euphemisms, double meanings, and innuendos**

Like English, Spanish has its euphemisms (*ay chihuahua, no manches, caray, joroba, ostras*, etc.), as well as double meanings and sexual innuendos. These also vary by country/culture.

> *Ej. hacerse una chaqueta, hacerse una paja, correrse la paja*, and *volar la cometa* can all mean *masturbarse. Echar un polvo*, among countless other phrases, means *tener sexo*.

Some foods in Spanish are euphemisms for genitals, like "nuts," "weiners," and "clams" in English. This will explain the chuckles you get when you say them completely innocently.

> *Ej. la panocha* (type of pastry), *el chocho* (little candy or pastry), *la papaya* (papaya), etc. *la salchicha* (hot dog or sausage), *el plátano* (banana), *el chile* (chile pepper), etc.

- **Espanglish y code switching**

"Espanglish" is a mashup of words like "*cheeseburguesa*" and "*no me toches*." Code switching *es cuando personas* alternate between *idiomas durante* the same conversation. *A veces*, it's because they don't know certain words *en los dos idiomas*, and sometimes *se hace porque* one language captures a sentiment *mejor que el otro*. To language purists, *es una aberración, pero para algunos*, it's part of their culturo-linguistic heritage y *se expresan mejor así. Curioso*, isn't it?

Apuntes

Apuntes

Apuntes

About the Author

David Faulkner holds bachelor's and master's degrees in Spanish, with an emphasis in teaching, and has taught Spanish in every grade from fourth to the university level. He is passionate about the fundamentals of language, as well as interpersonal communication and personal expression, particularly where their practical application has a positive impact on people's lives.

Faulkner opened up about his childhood in his memoir, *Superheroes* (2015), and has since shifted his focus back to his true calling: teaching Spanish and inspiring others to practice it in their daily lives.

Faulkner enjoys spending time with his family, public speaking, traveling the world, and staying active. He is an idealist and a relentless dreamer, reveling in the happiness of pursuit. *De cabo a rabo* (*Gramática*, *Vocabulario*, and *Actividades*) comprises his second, third, and fourth books.

To schedule David Faulkner for a curriculum presentation to see how his Spanish guides could benefit your language program, or to hire him for private lessons or as a guest teacher at your school, please contact him through DavidFaulknerBooks.com.

Flashforward
Publishing

Made in the USA
Las Vegas, NV
13 March 2022

45570015R00111